ME AND KIT

ME AND KIT

by

Guthrie McClintic

With Illustrations

An Atlantic Monthly Press Book

Boston · Little, Brown and Company · Toronto

The author wishes to thank A. D. Peters, literary
agent for the estate of Hilaire Belloc, for permission to
quote four lines from Mr. Belloc's "Dedicatory Ode."

ATLANTIC–LITTLE, BROWN BOOKS
ARE PUBLISHED BY
LITTLE, BROWN AND COMPANY
IN ASSOCIATION WITH
THE ATLANTIC MONTHLY PRESS

Published simultaneously in Canada
by Little, Brown & Company (Canada) Limited

PRINTED IN THE UNITED STATES OF AMERICA

FOR KIT

Author's Note

To any whose eyebrows may be raised by the title of this hegira into my past I venture to express I had title trouble from the start. It has run a whole gamut of names until my distinguished editor, Edward Weeks, suggested we call it KIT AND I, I dare say secretly hoping the other name would boost the tome's box-office appeal. I am all for that; but as this story begins with me, I decided for once to take first billing and possibly keep the box-office appeal as well. Hence ME AND KIT.

And last but not least I want to say that any merit the ensuing pages may possess is entirely due to the guidance of the above-mentioned Edward Weeks.

GUTHRIE McCLINTIC

May 19, 1955

Contents

4 L. 1893 Berlin

Contents

Illustrations

ME AND KIT

I

West of the Mountains

WE HAD a tomcat that was born in 1905. The day his eyes opened was the day that the victorious Admiral Togo, hero of the Japanese Navy in their war against Russia, passed through Seattle on his triumphant journey home from Portsmouth, New Hampshire, where, with President Theodore Roosevelt as mediator, he had attended the signing of a peace treaty by the representative of the Mikado and the envoy of the Czar. The Seattle city fathers declared a holiday and there was a big parade down Second Avenue in the Admiral's honor. All the Japanese population along with the rest of us, lined the streets waving the flags of Nippon and yelling *"Banzai!"* to the conquering hero. My mother, exhilarated by this event, named our cat Togo. He lived to a great old age and saw many changes take place. Although I was not born in 1905 I think it is not a misstatement to say my eyes opened that year, too.

I was twelve years old that summer, and I was wearing my first long pants. In those days that was something — knee pants were usual till you measured over 5 feet 5. I was definitely not the athletic type (I am still definitely not). I was scrawny and underweight, with a mop of dark brown hair and large eyes that seemed larger because of my extreme thinness. My clothes were on occasion neat but never snappy. I had neither the means nor aptitude to be slick.

Automobiles were just beginning to be seen on the streets of Seattle but they produced no excitement in me at all. They still don't. I ride in them but I don't drive. Once when a horseless buggy broke down in front of our house and all the neighborhood were gaping at the driver's attempt to fix it, I remained on our front porch absorbed in *David Copperfield*. Mrs. Woods, a childless party who lived next door, commented to my mother with neighborly acrimony in her voice: "Mrs. McClintic," she said, "I just don't understand a boy who isn't interested in mechanics." Well, since she didn't understand there was nothing I could do about it, so I turned a page and went on with *David Copperfield* — leaving my poor, patient, gentle mother to face the fact that her one and only was "different," to put it mildly — a nonconformist you might say.

I think I was brighter than the average — nothing sensational but just a little bit brighter, that's all. I was never a teacher's pet. Many years later, when Kit (the first time I met Bernard Shaw he said that "Kit" was a very undignified way of referring to such a distinguished actress as Katharine Cornell — I don't agree, so I'll repeat) when Kit was playing in Seattle, some of the surviving old girls who had taught me at Lincoln High School attended a matinee and afterwards came backstage to meet her. Since I was her husband and her director I assumed an unwonted importance in their eyes. As I was also a former pupil of theirs, they all agreed that *I* was the *one* in school they always knew would "amount to something." However, they skillfully managed to keep it from me when I was in class. I suppose they thought my head might be turned. Well, my head was turned. It began turning in 1905. It happened this way.

One Saturday morning, toward the end of May in that year, I was on my way to the public library; as I passed the Third Avenue Theater I came upon a small group laughing at a little boy in a pink Buster Brown suit who had dashed out of a doorway — which I found out shortly after was a stage entrance — pursued by an elephant. Swiftly after them came a youngish dark-haired woman whose cheeks were so red that I felt sure they must be painted (and they were), who called out: "Hey boys, he's in a bad temper, so quit your horsing and come back on stage. They are doing the end of the act over again." At this the elephant took off its head and said, "Don't be scared, Dwight, we were just funning." The two men who were its front and hindlegs then resumed their impersonation, and all of them went back inside, the dark lady leading the little boy by the hand.

I followed after with a couple of other stragglers. Going out of the bright sunlight it seemed quite dark when I had crossed the threshold. I looked about. Many things were going on. What seemed chaos to me evidently was quite normal to the people around me. . . . I was in a theater for the first time. I had entered through the stage door. I was "backstage." . . . I was agog at the painted trees, the rock flats and the rows of lights overhead. Against the back wall, two men in dirty white overalls stood on a scaffold painting what looked to me like a Moorish scene. There was a strong smell of glue in the air. A yellow-haired woman with a Gibson Girl pompadour and a lively perfume was walking up and down with a little book in her hand, repeating over and over in a low elocutionary voice "Who goes there? I am

Kenume, Countess of Ogawa." Two men in shirt sleeves were likewise pacing up and down with their books, and they were also repeating lines. "How many sides you got, Verne?" said one in passing. "I don't know," replied the other, shuffling the pages of his book, "maybe thirty-five." In the center of the stage a young woman ran up a ladder and stepped from it onto the back of the elephant, which promptly started to trot off to the left. "Cholly," protested the young woman, "I'll fall off if it goes that fast." "You're escaping from a harem, aren't you? It can't amble. Go on," said Cholly, frantically. "Never stand in the way of the U. S. Navy!" thundered a man with a big bass voice, and at that he struck down a cringing little fellow, and ran after the young woman on the elephant. Someone called "Curtain!" The ladder was brought back; the young lady got down off the elephant and Cholly, a nice harassed-looking man in his late thirties, announced: "Half an hour for lunch, then we start with the last act." Everyone relaxed. The actors filed out the stage door, leaving me wide-eyed and vaguely disturbed. I forgot the books I wanted at the library but I knew I was coming back. I made for the front of the theater to see what this was all about. A vivid poster showing a young woman atop an elephant being pursued in the moonlight by what looked like East Indians carrying long spears had this lettering on it:

CHARLES A. TAYLOR'S NEW YORK COMPANY
in the sensational melodrama entitled
ESCAPE FROM THE HAREM
IN 4 ACTS AND 7 SCENES
WEEK COMMENCING SUNDAY, JUNE 4, 1905
MATINEE SUNDAY AND SATURDAY

At the ticket window I was told I could gain admittance for ten cents at the Saturday matinee, but the seats weren't reserved so I would have to arrive early to be sure of getting in.

I returned to the stage door and hung around until the actors came back from their lunch. There was a curious musty coolness backstage. As the rehearsal proceeded I was fascinated. As far as I was concerned it was the Lorelei. Thereafter, every nice day that summer, when the barnlike stage door was open, I was there watching the company rehearse. And every Saturday matinee during the Taylor season found me out front to witness the result of what I had seen in work the week before. I was beginning to hear a melody, distant but penetrating. The melody was theater. I was to hear it the rest of my life.

The Third Avenue Theater was on the northeast corner of Third and Madison, one of the noisiest spots in town. Cable cars clanged up and down Madison Avenue Hill, while the electric streetcars on Third ran them a close second, ringing their bells as if they were going to a fire. It was a weatherbeaten wooden building with a cupola, a "family theater," it was called. Russell and Drew were the managers. "Pop" Russell was quite a figure. I can see him now, pushing in front of the curtain covered with advertisements — a rotund and red-faced little man sporting a great handle-bar mustache, with his derby hat in his right hand held against his chest. This would be immediately after the big scene at the end of Act Three. I can hear him, too, announcing the next week's attraction — "The greatest melodrama ever written, Charles A. Taylor's *From Rags to Riches*," he would bleat. This was before the days of microphone and, believe me, he didn't need one. His hash-house voice would continue: "It has been pronounced a marvel in stagecraft, a melodramatic gem deftly woven with a web of tears and a woof of smiles. This great play will be seen for ten performances only, beginning Sunday matin-knee [his pronunciation] June twelfth." And he would always wind up with the threat, "Don't wait until the day of performance and expect to get what you want!" After this, he would adjust his derby and squeeze offstage, right, distending the advertisement on the curtain, and disappear.

Then the audience would start to buzz and the orchestra would liven up the intermission with a rendition of "Please Go Away and Let Me Sleep" while the candy vendor forged up and down the aisle hawking his wares at the top of his lungs: "Chocolate chips, salted peanuts, lemon drops and chewing gum!" And he would throw a handful of lemon drops first to the left then to the right with the customers falling over each other in an attempt to grab a sample.

That first matinee had me sitting on the edge of my seat, trembling with excitement. The play was about a fair young choir singer who is persuaded by a seemingly charming older woman to have a lemonade with her — but the lady has sinister designs: the drink is drugged and the poor choir singer is sent to far-off Siam, alas not to sing hymns but to be the plaything of the Imperial Prince. However, her sister, who has a suitor in the Navy, puts the Marines on her scent — and presto they locate her, luckily before she has been deflowered, and her escape is contrived by way of that friendly elephant.

With the exception of his wife, the Charles A. Taylor Company did not represent the peak of Thespian achieve-

ment. But they had zest, vitality and — in Seattle — success
. . . thanks largely, I would think, to Mr. Taylor himself —
"Cholly," as his young wife called him — who directed with
energy and frenzy and wrote most of the plays to boot. They
were really blood-and-thunders with titillating titles, such
as *The Queen of the Highway*, *The Girl Engineer*, *The Fe-*
male Detectives and many others. Also, as I have said, there
was Mrs. Taylor — wife of the producer, mother of Buster
Brown, the boy in the pink suit — a young actress whose long
blond curls framed a face of peculiar loveliness, with great,
deep-blue eyes that reflected her Irish moods and a radiant
smile that seemed to give the lie to the haunting melancholy
of her voice. She had for me an inexplicably disturbing appeal. She was the soubrette of the company. It was she who
escaped on the elephant. She was different. I couldn't say
she was a better performer than the leading lady, Ailleen
May — but she was enchanting. Miss May was winsome, with
a bleached blond pompadour that never varied no matter
what part she was playing — and an off-stage wardrobe of
big hats with waving ostrich plumes and dresses with peeka-
boo tops (very daring), mostly in baby blue, that made the
stage-door mob gasp when she came out after the matinees.
She spoke to all of them and they followed her up the hill
to her hotel. She was a great favorite. Mrs. Taylor was not
nearly so popular, perhaps because she was concerned more
with her acting than with hobnobbing with the customers.
For me, magic hovered over her like a halo. I forgot to say
her first name was Laurette: Laurette Taylor she was
called. . . . When that summer was over, my indoctrina-
tion was complete. It was the theater for me, for better or
for worse.

*   *   *

Seattle in 1905 was just recovering from the Gold Rush of '97. Its boosters called it "The Queen City of the West Coast." On those too infrequent days when our incessant drizzle ceased and the fog lifted and we could see the incomparable mountain ranges — the Olympics over Puget Sound, the Cascades over Lake Washington, and Mount Rainier to the south of us — even I, a native son, felt a certain amount of awe. Like Rome, it was built on seven hills. That's what our Chamber of Commerce said. What they didn't say was that it had a kind of frontier lawlessness. Who besides myself, I wonder, can remember the Holy Roller murders when members of that religious group were popping each other off like ninepins in King Street Station, or the family feud that ended in the fatal shooting in Guy's Drugstore at the corner of Yesler Way and Second? And the alarm that seized all outlying districts when the two famous "bad men," Harry Tracy and Dave Merrill, escaped from the penitentiary and kept the countryside in terror until they were killed some eight weeks later? In our town of maybe 100,000, we did not lack for excitement. Boats from Alaska . . . Boats from the Orient . . . And over all the smell of pine woods, spiked with the salt air of the Pacific . . .

I can still see Chinese women in black silken trousers with tiny bound feet mincing along on Second Avenue, attracting a group of the curious, and "Chinamen" with cues (pigtails, we called them); there were Japanese girls, too, with chalk-white faces and elaborate pompadours, in brilliant-colored kimonos. Sometimes you ran across Alaska-bound prospectors with a team of Eskimo dogs, on their way to the wharves on Western Avenue; and on street corners sat Siwash Indians — the town was named after the dead chief of their tribe, Seattle. These Indians, inscrutable and wrinkled, would be squatting on the sidewalks with their blankets and woven baskets, beads, and miniature totem poles for sale. From below the "deadline" would saunter ladies of the evening — usually in pairs, holding their trains a little too high and walking with an exaggerated kangaroo bend — "fast women" they were called by the more refined. They seemed glamorous to me, with their painted faces and potent perfume. But my mother always gave them a wide berth whenever we passed them on Second Avenue. A fact the Chamber of Commerce neglected to publicize was that Seattle had one of the biggest and most flourishing red-light districts in the country. I remember the newspapers' attacking our mayor, who was in cahoots with the whoremasters and vice overlords, and who was ultimately impeached by the virtuous and indignant women of the town — who, in the Year of Our Lord 1910, had just won the power to vote and were "cleaning house."

All in all it was quite a town, but I was an alien there although I was born in Seattle and had never been anywhere else. It was exciting but it wasn't home. Home was over the hills and far away — "East of the mountains," my mother would say longingly as she looked at the Cascades as if they were prison walls, "east of the mountains, son, it's nicer." In a very few years I was going to *look* for that home.

Mother and Father were third cousins. They were both born McClintic, and had a common ancestor, also a McClintic, who came from the North of Ireland in 1740 with a land grant in his pocket from George the Second of England.

He was a peasant who could neither read nor write. His signature was an X. He settled in Virginia colony where his family flourished and multiplied. My mother was born on a farm outside of Staunton, Virginia, one of fourteen children. She was christened Ella Florence. Her older brothers had fought with the Confederate Army in the Civil War, and both my parents had a passionate devotion to the memory of the old South. Jefferson Davis's picture adorned my mother's bedroom; and if there had been a likeness of Abe Lincoln around the house, Father would have used it for target practice. When I showed him my history book account of the War between the States he pronounced it "a pack of damned Yankee lies" and wrote to his mother, who promptly sent him a copy of *The Southern Story of the Civil War,* which I was told to read. I did so, wondering at the disparity of the accounts; and later I had the temerity to bring it to the attention of Miss Rucker, our teacher; her face darkened and, scenting sedition, she said that if I ever mentioned such a thing before the class again she would send me to the principal to be whipped. I took the hint and clammed up.

My father was born in Marlinton, West Virginia, one of five sons. He was christened Edgar Daggs, both surnames of his two dour-looking grandmothers. His family was financially better off than my mother's; this was principally due to my father's mother, who as Mary Matthews — great-grandniece of George Matthews, second Governor of Georgia — brought a considerable sum of money to the marriage.

Mary Matthews McClintic was a devoutly religious woman — a fanatical Presbyterian. Such was the vigor of her enforcement of Mr. Calvin's precepts, if not God's, that all

of her sons on reaching maturity became atheists or next
door to it in a tardy revolt against the religious tyranny they
had been exposed to as children. She was a forceful woman
and a generous one and her sons held her in great respect.
So did I, for every Christmas and every birthday she would
send me five dollars with a note that always ended "trusting
that you will grow up to be a true Christian is the constant prayer of your devoted grandmother Mary Matthews
McClintic." I never saw her. In fact I never saw any of my
relatives until I was nineteen years old.

My father, with a greater power of persuasion than I
should ever have believed him capable of, induced my
grandmother into giving him a considerable sum of money
while he was still in college, on receipt of which he re-
nounced all rights to share in her estate at her death. With
this ready cash in hand he left school before graduation
and went to Texas where he invested in a cattle ranch. Now
there are some people for whom luck is *never* a lady. My
father was one of them. The draw was never right for him
during his entire life. The following winter a great blizzard
obliterated Texas temporarily and all of his cattle perma-
nently. Discouraged, he disposed of whatever he could sell
and moved on. He was young, fine-looking, with an adven-
turous bent and like many other young men was seeking
that magic moment when he would "strike it rich." Out in
the Northwest there was a growing town which had *just*
been stricken with a great fire that had practically destroyed
it — Seattle, situated in Washington territory soon to become a state. My father, who quite rightly thought there was
a future in Seattle, set forth and arrived there in the winter
of 1889. I believe that with what he had left of my grand-

mother's bounty he could have bought a sizeable parcel of valuable land in that virgin territory. But that was not to be. Whatever voices advised him were the wrong ones and he purchased acres and acres near a place called Kent of which sea and tide took their toll and acre by acre they disappeared altogether under water. But at the outset Seattle seemed promising and it was in this interlude that Dad returned to Virginia and married my mother.

Mother was little, charming-looking, and had a lovely speaking voice. (I am allergic to voices. I am married to one of the most beautiful voices in the world.) I don't believe my mother and father were happy for long. They had little in common. The promised land turned out to be unyielding. I was their only child, born when Father was in his mid-thirties, and when I was five years old he made his final push for Eldorado, mortgaging the last negotiable possession he had — the house in which I was born — to join the throng that was Klondike bound to find gold in Alaska. Gold there was, but not for him, and he came back home after eighteen months empty-handed, to start again — this time from scratch — and scratch it was. Our house was sold for the mortgage to the husband of the woman who had done our washing. (HE *had* struck gold up North.) My father became bitter and subject to violent rages against a fate which he felt was constantly giving him a raw deal.

Mother, who was gentleness personified, found herself unable in any way to alleviate Dad's frustration; she developed a philosophy of her own and lived more or less within herself. She could draw remarkably well, had a keen sense of humor and was deeply interested and informed about *all* religions. Early in my life I was snatched from the doors of the Presbyterian Church of my baptism to hear the truth and light as it was dispensed at one time or another from the pulpits of the Unitarian, the Theosophist or the Ethical Culture group.

My arrival helped matters not at all. From the start I was an odd one. To my father, who was a big man of over six feet with a powerful bellowing low voice, I was an enigma whose every act was done on purpose to annoy him. My mother was far more sympathetic to me, partly because I had been what is known as "a frail child," having survived through my earlier years every illness that children fall heir to. The thrashings my dad administered to me in the woodshed with a sturdy leather strap I am certain were deserved but they in no way curbed the qualities in me which were irritating to him. Rather they set us poles apart and made me more a lone wolf than ever. God knows, while I never tried to please him I never tried to offend him either. I hated to see my mother's grief in the violence I caused in him but I just couldn't help it. It developed in me an independence and also, I am afraid, a surreptitious trait that I can't say I am proud of. I am not excusing or blaming anyone. These things happen. When you mix red and yellow you get orange and that's that.

In May of 1905 I finished the seventh grade and had one more year of grammar school ahead of me before I would be ready for high school. At times there were vague discussions in the house as to what my profession should be when I grew up. That was something I had never thought about. Law was my father's choice, with a rosy vista, to him, of a place for me in the office of his successful brother, my Uncle

George. My mother did not crave Uncle George. She suggested my being an editor. As far as I was concerned, it would have been more to the point if they had suggested I be an acrobat. Then I would have known exactly what they were talking about and could have said "no," thereby precipitating another family *crise*. In our family arguments I must pause to say that my father's profanity was the most colorful and expansive I had ever heard. He never descended to four-letter words but what he did to the Holy Family would have made him today an honored comrade in the Soviet Enclosure.

One of the loudest of these crises arose when I was caught in a whopping big lie. At that time we lived on Beacon Hill. On my trips to the public library I would walk down and ride back to avoid climbing two hills home. I journeyed there on the average of once a week. My reading had varied all the way from Henty and Jules Verne to Thackeray and Dickens. Dickens was my favorite. I read and reread *David Copperfield, Oliver Twist* and *Nicholas Nickleby*. I had an allowance of twenty-five cents a week, which up to this eventful summer more than took care of my cable-car rides and ice-cream sodas. But, when the open stage door of the Third Avenue Theater revealed that glimpse of a new world to me and I decided to go to the Taylor Company's Saturday matinees, my twenty-five cents allowance began to look mighty small. At the beginning I sat in the ten-cent "rush" seats at the back of the balcony. In those days women wore pompadours and, on top of those, hats; and many of those hats were monstrous not only in style but in size. And in a theater they didn't always take them off. When in front of me, it seemed they never did. So I made up my mind to oc-

cupy a reserved seat in the front row of the balcony. It cost
a quarter — my whole week's allowance! — which, obviously,
I could not afford.

Now my father had a stamp collection. He never gave it
much time, but on occasion I had seen him show it to
some friends. Being a Southerner, he had many Confederate
stamps, even duplicates — so I figured these would be missed
the least, and took a few. Down on Third Avenue I had noticed a sign: STAMPS, BOUGHT AND SOLD. When I went there
with my loot, a bifocaled, evil-smelling old man looked over
what I had brought with me and offered me a half-dollar
for the lot; said he would buy any others I could get hold of.
My theatergoing for the summer was insured! Some years
later I discovered that, singly, these unperforated ten-cent
Jefferson Davis Confederate stamps sold for two hundred
dollars apiece! Father had no idea of their value, I'm sure.
They were sentimental reminders of the old South only.

Theatergoing was not a habit of our house, so I never
told the family of my matinee excursions. But on Saturdays
Dad always wanted to know where I was going, so I supplied him with a variety of likely stories: I was going "over
to Queen Anne Hill to play with the Wilton boys" or "up to
Harold Black's at the top of Beacon." He never doubted me,
and things went swimmingly until the day of the last matinee of the Taylor season. I said I was going to play with
Harold Black and tripped blithely downtown to see *The
King of the Opium Ring*. At the end of the performance I
waited around with scores of others to get a final glimpse
of the actors as they left the stage door. I watched them as
they went their various ways with a positive ache and longing. It was the first time I had ever experienced that kind

of sadness. They were going away and my life would be emptier. Not one of them did I know and yet somehow they had come close to me, closer than anything in my life up to that moment. Blindly somehow I felt that world, their world, was where I belonged.

I was very late getting home. I was too absorbed in my own feelings to notice any tenseness in the atmosphere as I entered the house. My father asked me if I had had a good time. And I said yes. He inquired as to what Harold and I had done, and when I came through with some glib lie he played right along like some sharp attorney leading his witness deftly into a trap. I began to come to my senses when he told me what time it was — my parents had had dinner an hour before — but, saving the best to the last, he informed me that he had phoned Harold Black's house and found out that I had not been there at all. Caught red-handed, I had to tell the truth. Then he boiled — in fact boiled over: sounding not unlike the whine of a jet plane, he started by intoning our Savior's name as if to bring a curse down on the whole world. Meantime Mother had rushed to shut down our windows, while the next-door neighbors were opening theirs wider. It was the worst rage I ever remember seeing him in. I had nothing to say. I was in the wrong. There wasn't one extenuating circumstance on my side and, except for my mother's tears, I wasn't a bit sorry. In the stress of this tornado, thank God, he forgot entirely to ask where the money came from that bought the tickets. He was content to pronounce at the finish that he would see me burn in "hell-fire before he would let me hang around a lot of God-damned pimps and whores of the theater." It was all hideously unpleasant except, I suppose, for the neighbors.

That night, when I went to bed, I lay there hating my father. I hated the prospect of the eighth grade, of high school, of any further life in Seattle. I thought of that company leaving while I was a prisoner with no escape. I looked out of my bedroom window, and there in the darkness down the hill a long train was pulling out of King Street Station — its windows lighted — going East — east of the mountains. Lucky people to be going away. Would I ever be so lucky?

II

Forbidden Land

AGAINST Dad's ultimatum there was nothing I could do beyond biding my time and praying for the day of my deliverance. Since the theater was now forbidden land I had to cherish it in secret. On the news-stands I saw a magazine called *Theatre*. I found it was available at the public library. Afternoon upon afternoon I sat in the reading room there poring over its monthly issues, becoming acquainted with and assimilating a hero worship of John Drew, William Gillette, Eleanor Robson and Ethel Barrymore. I gazed at their pictures in wonder. They seemed as remote as the stars in the dipper. Every reference spelled NEW YORK. New York was three thousand miles away — five days by the fastest train. New York was where these people played, lived, worked — where there were scores of theaters. That was where Broadway was . . . where theater people were not "pimps or whores.". . . I came across a photograph of Edwin Booth as a young man, and I looked and looked at it — and the more I did, the more I became convinced I bore a striking resemblance to him. I learned he had died two months before I was born. I began picturing the day Mother would take me into her room and, after closing the door, would say: "Son, you will have to know this someday, it might as well be now — Edwin Booth is your father."

At the library, too, I began to read plays — *The Liars* by Henry Arthur Jones; *The Climbers* by Clyde Fitch; James Barrie's *The Admirable Crichton.* I waded through William Archer's forbidding translations of Ibsen, which I thought were written that way because they were saying something different. The climax of this secret life of mine came when I began reading Shaw. After finishing *Man and Superman* I was all but leaping. The mists had risen, the air was clear. I was nobody's joy but my own. I was thirteen.

The San Francisco "fire" occurred in April, 1906. We all held our breath for fear it might move north. Sometime in the following month I got a job as office boy to a firm of well-known lawyers, Peters and Powell. I had to report for work at 8:45 in the morning and began by making copies of the dozens of letters they wrote daily. Carbon paper was not in use then and those letters were put in a large book with a damp cloth on the other side of the page that they fronted. Many pages were laid out in this fashion and then the book was put in a press and I turned the handle down tight for three minutes or so and when I released it the copies were made. The originals were dried, put in envelopes and mailed. That was a chore I disliked intensely. Other duties I took in my stride, such as filing briefs at the courthouse at the top of First Hill — one of the steepest in town and nary a nickel was I given to ride up — serving summonses and numerous other errands. I had a half hour for lunch and was through at 5:30. My wages were five dollars (one gold piece, in those days) paid every Saturday morning. I liked the job because it gave me freedom and I guess I was satisfactory to them for I worked there five summers in a row.

Looking through the Seattle *Post Intelligencer* (*Pee-eye,* we called it) one morning, as I was waiting for those wretched letters to dry, I saw a large ad showing a grinning cat — and it read: THE C A T CAME BACK. — THE CHARLES A. TAYLORS' NEW YORK COMPANY RETURNING TO THE THIRD AVENUE THEATER FOR A SECOND SEASON. It was wonderful to know I would be able to see them soon again. Saturday afternoons I was generally off early so I could attend most of the matinees and on my own cash, with no questions asked. I learned that Ailleen May had signed with a new management and was to be established in a newly built theater (the Lois) to play in opposition to Mr. Taylor's company; her absence resulted in Laurette Taylor taking over some of the leading roles Miss May had played the previous season. For the first time in my life I saw the same part played by two different actresses. Vaguely I had sensed that Laurette Taylor's acting was a great deal more than reading lines or putting paint on her face and trying to look glamorous. Seeing *Stolen by Gypsies* for the second time confirmed my intuition and left me dimly aware of how creative imagination could illumine a part.

"Cholly" Taylor had the happy faculty of taking front-page headlines and turning them into rip-snorting melodramas. The previous year Seattle had been favored with his play *The White Tigress of Japan,* which cashed in on the Russian-Japanese War then raging. *Held for Ransom* told in his inimitable way the story of Ellen M. Stone, a missionary who the year before had been abducted by Macedonian brigands. *Stolen by Gypsies* was a slice of life that dealt with transmigration of the soul. Theosophy, thanks to Annie Besant, was just gaining a toehold in the Northwest;

transmigration of the soul was a profound topic of discourse with the advanced few.

Mr. Taylor's play concerned a cruel Mexican bandit, Yosemite by name, and Mercedes, his beautiful Spanish bride, who flees from him with her only child, a wee papoose of a girl called "Lone Star." How long this flight took her was never stated, but she did it on foot, finally stumbling onto a group of ten-gallon-hat he-miners whose voices were lower than downtown Manhattan and whose hearts were finer than the gold they were seeking. They took her to their hearts. But nemesis, in the shape of her husband Yosemite, caught up with her after three acts when he plunged a knife into her unsuspecting back. Meanwhile the papoose, little Lone Star, who had reached the age of six but was mysteriously ailing despite the care of her Aztec nurse, becomes a miraculous example of transmigration as her dying mother's soul enters her frail body and takes over. The audience didn't see her again until the final act, when there she was — a young woman, the spitting image of her dead mother, the beauteous Mercedes. Miss May had a whale of a time playing both parts the previous summer, and Laurette Taylor fell heir to this toothsome assignment fifteen months later.

As I recall Miss May's entrance down a painted rock runway, her bleached-blond hair was exquisitely marcelled, her make-up was impeccably pink-and-white, her costume of red china silk was jingling with Chinese yen, and her gold sandals were immaculate, a great tribute to the roads over which she had traveled — she obviously had not run, even from her dressing room. Her first request was for a drink of water, of which she took two dainty sips from the miner's dipper that eager hands had rushed to her; and then one of the miners, removing his hat, asked the name of the wee bairn. Miss May, grasping the prop papoose, vocalized thus: "I call her Lone Star because she is the only star" — and left it at that, while the miner wiped away a tear.

Laurette Taylor's performance was as different as chalk from cheese. On her entrance, you saw a dark hand grasp a rock for support as slowly she pulled herself into view. The rocks became real. Her natural blond curls were obscured by dark hair that had been in wind and rain. Her clothes were torn and soiled; her sandals revealed feet that were dirty and bloody. She literally collapsed. Her speech was incoherent. (No dressing-room trek, this.) When she got her drink of water it was as if a thirsty plant was absorbing it and gradually showing signs of life. And when she was asked the name of the child, she looked at the prop she was holding and it became alive. You felt her heart beat faster as she held it close. She transformed that "Lone Star" speech into something that was motherhood and longing and desperation. The actors around her, with their assumed Western accents, were forgotten. We were in the presence of a dimensional person wracked with emotion, her great eyes haunted with the image of what was to be her destiny — her husband and the knife! That moment Laurette Taylor opened my eyes to the facts of acting.

Miraculous changes were taking place in Seattle. The city fathers, who were intent on making our town bigger and better in every way, decided that it would be more navigable if a couple of hills were sluiced away so that the business and shopping districts could expand on level ground. This enterprise was called "the Regrade."

Among the houses that were marked for demolition in the Regrade was the one we lived in, on Beacon Hill, so Father moved us to a district called Fremont — out by Lake Union, with the Green Lake electric cars conveniently running right by our front door. When I enrolled in high school it was at Lincoln High, which was a ten-minute walk from where we lived.

The Lincoln High School was a new building when I first roamed the corridors as a student, trying to look as if I shaved every day. It seemed more formal than grammar school. For one thing, I was addressed as "Mr. McClintic" for the first time in my life. I had stimulating teachers: Mr. Anderson, meticulous and lame, for Latin; Elizabeth Willcox, sharp and snappy, for Algebra; Juliette O'Hearn, her ancient features topped with a glossy, elaborately pompadoured auburn-hued wig, teaching English with a gusto that was not exactly infectious; and Rose Glass, with her red, red hair and a warm smile, for History. Miss Glass was a good history teacher, but she was much more than that. What she might have been, differently placed in life, it is impossible to say. I must hastily add that this is in no way a comment on her present considerable stature. She was the daughter of a Methodist minister, a member of the Epworth League, a young woman, a suffragette sympathizer who saw in emancipation for women something more than the indulgences that were granted the sterner sex. To this day I don't believe she has ever smoked or touched a drop of hard liquor. I remember it used to irk me to see her freeze up at

the mention of someone having a drink or smoking a cigarette, but underneath this patina of what seemed to me then
narrow-mindedness she possessed an extraordinary understanding, sympathy and warmth for young people. She
sensed your barriers, your problems, and without ever being
aware it was happening to you, you found yourself quite
naturally confiding in her, things that had been impossible
to talk over with your parents or even your friends. She
visited my family and talked with eloquent sympathy about
my desire to go on the stage. This impressed them. That
she would attend the theater with me reconciled them somewhat to my going.

The Jamestown Exposition, in the summer of 1907, which
celebrated the founding of Virginia Colony, seemed to draw
Mother and Father closer to each other — bound as they
were by a common longing to be once more in their own
homeland but thwarted by the lack of funds to take the
three of us there "in style," as I heard them say over and
over again, and not as "poor relations." That phrase "poor
relations" I am afraid left me with a faint Freudian bruise —
I had to face it, that was what I was: a poor relation. That
was what I determined not to be. It strengthened my resolve
of not following in the footsteps of my uncles — of not being
accepted at Uncle George's law office, which was Father's
dream, as a gracious act of charity on his part because I was
Brother Ed's son — a poor relation. Not for me! Not ever!
Dad never stopped harping on the time when I would be
ready to take up law. I think, really, he was trying to save
me from what he thought brought misfortune to him, namely
not finishing college.

In my early weeks at high school I found a great friend

in a boy named Harold Harshman, who was blond and Teutonic-looking. We went to see Laurette Taylor together and we were both depressed when her company folded and she left Seattle. Harold held a particular fascination for me, because as a child he had been an actor with the Pollard Lilliputians, a juvenile troupe that originated in Australia and toured the West Coast. At last I knew an actor! He lent a willing ear to my passion for the theater, and told me he had decided to give up acting (I think his experience was of less than a year and sometime before he was ten) as he intended to be a writer instead. We solemnly agreed that he would write plays and I would act in them.

Rose Glass was our confidante in all these plots and plans and dreams we had against the future. She took it as a matter of course that I would be an actor and Harold a writer. She listened to the gripes and hopes of all our group. She was a great friend and pal, and her classroom after school was more like a club than anything else. We went to the theater together often — Rose, Harold and I — standing in line for the rush gallery seats. Later I discovered a fire exit by which I could scramble unnoticed into the peanut gallery, without the bother of paying admission. Harold and I used it exclusively and so it became possible for me to see more of those lustrous stars who up to now had only looked at me from the pages of magazines. Mrs. Fiske was the first two-dollar star I ever saw (two dollars was the top price in those days and no tax). The play was *Leah Kleschna*. It very likely was no great shakes, but compared to the thrillers I had seen at the old Third Avenue Theater it seemed infinitely superior. Laurette Taylor alone remained in a niche by herself. There was no possible way of comparing her with Mrs. Fiske, but there was no doubting the fact that they were both in their own way very special. Grace George was sheer enchantment in *Divorçons*. Mrs. Leslie Carter's redheaded *Zaza* — and, may God forgive her, her redheaded *Dubarry* — left me wondering what the critical huzzas had been about years before. William Faversham I admired enormously in *The Squaw Man*, but the one I was waiting for with bated breath was E. H. Sothern. From all I had read he was the one I thought I would model myself after. I had read certain details of his interpretation of *Hamlet*, such as his sitting by a brazier of coals when he did "to be or not to be." So, accordingly, when I had committed the famous soliloquy to memory, I would recite it to myself — after Father and Mother had gone to bed, leaving me to do my homework at the dining-room table — crouching by our coal-stove, banked for the night. I would do parts of it again and again, in what I thought was barely a whisper, when my dad's angry voice would interrupt my flight into art.

"Guthrie! Who the hell are you talking to?"

"Nobody, Father," was my truthful reply.

"Then what are you mumbling about?"

"I am learning a poem for my English class."

"Then learn it to yourself. You are keeping your mother and me awake."

Thank God I could really let myself go in the woodshed in the afternoons when I did portions of François Villon from Justin Huntly McCarthy's romantic play *If I Were King*, in which Sothern also had made a great success. In the woodshed I disturbed only our neighbors' chickens. I was not sure I was too good, but I didn't want it confirmed by

anyone in the family. I was obsessed with a certainty I had
something — something for the theater — and I would find
that something when I escaped East. Sothern came to Seattle. I spent two dollars to sit down close for his *Hamlet*.
It was a great disillusion. I suppose technically he was fine
and that his readings were scholarly, but he had no inner
fire, no smell of humanity about him. As an actor I never
wanted to see him again. And I didn't.

When the Regrade was finished, Seattle looked so handsome and different that the city decided to give a party.
They called it "The Alaska-Yukon Exposition." Everybody
put his best foot forward that summer of 1909.

Father got a raise in salary and made a first payment towards buying the house we were living in. I mooned over
a girl named Eva Davies, and we used to hold hands while
at the theater when the orchestra played "Love Me to That
Ever-Loving Springtime Melody." Each summer Peters and
Powell continued to employ me as office-boy and occasionally I saw a moment or two of Ailleen May's rehearsal at the
Lois where her successful and lengthy engagement was
drawing to a close. Summer nights I spent mostly at the
Fair Grounds listening to the open-air concerts and wondering if I would ever get away from Seattle. High School that
in the begininng had been stimulating with its Latin, Geometry and Ancient History was beginning to pall. Everything
seemed far away and implacable — graduation — then the
University! Would I be able to hold out? LAURETTE TAYLOR
A STAR — *Seattle Actress Hailed On Broadway* was a head-
line in the local paper. My God, I thought, they have their
nerve. . . . Seattle actress indeed! Seattle never acclaimed

her; never appreciated her magic. Seattle let her starve, while they flocked to the Lois Theater. SEATTLE! If I stay here I will dry up, disintegrate. . . .

I ran to Rose Glass with my gripes.

"Can you tell me what good it will do me in my future life to know the date of the Diet of Worms?" I demanded.

"History is only a road to understanding the things that are happening around us now. It will certainly do you no harm to finish school."

"I don't agree," I argued; "I don't agree at all. I bet you a dollar there isn't one great actor in the world that can do a trigonometry problem or read Virgil in Latin."

"Well," she replied, "I don't think your *not* being able to read Virgil will insure your being a great actor, either."

"That has nothing to do with it. I am wasting my life going to school. I loathe it. I'll rot here. I've got to get away."

"Well," said she, "if you feel that strongly you should speak to your parents. But be sure you are right. You can never get these years back."

"I know it," said I. "That's what's worrying me."

When I tackled Mother and Father on the subject they were flabbergasted at the idea and shocked that Miss Glass proposed my taking it up with them. I was very quiet and firm as I proceeded, and my manner, I think, prompted Mother to suggest: "If you feel you have such talent, son, why don't you find someone in Seattle that knows about such things and let them hear you do something — and they can tell you whether it is worthwhile your going ahead."

"There is no one in Seattle who would know anything about it," I replied rather loudly.

"Don't raise your voice to your mother," shouted my father.

"I am not raising my voice to Mother. It is to the idea," I replied, a good three tones lower.

"The trouble with you, Guthrie," said Dad, "is that you know everything. No one else knows a damn thing, only you. How would you live in New York? Answer me that."

"I'll get along. At least I'll be around people who understand me."

"Understand you?" bellowed my father. "Good God, what have I ever done that I should be cursed with a son like you? I am warning you. If you keep on the way you are going you will end in the gutter, and don't think I will help you then. Oh, no!"

"I wouldn't take anything from you," I started blazing. "I —"

"Son," interrupted my mother, firmly taking hold of me. "Leave the house and don't come back until you can be civil to your father."

Thus ended the interview.

III

East of the Mountains

HAVING vigorously rejected Mother's suggestion that I consult someone in Seattle about my histrionic capabilities, I turned right around and waylaid T. Daniel Frawley on the street as he was leaving a rehearsal at the Lois Theater. Frawley, who was probably the foremost stock director in the country, was then co-starring with Ailleen May. I suggested that he hear me read a soliloquy from *Hamlet*. He gazed at me oddly, as if I reminded him of something unpleasant, and said: "Don't go on the stage, son. I can tell from talking to you that you have nothing to offer."

I was unprepared for this pronouncement. "You can?" I gulped.

"Sure," he replied, as he turned away. "Anyway, you're too skinny."

Plainly there was no help in the neighborhood, so chagrined but not discouraged I resumed my reading of the *Theatre Magazine*. I studied photographs of Mrs. Fiske, Holbrook Blinn, George Arliss and others. If I could only get behind the stillness of a photograph, I might discover what made these celebrities tick! Why were they what they were? If I could only get to know one of them it would help. Perhaps I could. At the Moore Theater David Belasco was presenting Blanche Bates in a drama called *The Fighting Hope.* After her matinee I saw her leave the theater and go into the Washington Hotel next door. She was a handsome, dark-haired woman in her thirties and completely un-actressy in her manner. Miss Bates was with another woman. I followed on their heels. They went directly to a waiting elevator and the door closed, cutting off further view of them. I hurried outside to a nearby drugstore, telephoned the hotel, and when the operator answered I asked to speak to Miss Blanche Bates. "Who wants to speak to Miss Bates, please?"

"Mr. George of the Seattle *Daily Times,*" said I. The call was switched to Miss Bates's room and a woman's voice, not Miss Bates's asked what I wanted. "An interview," I replied.

After a brief pause I was told to come to the theater that night during the intermission between the second and third acts. I got hold of Harold and asked him to stand by in case I was detected and got in trouble. At the appointed time, armed with a notebook and pencil (the authentic reportorial touch I thought), I arrived not without apprehension at the stage door. I was expected and Miss Bates's colored maid took me directly to her dressing room. In a smart afternoon dress, she was seated at her dressing table with a large mirror above it framed with gleaming electric light bulbs. She was the first actress I ever saw close to in full make-up. In her low vibrant voice she asked me to be seated. Her keen, shining goodness made me feel a louse — which I was — in the perpetration of this hoax. The interview was a shambles.

"Do you like Seattle?" was my stumbling beginning.

"Not the climate," she replied.

"Has Mr. Belasco ever thought of presenting you in one of Ibsen's plays?"

"Definitely no," said she and so on until the next act was called. I left not exactly elated by my reportorial skill, but acutely impressed by Miss Bates. It might be worth trying again.

Next time I descended on Minnie Maddern Fiske. She received me in the mezzanine of the Washington Hotel. Mrs. Fiske was oversensitive about her face and took refuge by hiding it behind more veils than Salome used in her famous dance. And from behind this barricade she greeted me. With no prompting she launched into her favorite topic — the crusade against vivisection. I am afraid I missed much of her eloquence on behalf of our canine friends as I was more engrossed by her eyes burning through her veils like X rays and her low voice and jerky, rapid speech. When the meeting was over and I was out on Second Avenue, a little unsteady from the impact of her personality and the force of her conviction, I knew these indulgences were getting me nowhere. I had been face to face with the real thing (no photographs) but the talks gave me no real clue — they didn't lessen the distance I had to travel.

Sometimes at night I would walk about in the more opulent residential districts of Minor Hill or Capitol Hill. The houses there seemed to exude the kind of success my family wanted for me. Their lights would be on, the plate-glass windows shining, no shades or curtains drawn; there was a similarity about all of them — parlor, library, dining room, big downstairs hall . . . all well ordered. In one house they would be playing a game of whist . . . in another the father was reading the evening paper . . . the mother was at her embroidery and, while Junior was studying, Sister was practicing Rubenstein's "Melody in F" on the upright piano in the parlor. House after house was the same: all anchored . . . frozen in security. I could see all their futures. The son would go into the father's business, Sister would get married, both would have houses like this. . . . And the vista went on and on. Everyone was a duplicate. Everyone an automaton. However wrong, this was my idea of them and it was against this that I rebelled. I was stubborn, self-centered and cared for nothing in the world but the theater and getting away from home. Though I didn't realize it, my moroseness was even having an effect on Father. Perhaps he was beginning to realize the truth of the old saying "You can lead a horse to water but you can't make him drink."

Then the miracle happened. A Mrs. Wilkins arrived in Seattle to live. Mrs. Wilkins came from Roanoke, Virginia, and had known my father when he was in college. There was general rejoicing at our house and, when they had exhausted the Old South with its sisters and its cousins and its aunts, Mrs. W., whose roving eye had appraised everything else in our modest domicile, lighted on me and asked what I was going to do when I finished school. I replied that I wanted to be an actor. She seemed undismayed and asked where I was going to study, and without waiting for a reply she went on to say that "Bessie" had gone to the American Academy of Dramatic Arts and had a very successful career and was a star when she married "Jim" and retired.

"That's a really wonderful school!" she concluded.

And when Mother, who did not come from Roanoke, cautiously inquired as to the identity of Bessie and Jim it turned out that Bessie was Mrs. Wilkins's sister, Elizabeth Tyree, who was indeed a star when she retired from the stage in 1902 to marry James Metcalfe, the well-known critic of the old *Life* magazine. All of this made an impression on Father — that an old friend's sister had risked the whirlpool and came out whole.

That week Father asked me to write the Academy for a catalogue. I had seen their ads in *Theatre* but never in my wildest dreams had I entertained the idea of my going there. The catalogue arrived. It was very handsome and impressive. The family pored over it. They reasoned that if I must enter an illegitimate profession I should do it legitimately. It might be the right way, but first there was the question of money. It was expensive — two terms, Junior and Senior, four hundred dollars each, plus my living expenses in New York. I didn't think they could afford it and I could see they had misgivings. Then one day Father asked quietly if I really thought I could pass the entrance examination for the Academy. According to the catalogue, this would consist of a series of questions to determine my fitness for a career in the theater, and, in addition, two recitations, one classical, the other modern. Without hesitation I answered yes. He then told me I could go. I could not believe my ears. Once they made up their minds, both my parents faced the decision with a Spartan stoicism. I know, now, it entailed every kind of economy on their part, this sending me to a school three thousand miles away to prepare for a career of which they heartily disapproved.

The tension on the home front was eased. I worked like the devil at Peters and Powell in the daytime (saved every penny too) and my hours away from there were spent in selecting, memorizing and practicing classical and modern parts for that all-important Academy examination. I was elated when Rose told me she was going to spend the following winter in New York, taking her master's degree at Columbia University. She hoped to leave in early summer to visit her younger sister, Mabel, who had married a former principal of a Seattle school, John A. Kingsbury. John at that time was Commissioner of Charities in New York City, on the staff of Mayor Mitchell.

When September 1910 rolled along I was living in anticipation of what lay ahead. I bought a new suit and overcoat and a trunk. Women friends of Mother would call and commiserate, "How can you bear to let him go, Mrs. Mac? — your only child, too." And they would end up by having a good cry. In early October, when my departure was imminent, I wrote Rose in New York telling her the time of my arrival, hoping she would meet me — and then began to count the days until I would leave.

I left Seattle from King Street Station. My father and Harold Harshman saw me off. Mother did not go to the station. She was quietly weeping. I can see her now, waving good-by to me from our parlor window as I was waiting to board the Green Lake car which would take me downtown. My father's face was set. He talked hardly at all. Once on the train he gave the porter a two-and-a-half dollar gold piece and asked him to take good care of me, as this was my first journey in a sleeping car. I wished he hadn't said that. It made me feel like a little boy. Then he told me to tip the porter again an extra dollar when I left the train at Chicago. He cautioned me to be a good boy — work hard — and write home every week. Then he shook my hand and abruptly left. Except for thrashings, that was the first time my father ever touched me. I felt rather odd for a moment.

But the train started moving and I became totally absorbed in myself. It was I — me — myself who was aboard this express, which was taking me east of the mountains and on to New York. Those trains that I had watched from my bedroom window on Beacon Hill, pulling out for points East — I was at last on one of them. Only it was morning, not evening; and nobody was watching this one go with any longing, I thought. I felt for the ninety dollars in gold hidden away in a chamois bag which my mother had sewn on the inside of my flannel undershirt. I looked at the small change and two five-dollar gold pieces in my pants pockets. I was on my way at last.

There were three types of travel in those days west of Chicago — Pullman, Tourist and Day Coach. You could travel Tourist Class on a Day Coach ticket plus the extra you paid for your berth. Tourist passengers were allowed no Pullman Class privileges, that is they could not use the diner or the observation car. Many that were going on the journey from Seattle to Chicago would bring their lunches with them: cold ham or chicken and potato salad — and brew their own coffee or tea on the stove in the car — which also furnished tin cups and plates, coffee pots, and so on. As Tourist was my class, Mother had fixed me a sumptuous lunch, the principal item of which was Southern fried chicken — and no one could do it better.

We arrived in Chicago on a Sunday and I changed stations in a horse-drawn Parmelee bus. The day was dark and overcast, and as I looked out of the window of the bus at the deserted, drab, endless vistas of brick and stone, I suddenly became panicky. I grew scared — I don't know why — but I bucked myself up thinking of New York. That would be different. The next day I spent at Niagara Falls — had my picture taken at the Rapids and sent it home. Then began the final twelve hours of my pilgrimage. There were no sleeping-car accommodations for people traveling Tourist Class east of Chicago, so I sat up in a day coach the final night of my journey. New York, I was convinced would be real cold in late October and I, accordingly, dressed for it. I made for the two-by-four men's toilet and was so busy washing, brushing and dressing for winter that I failed to see those sordid dwellings that can still be seen from the New York Central's approach to Manhattan. My 117 pounds was already insured against draft by long flannel underwear. Now as an extra precaution I put on a turtleneck gray sweater over my outer shirt and then, donning my brand-new overcoat with a velvet collar, I stepped off the coach, suitcase in hand — to find myself sweltering in one of the hottest Indian Summer days I have ever experienced.

All the early morning locals from Bedford Village, New Rochelle, Harmon and points adjacent were disgorging their passengers — white-collar workers who were scurrying to the nearest exit, falling over and cursing me for being in their way every time I rested that wretched suitcase, which was getting heavier by the minute.

No sight of Rose Glass anywhere! I had mailed the letter advising her of the time and place of my arrival. But there wasn't a redhead in the station that morning. . . . The nightmarish aspect of my arrival was partly due to the fact that in 1910 the Grand Central Terminal was not the noble reception room to a great city that it is today. It was under construction and was a great mass of scaffolding and temporary exits and entrances. Finally, in a moment that bordered on intelligence, I resorted to the telephone, and the operator, when I told her the address of John Kingsbury, explained to me that Yonkers was not a part of Manhattan, then rang their number and Rose answered. The mistake had been mine. I had addressed my letter wrongly. And now, without much urging, I found myself on a train again — sweating it out for Yonkers.

The Kingsburys, Mabel and John, were hospitality itself! I bathed — ate — divested myself of all surplus apparel — and visited. Since she was taking her master's degree at Columbia, Rose had decided to live in the neighborhood of the University around 116th Street and Morningside Drive, and she thought it might be nice for me to live nearby, also probably cheaper. We arranged a meeting for the next day and John took me into Manhattan after dinner. Looking west from Fourth Avenue and 23rd Street, as we left the subway, I saw the Flatiron Building for the first time. . . . I had seen many pictures of it. Now I knew I was in New York!

I spent my first night in New York at the Columbia University Club, at that time on the south side of Gramercy Park adjoining the Players', where seventeen years before Edwin Booth had died. John Kingsbury put me up. After he had left me I ventured forth, a little cautiously I'm afraid, to the Flatiron Building. This I knew was the intersection of Broadway and Fifth Avenue. And Broadway I couldn't wait to see.

It was around ten o'clock at night. Fifth Avenue was dim and well-mannered, while Broadway was gay and twinkling

— the Great White Way in fact! I walked slowly up the famous street. As I passed the old Fifth Avenue Hotel, I noticed to my right across the park the lovely illuminated figure of Diana atop the building of Madison Square Garden; I remembered that it was there on the roof garden that Stanford White, the architect, met his death in 1906 from a revolver shot fired by a demented young millionaire from Pittsburgh.

At 28th Street was the Keith & Proctor's Vaudeville House and from there on — to me — I was treading a magic carpet. I passed Weber and Field's famous Music Hall; Daly's Theater, where Ada Rehan, the toast of two continents in the '80's, once reigned; the Bijou; Lester Wallack's; the Herald Square Theater where Marie Dressler was appearing in *Tillie's Nightmare;* Harrigan and Hart's Garrick on 35th Street (which was to be the birthplace of the Theater Guild); the Knickerbocker; and at 39th Street a great Moorish edifice, the Casino, dedicated to light opera; I sauntered over towards Sixth Avenue on 39th to see the charming new Maxine Elliott Theater, where the beautiful lady herself was then appearing; and next door to it I found Nazimova's 39th Street Theater.

Then back on Broadway I came to that aristocrat of all New York theaters, Charles Frohman's Empire, where the one and only John Drew was playing in Somerset Maugham's comedy, *Smith.* Its spacious lobby was brilliantly lit. I ventured in on the red velvet strip of carpet that began as you stepped from the sidewalk and went beyond the ticket-taker's enclosure at the entrance to the inner lobby. On the left was the box office, with its substantial highly polished brass rail that automatically herded the patrons into a sem-

blance of order as they clamored for seats. It was closed.
Just beyond it was the alcove with its red leather seat above
which was a painting of Margaret Anglin, and facing her on
the opposite wall were glamorous pictures of Maude Adams,
Ethel Barrymore, Billie Burke, John Drew, William Gillette,
all of whom were from the top drawer of Mr. Frohman's
collection of stars. I walked with a feeling of reverence. This
was the real thing.

At Times Square I stopped. I gazed up and beyond the
Astor Hotel at the great electric sign high above a building
with its chariot horses galloping right at me. And 42nd
Street had some beckoning lights too; looking through the
windows of the Knickerbocker Hotel on the southeast corner
I thought there couldn't be another such luxurious hotel in
the world. Then I started back down Broadway towards
Gramercy Park. Many of the plays were just over, and the
audiences coming out were peppered with gentlemen in
white ties and tails popping open their opera hats, escorting
bejeweled ladies in chinchilla and ermine. The carriages
waiting for them were to me the acme of elegance, the
horses shining; and swanky motor cars were there too, the
drivers and chauffeurs all in livery, while lesser folk were
being solicited by hansom cab drivers' "Hansom, lady?" —
thereby shaming the helpless males into taking one. All very
different from Seattle! New York hadn't let me down.

I slept soundly on the satisfaction of having taken the
first big step and was awakened in the morning with Rose
on the telephone, asking me to meet her at Columbia and
giving me directions of how to get there by subway. Before
going to the subway I went again by the Flatiron Building
to look up Broadway in daylight. It was very different —

like a house after all the company has gone. I tensed up, and my journey to Columbia University by subway dampened my spirits still further as I breathed the stale air, took in the dirty cars — and contrasted the passengers with the theater crowds of the night before. I was surprised to feel a twinge of homesickness. These daylight people of Manhattan were pale and anemic when compared with those of Seattle.

Rose and I spent a long, strenuous day of looking at small, unattractive rooms shown by dreary, untidy women before we entered 403 West 115th Street to inquire for Mrs. Heinsohn, who had two rooms for rent in her ground-floor apartment. Mrs. Heinsohn turned out to be a dark, attractive woman with a Southern accent and a winning smile. The effect of her personality was such that though her rooms were small and on a court they seemed large and sunny. We took them immediately. Three dollars a week apiece! I moved in that night. My room was next to the parlor where Mrs. Heinsohn and her husband slept on a sofa that turned into a bed at night, while Rose's room was down the hall.

The next day in my Sunday best, I presented myself at the American Academy of Dramatic Arts, then located above Carnegie Hall, to take my entrance examination. Carnegie Hall! The mecca of all music lovers then . . . the mecca of all music lovers now. The memories the mere mention of its name awakens! Toscanini . . . Kreisler . . . Sembrich . . . Flagstad . . . and old Gustav Mahler, who conducted the Philharmonic when I first attended a concert there. In the building above it were the various studios on different floors that served as classrooms for this dispensary of dramatic art that I was hoping to attend, also many studios used by singing teachers. My first impression on entering the building was one of discordant sound . . . like the inside of a zoo. Down the caged elevator shaft came the frantic efforts of a score or more sopranos, bassos, contraltos, and tenors limbering up or in pursuit of an elusive note.

Franklin Sargent, the head of the school, received me in his roomy office. He was a charming, distinguished elderly man, slightly stooped, with a whispering voice that sounded as if he were talking from beyond the pale. He asked if I was ready to do my examination pieces, and taut and apprehensive I began: "Once more unto the breach, dear friends . . ." from *Henry V* and followed it with a bit of John Tanner from *Man and Superman*. When I finished Mr. Sargent congratulated me, sent for Emil Diestel, the treasurer, and told him that in me the school had extraordinary material. It was music to my ears. I was being appreciated at last. . . . It never occurred to me, as I was handing over my tuition fee — a draft for four hundred dollars — that, for that amount, they would have taken me had I been crosseyed, harelipped and spavined. You see, I had not yet seen the Junior Class!

IV

Dramatic School

THE FIRST day of dramatic school found my knees wobbling and my insides turning over. All the incoming students and the faculty were herded into a largish room, where we sat on folding chairs, gilt chairs, and falling-apart upholstered ones, listening to Mr. Sargent's long and rather pointless speech while our eyes traveled around the class appraising each other. It would be difficult to say which depressed me more, the students or the faculty. The class was, to my eye, a conglomeration of misfits, myself included, from all parts of the States and Canada, I being the only refugee from the Evergreen State. I suppose what was really troubling me was that I expected these people to be different — theater material had to be! But they were not. They were just like what I had left behind at Lincoln High. Their ages were varied, from myself who was one of the youngest to some of the girls who seemed depressingly old — over thirty; and out of this group of a half hundred or more the possibility that any of them could act, or *ever* would, seemed to me as remote as the possibility of my being an offspring of Edwin Booth. And then suddenly the hideous thought struck me that all of these students I was presuming to pass judgment upon had all been, like me, examined and questioned by Mr.

Sargent! They had read for him and they too, had passed! I was shaken for a moment.

As Mr. Sargent's tired voice continued droning out his speech I turned my eyes from the students to the faculty. Help! As grim a looking bunch as I had ever seen. The women seemed dowdy, in their shirtwaists and skirts, looking not unlike Mrs. Pusey or Miss Goodspeed who had taught me in grammar school. The men with two exceptions, Edgar Hart and Charles Jehlinger, could have worked with my father in the Assay office. Mr. Hart suggested more a helper at a bar, while Mr. Jehlinger was intense, dark, with burning eyes, and dilating pupils. He, who I learned later was the big noise there — and that was true in more ways than one — tiptoed out before our welcome speech was over. When Mr. Sargent sat down we were divided into groups and given a schedule as to when and where we would assemble for instructions in dramatic readings — pantomime — voice — action — make-up — and so on.

Mrs. Carter (not Leslie) was to coach us in dramatic readings. I was her first victim. She asked me if I had anything I could do and I very confidently burst into "Once more unto the breach, dear friends . . ." When, exhausted and breathless, I finished, she smiled sweetly and proceeded to tell me and the class how badly I had done it, pointing out my many errors which they must never commit and which she hoped in time to correct in me. She was more than likely right — but inasmuch as that was the very recitation which prompted Mr. Sargent to tell Diestel I was extraordinary material, I found myself unable to make two and two add up to four.

✻　　✻　　✻

Mme. Alberti gave us pantomime and action. She was a New Englander, despite her name, and a sympathetic motherly soul with a gentle voice. Not then nor to this day have I been able to suggest by pantomime whether it was an orange, a lemon or an apple I was peeling nor has anyone else been able to do it for me. But hours were spent trying to master this elusive feat. We had exercises to make our bodies more flexible. We learned that in a drawing room, for instance, no gentleman stood in the presence of ladies with his legs straight or far apart; always, the right knee was slightly bent. I can't say that knowledge has helped me socially. Maybe I don't bend my knee right! We were told that in a restaurant one did not speak to the waiters. I have sometimes found it very difficult to get the waiters to speak to me. We were sent to the highways and byways to observe any character that might intrigue us and then present said character in pantomime before the class. Dillon Deasy took the prize one day by wielding the baton over an orchestra. Some of the more enthusiastic girls swore that they knew what he was conducting! "Life study," that was called.

Edgar Hart told us where to buy make-up boxes and grease paint. A couple of forgotten faces took care of our fencing and dancing, and Mr. Putnam, our voice teacher, started us working on "resonances."

As I rubbed shoulders with the class during the months to follow, I found that a lot of us were genuinely eager to go on the stage. A few were just plain duds and some of the older women were taking the course with the intention of teaching dramatics later. As the weeks passed it was obvious that one young fellow was going to be a very good actor. His name was Minor Watson — and he did go on to success. He was tall, good-looking, and had a nice voice.

I did not mix with the students much that Junior term, partly because I was standoffish and partly because I was weighed down with the idea they were "better off" than I was, and I was sensitive about having to count my pennies. My budget was ten dollars a week and I managed. I had my breakfast and most of my dinners in the restaurant on the campus at Columbia University with Rose and when anyone went to the theater with me it was usually she. Mrs. Heinsohn's cordiality took some of the strangeness out of my rented room. Whenever I had a meal downtown (in the theater district, that is) I went to a Child's restaurant, which was cheap and in those days not fancy. I loved their baked apples and longed to have cream with them, but that I had to deny myself as it was five cents extra. I had quite a shock early in my stay in New York when the cashier at a Child's pushed back at me the ten-dollar gold piece I had given him to pay my lunch check, with a suspicious "What's that?" When I answered, "Ten dollars," he summoned the manager, who listened wide-eyed while I told him gold passed for money out West.

Despite the disillusionment and disappointment of those first few weeks, I bolstered my morale by looking at the pictures of some of the academy's distinguished alumni — Grace George, Grant Mitchell, Jane Cowl — which adorned the walls of all the classrooms, and I made up my mind to try to acquire whatever they had acquired from their attendance there. I was painfully conscious, too, that my parents had made a great sacrifice to send me there and it was up to me to prove myself.

But why was nothing ever right — not even at the Academy? Looking back I think I must have been a precocious horror; but at last self-preservation came to my rescue and cut me down to the realization that I had to adjust myself to the fact that I *was* in NEW YORK, at last — that any romantic illusions I had about it or myself out in Seattle were just that, and no more; and that at this point it wasn't a question of the theater or New York conforming to any preconceived notion of mine, but whether I could find my solution in being a part of both. This solution was not immediate nor was it easy. All of my life no one has been more aware of my own shortcomings than myself and, odd as it may appear, few have been as conscious of my good points. When the first glimmer of this reasoning had restored my equilibrium I embraced what New York had to offer with enthusiasm and was solidly sustained during that first year by Rose Glass, who ironed me out many a time in my gripes about the school.

In the Family Circle of the Metropolitan Opera House I listened to Wagner, Puccini, Bizet or Gounod, with such interpreters as Fremstadt, Farrar, Destinn, Scotti, and Caruso; and, when she was on tour, Mary Garden sang there with the Chicago Opera Company on Tuesday nights in *Thaïs* and *Louise*. I saw Pavlova dance for the first time that year, and a little bit later Isadora Duncan — the pioneer and high-priestess of all modern dance, I suppose. Some of the performances are a far echo in my memory: Farrar's beauty — Fremstadt's *Kundry* — Caruso's voice — Garden's *Louise* — Pavlova's "Dying Swan" — Isadora's interpretation of "The Blue Danube." I am not a balletomane, but today when I see Martha Graham dancing "Letter to the World" I know she has a secret I should like to share.

During that autumn Mme. Sarah Bernhardt had a short season at the Globe Theater. This was some five years before she had the operation that removed her right leg, and it was the last time she ever played plays in their entirety in this country. The school was given complimentary tickets in the front part of the first balcony, and we saw on various nights *Adrienne Lecouvreur, Camille,* and *La Samaritaine;* the latter was rather daring in view of the fact that Jesus — with his back to the audience — appeared on the stage during the first act.

On the night Rose and I saw Sarah's matchless performance of *Marguerite Gautier* we waited in the drizzle, with many others, to see her come out of the stage door. After a half-hour or so she appeared, heavily made up, her henna hair frizzled under a toque with aigrettes that spiraled. She was enveloped in a voluminous chinchilla coat and leaning on the arm of her leading man, Lou Tellegen. She smiled and murmured something indistinguishable to the worshipers on the sidewalk as she was helped into her car and drove away. That was the first of the only three times I waited at a stage door in New York, and each time it was to see the "Divine Sarah."

When next she played she was in vaudeville at the Palace (two a day and her age just under seventy). At her first matinee, when she entered as Phèdre, Laurette Taylor, Jane Cowl and Marguerite Clarke were her honorary handmaidens. At that time each of these lovely young women were stars in their own right, and as a gesture to Bernhardt, who was making her debut in vaudeville, chose to do this. Whatever one expected of these oncoming pillars of the American theater, they turned out to be as wooden a threesome of supers as ever hovered around a great star. Sarah, whose costumes at all times were to say the least individual, as Phèdre wore a dress of what appeared to be chiffon. It was form-clinging and weighted with embroidery of rhinestones, turquoise, brilliants of all kinds — in fact everything was on it but cowbells. Her sleeves were skin tight over her thin arms, and made of the same material as her dress with panels of material fastened from shoulder to wrists; and when she raised her arms in an emotional gesture these winglike sleeves swept the floor with the aid of their weights, also of brilliants and rhinestones. At the end of one of her great speeches she opened her arms wide with passionate fury, and as the audience acclaimed her in an ovation she kept her pose; it was fascinating to watch our young American beauties trying to disentangle themselves from the suffocation of her costume as it was tangled around them.

In the autumn of 1916 Mme. Bernhardt was sufficiently recovered from the amputation of her right leg to journey once again to America for a season that was really her final "Farewell." Her opening night at the Empire Theater was an electric occasion. The United States was not yet in the war that England and France had been waging for two bloody years against Germany. Sarah had become a symbol of France. Although she had appeared in practically every other part of the world, she had never played in Germany after the Franco-Prussian War of 1870. It is reported that when asked by the Kaiser what inducement would persuade her to, she replied, "Alsace and Lorraine!"

The French Ambassador came up from Washington to

attend, and every stellar personality of the artistic, politi-
cal and social world that was able to crowded the theater
that night. She played three acts from different plays she
had made famous. When the curtain rose on her as Cleopatra in the last act of Sardou's play, she was breathtaking
to see. Her famous smile acknowledged the thunderous
never-ending applause and then, as the ovation subsided,
with the vitality of a young woman she suddenly rose on
her one leg, unaided, with arms uplifted, as an ultimate gesture of thanks for her reception — whereupon everyone in
the theater from the last row in the gallery to the front of
the orchestra stood up too. When she sat down we sat down
and the performance began.

At the end of the act there were countless curtain calls,
a carload of flowers was passed over the footlights, and
from out of the wings Rose Coghlan appeared in a pow-
dered wig, wearing what might have been the costume she
wore when she made her debut at Wallack's Theater in
1882 as Lady Teazle, and launched into one of the longest
speeches I ever heard, welcoming Sarah back on behalf of
the American actors. From offstage, as Miss Coghlan's
speech droned on, you could hear frantic warnings of "hurry
up" as Sarah stood leaning heavily on two handmaidens
through it all. When Miss Coghlan finished she reached into
what looked like the placket of her dress and pulled out an
ordinary laurel wreath, which she presented to Mme. Bernhardt as the curtain, along with the wreath, fell and Sarah
leaned precariously over to kiss her.

I am sure the audience did not know that that wreath was
a substitute for one that a great jeweler was making with
gold and platinum leaves, each leaf being engraved with

the name of a part she had made famous. Well, it seems when the wreath made its tardy appearance some ten days later, during a rainy Wednesday matinee, it was brought into Sarah's dressing room at the Empire with its windows facing onto 40th Street; the embossed case was opened and the resplendent wreath, I hope, was being admired when a knock on the door admitted a smartly uniformed man from the jeweler who said he had been told not to leave until the wreath had been paid for. Bernhardt, whose fiery temper was the talk of two hemispheres, is said to have reached a new high as she hopped on her one leg to the window, opened it, and imperiously flung the offending tribute into the drizzle and hurly-burly of 40th Street. There was great excitement outside as the immaculate messenger, unmindful of mud, endeavored to uncover the wreath. While inside the diplomacy of everyone attached to "Madame" was working overtime in an effort to appease her into continuing the performance. That there had been a mistake was obvious. I never knew what became of the wreath.

When the final curtain was rung down on that opening night with the Divine Sarah receiving another ovation and another carload of flowers she must have been all but dead. I, along with a hundred or more, waited outside the Empire stage door on 40th Street to see her come out. We watched the world and his wife who had gone backstage to pay homage to her leave, and at two in the morning this seventy-two-year-old woman — still heavily made up, still swathed in furs, still turning on the famous smile, and in a hat that would have made Gaby Deslys jealous — was carried in a sedan chair to her waiting automobile and, with the jauntiness of a young woman, pulled herself into the car, while the crowd on the sidewalk cheered *"Vive Sarah!"* *"Vive la France!"* And a few were just plain weeping. Her maid and companion clambered in beside her and as the machine pulled away she turned and waved to us. It seems a pity that this generation should have to judge her from those brutal films that are shown in the Museum of Modern Art. Read Arthur Symons's *Plays, Acting and Music,* or Max Beerbohm's *Around Theatre,* if you would know her true greatness — for great she was; one needed no knowledge of French to appreciate that fact.

Language was no barrier, either, in December 1910, when I wandered downtown to Irving Place to witness the acting of the distinguished German, Von Possart, and shortly after went even further downtown to see the great Yiddish actress, Mme. Kenny Lipzin, at her own theater on the Bowery, where her emotional genius reduced her uninhibited audience to loud sobs.

Far away from the Bowery and the Third Avenue El, far uptown at 63rd Street on Central Park West, facing the park, was one of the most beautiful theaters I have ever been in any time, anywhere: The New Theater — at that moment teetering on the edge of disaster with its second season of repertory. It was there I saw Winthrop Ames's sensitive and lovely production of Maeterlinck's *The Blue Bird.* As I was strolling through its spacious foyers, lost in wonder at the magnificence of it all, I could not know that the distinguished head of the theater, Mr. Ames, rebellious at certain impracticalities which this new house presented, was already dreaming of the exquisite Little Theater which he planned, built and opened in the spring of 1912. Nor did any psychic sense reveal to me the decisive part that Mr. Ames was to play in my life in the theater.

I thought Riverside Drive at 116th must be the handsomest thoroughfare in the world. Once or twice I grew extravagant and rode on top of the bus all the way down to Washington Square. It cost ten cents. Most of my moving about was on the subway (five cents). I used to marvel at getting on at 116th Street and off at 59th — to think that all this great city was above us, and we were seeing none of it!

Broadway at night was my elixir. Its theaters extended farther up and downtown than they do today — from the Colonial at 63rd Street just above Columbus Circle to Keith and Proctor's on 27th Street, both first-class vaudeville houses standing as sentinels to the sacred alley of "the legit." I never tired of walking along it in the evening, gazing at its myriads of lights, being elbowed and jostled by the slow-moving crowds, listening to the popular tunes of the day being pounded out by the pianists in the sheet-music stands, tinkling pianos playing Victor Herbert's "I'm Falling in Love with Someone" against "Day Dreams" from *The Spring Maid* across the way. And farther along you would hear the *Madame Sherry* tunes. To cross the threshold of one of Broadway's stage doors as an actor was the ambition of all of us.

I was the only one of the class who took special pride in the announcement that at the Lyceum Laurette Taylor was soon to appear with Charles Cherry in *The Seven Sisters*. She had made the grade all right, from the humble, made-over church where she had last acted in Seattle — she had, in a remarkably short time, and in a series of quite ordinary parts, risen to be a star. From the front row of the second balcony (in New York, thank God, reserved) I saw her in *Seven Sisters*. She was radiant and dominated the play, although she was what is known in the profession as a "supporting player" to Charles Cherry. I swelled with pride as if she were my childhood chum at the warmth with which she was received by the New York public.

In her entire life in the theater Laurette Taylor appeared in only four plays of any distinction. They were Philip Barry's *In a Garden,* Sutton Vane's *Outward Bound,* J. M. Barrie's *Alice-Sit-by-the-Fire* and *The Glass Menagerie* by Tennessee Williams. But in the English-speaking world I am sure she will be remembered as one of the finest artists this century has produced. Her beginning was vaudeville, where as a child she was billed as "La Belle Laurette," doing imitations which were much in vogue then. Her training was cheap melodramatic stock. Her teachers, audiences. The great repertory houses of Europe produced no better. To her, acting was not a passion or a malady, but a joy.

Despite my bellyaching and general dissatisfaction about the academy I worked earnestly and hard, lapping up every morsel that was dispensed there. I wished I could have been in the class ahead of me, because when I saw those Seniors doing their plays at the Little Carnegie and later for special matinees at the Empire they seemed practically professionals. But there was nothing I could do about that. Meanwhile, as the trees were budding again in Central Park, we of the Junior Class, with capacious and shiny make-up boxes filled with sticks of grease paint and ropes and ropes of crepe hair, were making up at class, learning the formulas of make-ups not one of us would ever use again. In the voice section we would drown out the singers in the building with our practicing of nasal and lip resonances. With Mme. Alberti we were practicing a collapse à la Delsarte. I was fascinated when she solemnly told me that when one is dead the thumb is inert in the palm of the hand. I've never checked on it so I don't know if it is true. As for dramatic readings, we were worrying over a tremolo finish to big speeches that Mrs. Carter called "final stress" — which God forbid I should even try to remember. We were progressing now towards rehearsals of scenes from famous old plays which were to serve as examinations to determine our fitness to be a part of the Senior group of the following winter. It did not seem possible to me that I would not pass, as I could not believe I knew less than when I enrolled there six months before. And I was right. We did our scenes for examination at the Little Carnegie with make-up, dress and scenery before an invited audience. Two days after, I was declared eligible to be a Senior. There were several students that quite understandably were refused. One dull earnest young woman, who at a final rehearsal seemed to have no acquaintance at all with the lines she was supposed to speak, when asked by Mr. Sargent why she didn't know them replied with virtuous reproach, "I do know them, Mr. Sargent, I just don't know where they come." (I must say for the school that they *had* told us what a cue was.) Minor Watson, lucky fellow, got a small part with Belasco's production of *Nobody's Widow* starring Blanche Bates and did not stay for the Senior year. I envied him.

New York was beautiful that spring — the sun shone and

the world seemed full of promise. When I wrote to my parents that I had been asked to return for the Senior year, Father replied that he would arrange it and sent me the money for a round trip home. My mother wanted to see me, he said. All of us embryonic Seniors thought the following year would do the trick. We had come to know the talents of the class which had just graduated. It was comforting to think that maybe they had been as awkward and ill-at-ease as we had been. And the grapevine was buzzing with rumors of their various engagements in the professional theater.

V

Keeping in Touch

In Seattle that summer I was something of a curiosity. The mail carrier questioned me about the elevated railways in New York and was impressed when I told him I had sometimes ridden on them. Mrs. Albee, our sourpuss from next door, after looking me over carefully, said to Mother — who was just happy I was home again — that she couldn't see what good being at school in New York had done, as she noticed no change in me at all. Harold was disappointed to learn that I had only seen Rector's from the outside.

Father thought it "funny" the academy hadn't written him of my "promise" or issued any kind of report card. He asked me to "do something" for him and when I obliged with Hamlet's "Speak the speech I pray you . . . ," which I had studied with Mrs. Carter, he was singularly unimpressed. He thought my pronunciation was affected and hard to understand. In the quiz he conducted as to what I had or had not learned at school, my one tangible accomplishment turned out to be those damned make-up formulas we were given at Edgar Hart's classes. That impressed him! And night after night he would invite various friends in, and ask — Ask? . . . No, *bully* me into making up for them.

Chinese . . . Hobo . . . Jewish . . . Italian . . . Irish . . .
And the friends, poor devils, would sit there baffled, half-
heartedly, half-politely approving, probably in their heart of
hearts thinking it was a life of crime I was readying myself
for, and these were my various disguises. My humiliation,
thank God, was lost behind grease paint!

I found myself purring with exhilaration at being back in
New York in September. Even the subway smelled good.
No homesickness this time! Mrs. Heinsohn was glad to see
me. She had visited her home in Texas during the summer
and one evening, she told me, in the midst of a family argument she had gone into a trance, to the amazement of her
relatives to say nothing of herself; when she came out of it,
she knew the whereabouts of a document which had disappeared and which when found resulted in their all getting some money. She was modest about it, but impressed.
Nothing like this had ever happened to her before. So was I
impressed.

Mrs. Heinsohn had also discovered that she had the power
of levitation and nightly, after she had finished her dinner
dishes, when in my room I was learning a part or doing
some of Mme. Alberti's exercises to make my body limber,
I could hear Mrs. Heinsohn at the dining-room table endeavoring to get messages from the spirit world. She had
a relative with an overpowering Southern accent, Cousin
Lulu by name, who was constantly there, baiting the table
with questions; and Mrs. Heinsohn, anxious to help her out,
was exhorting the table to answer. "Tip once for NO and three
times for YES," she would coo. And then you would hear the

table resoundingly boom once on the bare floor of the dining room, and Cousin Lulu, never satisfied, would be back
with another question.

Across the hall from me Mrs. Heinsohn's two sons, students at high school, were slugging away at Latin and
Geometry, and I could hear them mumbling to themselves
while this was going on. "Is Mama nutty? Three times for
YES!" I am sure the fact that her apartment was on the
ground floor made possible the continuance of these sorties
in search of communicative spirits. The séances, if one could
call them that— for the lights were never out and the sole
means of contact with the "other world" was the tipping of
the dining-room table — these séances were strictly a family affair. Cousin Lulu was the most avid. She would be in
several times a week and occasionally another more important relative, Cousin Mercedes, who had been on the stage
and afterwards married and lived in Russia for a number of
years, would drop in to seek information.

One day in early October, as I was going to school, I ran
across Linnie Love in front of Carnegie Hall on 57th Street.
Linnie was a sunny soul, about my age, maybe a year older,
who was constantly around the theaters in Seattle working
as a super. She knew all the actors that had played in stock
out there. Although I had seen Linnie often back home I
did not know her, but on 57th Street I made bold to introduce myself and we subsequently became quite good
friends. Linnie had a lovely singing voice and she told me
Laurette Taylor was financing her music lessons in New
York. She brought me up to date on a lot of things. She told
me that Charles Taylor had deserted Laurette, and that as

as soon as Laurette was able to get a divorce she would marry J. Hartley Manners, who wrote plays also.

I worked hard at dramatic school, but I could not be sure to what purpose. They say you get from study what you bring to it, so possibly the fault was mine. But I was eager and receptive, yet somehow the school and I did not click. Try hard as I could, it held no excitement or stimulus for me. In our Senior year we had Mr. Jehlinger for the first time. He was the star instructor there, and was the only person I had ever heard who could match my father vocally when he was in one of his tantrums. In his classes he yelled at me continuously, "Nature abhors a vacuum." And when I would pause to try to figure that one out, he would spiral and finish up with magnificent emphasis, voice and breath control, pointing a scornful finger at me, hissing, "You are an idiot!" Just like home and father! So I can't truthfully say he helped me much. Mr. Putnam, our voice teacher, a muddy, squat, colorless man, now took up the problems of speech; he would warn us, for instance, that in pronouncing "knees" to be sure to give it the *z* sound at the end like "kneeze" — otherwise, if we had a line like "We found him in the woods on his knees" it might sound as if he were "on his niece," and that, he added with an unsavory grin, would change the meaning entirely. Well! Well!

Early in the Senior year I read an article written by Maurice Renaud, the famous baritone of the Chicago Opera Company, in which he attributed his vocal brilliance to his practicing in falsetto for two hours every day. It developed a false set of vocal cords, the vibration of which added to one's normal voice, he said. That was all I needed. Although I wasn't a singer, voice was the equipment of a fine actor;

so I began practicing in falsetto. It was quite strenuous and hurt a great deal. But I pressed on. As a cover-up I did it in the bathroom with the shower going and on the subway while the train was in motion. But there were times when a sudden stop between stations would find my face red and the nearby passengers rising startled by the strange sounds emanating from my larynx. Whether the Renaud method was right or wrong, the fact is I have a powerful voice which, after all, may only be my inheritance from the hot-tempered McClintics of the Blue Ridge Mountains. Or via Father.

Our Senior Class was a small one, numbering just over twenty, and there was a frightening earnestness about all of us. We worked like demons. Our first play was T. W. Robertson's *Caste*, which Edgar Hart directed, and it is wicked of me even to remember it. The first play we performed at the Empire was new. It had never been done before, and I believe our performance was its one and only. It was called *Captain Jo* and it was about a girl's basketball team; our class was topheavy with the feminine gender, and it was frightening to see them parading around in bloomers with their faces streaked with make-up sweat, trying to pump life into this tepid, unjellied horror.

Our Senior group did include one exceedingly pretty girl, Maude Eddy; a very cute girl, Harriet Rossignol; and an enthusiastic and intelligent girl, Dorothy Ellis. Mary Petticolas was our emotional queen — she cried real tears even at rehearsal, and blew her nose loudly to ease the pain, curiously enough when you had a good speech. She told all of us that our classmate Dillon Deasy, who was too good to be true, would be another John Mason (he was a big star then) and while that was depressing to contemplate, no one believed it except Deasy. There was also a male that seemed blessed with an overabundance of pulchritude, over six feet tall — with wavy blond hair and, if memory serves, wavy blue eyes as well, whom we feared would be successful, and he was for a while. We nicknamed him "Poison Ivy."

New York's theatrical season of 1911–1912 was crowded and colorful, with Ina Claire singing "Tony from America" in *The Quaker Girl;* Otis Skinner a big hit in *Kismet;* Mrs. Fiske, at the Empire, was giving a scintillating performance in a play that failed called *Lady Patricia* by Rudolf Besier — whose *Barretts of Wimpole Street* was to give Katharine Cornell one of her most brilliant successes twenty years later at the same theater; Ruth Chatterton romped into great popularity and acclaim with Henry Miller in *The Rainbow,* and the Irish Players, playing here for the first time, stirred some of their more religious fellow countrymen into creating a minor riot at their opening performance of Synge's *Playboy of the Western World,* an imperishable, beautiful and funny play (which I was to direct many years later with Burgess Meredith, Mildred Natwick, Maurine Stapleton and Julie Harris and, let's not forget, J. M. Kerrigan, who was in the original cast); I was enormously impressed with the well-known London star Lewis Waller's ability to hold an audience enthralled, as he plowed through a fifteen-minute speech in *The Garden of Allah;* fascinated at the technical agility of George Arliss as *Disraeli,* and moved at the emotional simplicity of David Warfield in *The Return of Peter Grimm.* Laurette Taylor had new candles lit at her altar for the witchery she endowed the part of Luana with, in *The Bird of Paradise.* And down on 39th Street Madge Titheradge, at the head of an all-English company, was nightly receiving an ovation in *The Butterfly on the Wheel.*

Now it happens that, while Miss Titheradge was nobly emoting each and every night, I was rehearsing a play in which I had the leading part — that of a young English Guardsman in Mrs. W. K. Clifford's *A Modern Way.* This was to be the Seniors' last performance of the year and of course was to be shown at the Empire Theater. Mrs. Clifford, a hearty type in tweeds, was over here from her native England and attended many of our rehearsals — which only goes to prove that the English are made of sterner stuff than most other mortals. She never winced once at those rehearsals while Mr. Jehlinger continually yelled in ear-splitting maniacal anguish at my effort to project the part. As this was my big opportunity, I could gladly have killed him.

The part was effective though the play was weak — a young man desperately in love who doesn't know it. I worked like a Trojan at it. I knew how I wanted to do it. It had a great deal of comedy that had to be put over with an intense sincerity, but what with Mr. Jehlinger's shouting I was in such a tizzy that half the time I didn't know what the hell I was doing. Mrs. Clifford ever so tactfully said my speech wasn't British, in which she was 100 per cent correct, and she also suggested that I find a better barber — to improve not my speech but my head. The last was easy, if expensive. As for speech, I remembered the performances the Englishmen in the *Butterfly on the Wheel* company were giving and paid it a couple of visits, finally fastening on the diction of a towheaded juvenile who certainly could never have qualified as an American; after several solo rehearsals in my room I turned up at school with a pronunciation that made "name" sound like "nem," "girl" like "gel," "game" like "gemm," "were" like "ware," "fame" like "fem," "sshedule" for "schedule," and wonder of wonders no one batted an eye when these sounds came out of me.

This matinee was an important event in my life and I felt that everything and everyone had conspired against its being what I hoped it would be. In the first act I arrived at a tea party, just off duty from Buckingham Palace. The costumer had fitted me out in a massive brass helmet — horse's tail and all — a shining brass breastplate over my red jacket with a great sword dangling against my white skintight doeskin trousers, and high-shining patent-leather boots that came to above the knee, with great spurs on the heels. For some reason they neglected to give me a horse. I presume this uniform is worn on duty, but I trust never in a drawing-room. When I demurred at the awkwardness of it at the dress rehearsal Jehlinger yelled: "Go on, you can't hold us up now." I went on. I sounded like an old-fashioned kitchen coal stove that was being shaken down as I clanked around that first-act set tripping over my sword as I was passing teacups with one hand while I clutched the helmet in the other. And nary a peep from Mrs. Clifford, who was concerned about my haircut and speech! On the day of the performance I thanked God when the agonizing first act was over and I could approximate what I hoped to do in normal clothes. As the afternoon proceeded I was more at ease, and in the last act I thought I was quite good. . . . When the matinee was over there were some nice comments, and Mrs. Clifford thanked me.

Mrs. Heinsohn, who saw it with Cousin Lulu, decided to celebrate my Broadway debut by treating me to a French table d'hôte dinner downtown. It was all quite gala. Eighty-five cents, with red wine. They were very impressed that I had remembered all my words. When we arrived back at 115th Street the phone was ringing — and strange to say the call was for me. It was Linnie Love. She said Laurette Taylor had attended the performance that afternoon and liked me very much. Miss Taylor had been trying to get me on the telephone with no success, and asked Linnie to call and invite me to see her new play, *The Bird of Paradise,* the following week and go backstage to meet her at the end. A date was set and I hung up, sitting on a cloud with no help from Mrs. Heinsohn or her powers of levitation.

Came the night, I arrived at the theater neat and newly pressed. The performance was a blur, an interruption of what was to follow, the imminence of which was putting me in a lather of perspiration: my collar, a stiff one, had wilted; my bow-tie drooped; the crease was out of my trousers. I had conceived so many effective ways of carrying off this meeting — they all left me. I only prayed I would not end up just laughing nervously. In her dressing room Miss Taylor, looking wondrous in her Hawaiian grass skirt and dark make-up, welcomed me with a brilliant smile and warm handshake. I could not have been too peculiar, for she said there might be a part for me in a play she hoped to do, and invited me to a dress rehearsal of *The Indiscretion of Truth* the following Sunday to meet Hartley Manners, the author, who was also writing the new play she had in mind. She was charming and direct, talking with simple eloquence while her searching, restless imagination reached out to find you. I came to know her very well in later years, and despite certain adversities that confronted her, as an artist in the theater she remained inviolate, untouched, always restless, always searching.

At that Sunday rehearsal I was introduced by Miss Taylor to several celebrities: Samuel Hopkins Adams and the lady who was to become his wife, actress Jane Peyton; and Anne Meredith, who was enacting the leading role and is now Lady Sackville, Mistress of Knole at Sevenoaks, England — before I met Hartley Manners and was led out on the sidewalk to let the light of day shine on me so he could get a better look. Manners was an attractive, genial Irishman. He explained that Miss Taylor was opening the following winter in New York in his new play, *Peg o' My Heart*, and in that there was nothing. But what she had thought of for me was the part of her son in a play he was writing for her to do *after* the run of *Peg*. He seemed pleased with me, and said they would certainly keep me in mind and on my side it would be advisable for me to "keep in touch." That was the first time I had heard "keep in touch"; it's a handy phrase and I've used it since. Disappointed I certainly was — but . . . the son of Laurette Taylor in the play to follow *Peg!* That was something, and only a season to wait! What a wonderful thing is optimism. That was March 1912. *Peg* opened in New York in December 1912 and closed in June 1914, after which Miss Taylor played it in London for two more years and did not appear in New York in the new play (with a son) until October 1916. But I kept in touch! Magic words.

When the curtain fell on *A Modern Way* that was "it" for all of us Seniors, whether we had done ourselves proud or not. We were now due a diploma, and a diploma we got. That formality occurred March 15, 1912, on the stage of the

Empire Theater, with all our friends and relations out front applauding like mad when we crossed the platform to receive the scroll. Sitting on the stage with us, two distinguished stars of the theater did us honor — Mrs. Fiske without a veil, revealing reddish hair and twinkling electric-blue eyes, and George Arliss, looking just like *Disraeli*. Mr. Arliss made a witty speech and darling, diffident Mrs. Fiske, when the crowd had left, agreed to answer any questions the class would like to ask. May the Almighty forgive us for those questions!

"What do you need to become a star?"

"Can an actress have a happy home life?"

"Do you like to travel?"

"Does a flop depress you?" (Not exactly tactful as she was closing a three weeks' engagement on Saturday.)

"Is it true that you care more about animals than you do about people?"

Mrs. Fiske bit her lips, wet her lips, but she replied. It was sad to watch that great actress floundering under the deluge of these vapid queries.

After that we wished each other "good luck" and went our various ways with plenty of misgivings about each other. As I look back at the Academy, I think its greatest lack was the utter absence of any personal touch (acting is the most personal of all the Arts); instead we were treated as so many automatons, subject to cut-and-dried rules. Possibly acting cannot be taught, but an approach can be suggested and that must be individual to you alone. That we were never given. Jehlinger, who was king of the roost, with his continual roaring at my every effort, almost completely undermined any confidence I had. So it was really a godsend when Laurette Taylor sent for me. It gave a lift to my sagging morale. My spirit had another boost when I read a nice notice of my final performance at the Empire in the *Theatre Magazine* of April 1912, which referred to me as an "actor with a future." Why something in print should impress one I don't know, but it does. It does me, at any rate.

Standing on the brink of professionalism was not what I thought it would be. In fact, I found myself being deflated again. The agencies the school suggested we go to were depressingly neutral as far as I was concerned. They took my name and told me to "keep in touch," which I did daily, meeting with the same singsong, dismal "Nothing today" at every office.

A month passed before my cheering section, Linnie Love, was again on the telephone. She had told Ailleen May of how impressed Miss Taylor had been with my work and Miss May, on hearing this, suggested my seeing a man named Edwards who was sending her out on a spring tour of Canada as Nancy Sykes in *Oliver Twist*. I made a beeline for Mr. Edwards; we met on the sidewalk, and he smiled a great deal. He thought me admirable not for one part but for two and proposed I play them both. The salary would be thirty dollars a week and I was to furnish my own costumes. It had happened. I had a job — acting!

The two parts were certainly a challenge to my versatility: Harry Maylie, the love interest, and the Artful Dodger, the cockney thief. They appeared in alternating scenes and that necessitated seven complete changes of costume and make-up during the performance. I burned midnight oil planning those quick changes. I knew Dickens's novel very

well and used the Cruikshank drawings as a model for the
clothes being assembled by the costumer. They were the
most effective part of my characterizations. We rehearsed
two weeks in a dingy hall and I kept repeating to myself,
"I am a professional now." We had no direction at all beyond being told where to enter and exit. The play was
stilted and unreal and so, I am afraid, was our performance.
Mr. Edwards dropped in from time to time and, if his be-
nign smile meant anything, he seemed quite pleased. Ailleen
May could not have been nicer. She worked hard and it was
too bad we were unable to give her better support. We
opened in Hamilton, Ontario, and the fact that it was just
before Easter was not the reason our business was bad.

Forty-odd years ago when stock companies flourished in
almost every hamlet in the country, actors and actresses
were designated as certain types. For instance, among the
men, there were "the leads" — that would be the Tyrone
Power type — and so on down the line through "second
leads," "juveniles" (that was me), "heavies," on to "character men" of which Charles Coburn would be an admirable
example today. The distaff side had much the same arrangement starting from the "leading woman" on down to the
"character woman" and "general business." The character
woman today would be the counterpart of the late Edna
May Oliver or today's Marjorie Main; they played a wide
range of parts — grandmothers, old maids, or servants, Irish,
Italian or colored. The character women were usually very
popular with the audience and less popular with the troupe,
because they were outspoken at all times and (possibly
because of sour grapes) never backward in their criticism
of other ladies in the company. They invariably fastened on

the young men of the troupe, God knows why — and I was
no exception.

In Hamilton our character woman, realizing I was a nov-
ice, advised me to ask the management to advance the
money for my hotel bill. I did, and an outraged Mr. Edwards reluctantly shelled out twelve dollars, after vigorously
commenting on the "unethical nature of my request." We
proceeded from there to London, Ontario, where we performed to empty benches for two nights and made the next
town, Brantford, by the skin of our teeth. Our performances
there must have hit the jackpot, for after it was over Mr.
Edwards, with an early-rehearsal smile, took me down a
long, dark corridor, put some folding money in my hand
and told me to take the girls out for something to eat. I
was amazed by this gesture, as in those days actors were not
paid until the Tuesday following their full week's work —
the idea being that Thespians were irresponsible fellows and
might imbibe too freely or even skip the show. So if they
were paid on Tuesday they would think twice before in-
dulging in any such wayward acts as would forfeit two
nights' pay. I thanked him, and when I got to the light found
he had slipped me two dollars! The next morning — a beautiful Sabbath — Mr. Edwards had disappeared. He told the
hotel manager to tell us that he would not be back. I wonder if he smiled as he said it. We were stranded in Canada.
Thus ended my first professional engagement. . . . But not
quite.

The troupe, together and separately, was racking its brains
for rescuers who on receipt of a telegram collect might send
the necessary mazuma to get us back to Manhattan. Solly
Cooper, a very fat old man who played the Beadle, went

out and sang in the street for pennies and collected enough
to buy himself a beer. At this point Ailleen May called the
company together and told us if we were all willing to stick
with her she would see that our bills were paid; her plan
was to transport us to Wilmington, Delaware, where she had
been a very successful leading woman two years previously.
She was confident she could put on a spring season of stock
there starting in two weeks. We all agreed immediately and
with great relief we sat around enjoying the nice weather
and pleasant prospects while Ailleen worked her head off
raising the money for the chore she had so rashly undertaken.
Before the week was over she had the funds. I remember
that as we left Brantford the headlines announced the sinking of the *Titanic*.

In Wilmington there was a boardinghouse near the theater, run by a Mrs. Buck, where some of the company, including myself, stayed. Now that formidable lady was quite
ample in size, quite untidy in person, but she kept an immaculate house, gave us splendiferous food, did all the work
herself — and our overall bill for the week was seven dollars
each. Mr. Buck was a rather dapper little man with gray mus-
taches who did nothing at all beyond explaining, if he could
get your ear, his days of affluence in the past. His industri-
ous wife spoke of him as being "too much of a gentleman
to work." She used to stand by the table as I was eating,
watching me stow away her delicious fare even unto the
second, sometimes third helping, and then with her hands
clasping her mountainous middle underneath her apron
she would say with a grim but not unkind smirk, the hairs
on her chin stiffening, "When my boarders eat as much as
you do they usually pay me extra," to which I could only

reply, "Oh," and finish cleaning my plate. She didn't know that my weekly stipend for performing was now seven dollars . . . sometimes with fifty cents thrown in for laundry.

We opened at the Avenue Theater, Wilmington, in the third week of April 1912, playing *Oliver Twist* before a house that was generously filled. Things were looking up that night, and the next morning after reading a couple of pleasantly neutral notices we started to rehearse *Faust*. Make no mistake, we weren't singing, although it couldn't have been funnier if we had been. Why *Faust* was done must remain a mystery. I played Valentine. It was awful. The following week was worse, when we put on *The Belle of Richmond*. I was conscious of an odd sensation. Here I was one of a company of stock actors not unlike those I had first seen seven years before in Seattle (the same leading woman), but we had none of that magic make-believe which once enveloped the Taylor Company. It disturbed me. Had I grown up? What was it? . . . When you are really close, is it always like that? I wondered.

Meanwhile, we rehearsed every morning and afternoon and performed at night. Business dwindled and dwindled. It wasn't too good to begin with. Following *The Belle of Richmond* we did the one and only respectable play of our season — Eugene Walter's sturdy melodrama *The Wolf*. The scene of the play was in the woods of French Canada, where the superstitious natives believed that the sound of a wolf cry at night meant death. Our audiences liked it. They also seemed to like me playing a young surveyor up from the States. They thought I was good and for the first time I thought I wasn't too bad.

For the fifth bill we were rehearsing *Madame X,* in which

I was to play the son (a great part). After the Saturday morning rehearsal my friend, the character woman, took me aside and warned me that if any of my belongings were in the theater to get them out because she "felt" the sheriff was going to seize everything in lieu of bills owed. I dressed in the basement at the Avenue and after the matinee I added some will power to my lack of brawn and dragged my trunk, with all my worldly belongings, up on the stage, out to the alley, onto the street and down three and a half blocks to Mrs. Buck's, where her gentleman husband helped me to get it into the house. The character woman was right. Sunday morning when we reported for rehearsal the sheriff was in possession of the theater and the performers were denied admittance.

We were closed irrevocably this time, but New York was not so far away now. Ailleen May paid all our bills and our fares back to the big city. This wretched, ill-starred venture was a black eye to her stock prestige, and her bailing us out ran her into debt. I can see her now, sitting on my hand-drawn trunk in Mrs. Buck's downstairs hall, counting out the money that paid our debts, smiling as she did so and wishing us luck.

Back to Mrs. Heinsohn's . . . back to the Rialto . . . quite a lot of experience in a little over two months. It was the end of May and I figured things ought to be easier now that I was a real "pro"! A short time elapsed, and Franklin Sargent sent me to see Stuart Walker, casting director for Belasco. He told me he thought there would be an opening for me when David Warfield went on tour in the autumn with *The Return of Peter Grimm*, as assistant stage manager and understudy. Walker added, "The prestige will be terrific for you to have been with one of D.B.'s companies, and your opportunity for learning limitless. Come back in early September. . . . Consider it as good as signed," he concluded. Don't ever borrow money on "it's as good as signed"! I believed him. Sargent advised me to wait, and I reasoned it would tide me over until Laurette Taylor's play was ready. No jobs of any kind were in the offing, so I wrote home that I had an engagement for the autumn and asked my father to lend me the fare to come home for the summer, which he did.

The summer passed quickly. I played several bits with the Baker Stock Company then appearing at the Seattle Theater, which occasioned no comment at all. Mother had my dramatic school diploma framed and hung in her bedroom just over Jeff Davis's picture. But a great wall of silence seemed to have come between my parents and me. I'll never know why. When it was time for me to return to New York, I think we were all relieved.

VI

The Table Talks

I REMEMBER the autumn of 1912 as being dark. William Barnes, Republican boss, blocked the nomination of Theodore Roosevelt, who split the party and ran on a ticket of his own creation, the Bull Moose, against his longtime friend William Howard Taft and a professor from Princeton who was the Democratic nominee, Woodrow Wilson. Letters from home informed me that Father was strong for "Teddy," but Mother, who was feeling her oats as an emancipated woman and therefore eligible to vote for a President for the first time, was "looking into" Wilson. He was born in Staunton, Virginia! In New York women spoke on the street corners in Times Square, arguing passionately for their right to vote in the Empire State, promising Utopia when it was once attained. Roosevelt was shot while making a campaign speech, but finished it just the same. Police Lieutenant Charles Becker was implicated in the murder of gambler Rosenthal, for which the four gunmen that shot him down were then on trial, and there was hell to pay.

Meanwhile every day I was going up and down the stairs of the Belasco office atop his theater hounding Stuart Walker, who was still holding out hope of my having a job with David Warfield on the road. For two weeks I climbed those stairs, and at the top was continuously reassured that it was all but settled. But it wasn't, because at the end of that fortnight Mr. Walker told me the job had been given to someone else.

The school then sent me to see Annie Russell, who asked me to come to the first rehearsal of *She Stoops to Conquer,* which was to be the opening play of her Old English Comedy season. I was punctual. Everybody seemed overjoyed in greeting everybody else. Nobody greeted me. When I returned after luncheon intermission Johnson Briscoe, the stage manager, told me they had decided against using me. Who the jury was and why they decided I never knew. I had not been asked to read a line.

Then I started going the rounds of the agents again. At 39th Street and Broadway, just below the Empire Theater, was a German restaurant, the Kaiserhof, which was the Sardi's of its day. In the office building over it the Messrs. Shubert transacted business (their theater was not built then). There, also, was Miss Ada Humbert's theatrical agency, known as the Packard Exchange. Marie of Miss Humbert's office never remembered who I was and soon gave up trying. Bijou Fernandez in the New Amsterdam Theater Building was less evasive. She said flatly that she could not register me until I had played in three New York productions! (But she didn't explain how I could get into them.) Wales Winter, who might be dubbed the official agent for the school, was kinder. He registered me and held out hope; but his receptionist, Miss Simmons, simply smiled and sang out "Nothing today!" every morning when I came in. Isabelle Prentiss in the offices over Shanley's Restaurant

— on the present site of the Paramount Theater Building —
smiled too, but she did get me my first job that season —
the Grant Mitchell part in a road company of *Get-Rich-
Quick Wallingford.*

This assignment came after weeks of brush-offs, and it
came just before Yuletide, so in my happy philosophy I interpreted it as a Christmas present. The part was good, and
I was to be paid twenty-five dollars a week.

Again no direction — no excitement — a group of people
approaching middle age or past it who were hoping to make
a living . . . On Christmas Eve we opened in Haverstraw,
New York. We struggled on for just over two weeks; and we
closed, without notice, in Mahanoy City, Pennsylvania —
there we were paid $52.17 and our fares back to New York.

If that autumn was dark, the winter was darker. When
leaving New York for the Wallingford road tour I had told
Mrs. Heinsohn to rent my room — which I had come to regard
as my very own — because I expected to be away until late
spring. On my unexpected return to town, I found that she
had. So I moved into an unappetizing but cheap hall room
in the Forties — which served as a parking place for me, my
trunk, which I religiously locked although it contained nothing, my wicker suitcase, and my battered dreams. The house
had a bathroom that was two floors below me. It also had
a telephone that was in the basement hall. When the phone
rang all the tenants stood on their various landings listening
to the other fellow's phone calls. I was on the fifth and top
floor. ("Better light," my landlady said. That might have been
true if she had had the windows washed once in a while.) In
any event I had plenty of exercise.

Remembering this low-ceilinged room — with its discolored wallpaper, iron cot, one chair, and one window opening onto a fire escape — gave me the idea years later for the last-act set and atmosphere of Mrs. Gorelik's rooming house in my production of *Saturday's Children*. That incarceration left me with a nostalgia for Mrs. Heinsohn's and 115th Street. I missed the sound of her warm, gentle voice — the sound of a table tipping — the boy's studying.

This was at a time when all of us lesser actors had cards printed which enumerated our more recent engagements (and some we hadn't we'd tack on for effect) and on the early nights of the week, Monday or Tuesday, in quest of passes, we would seek out the company manager in the lobby of the theater, present him with this imposing card, and, while he was still assimilating the details, press him with the traditional query, "Do you recognize the profession?" This question once brought from Brock Pemberton the cutting reply, "A mile away." However, in my day, the managers were generally courteous. And when they had written "O.K." across one of these cards, we handed it to the box-office treasurer, who punched it and gave it back with two seat-location stubs. So we were admitted. These cards were called "Annie Oakleys" for the famous markswoman could shoot two holes in a card tossed in the air before it hit ground. And in U.S. slang, theater passes have borne her name ever since. I saw many a play that otherwise I could never have afforded for the investment of one dollar for two hundred and fifty of these printed cards.

Of necessity I was pinching every penny. I pressed my pants by putting them between the mattress and the springs when I went to sleep — shined my shoes, of course — washed my socks and underwear — walked instead of taking the subway — et cetera, ad infinitum — but the miracle of miracles was my discovery of the bar of the old Knickerbocker Hotel at 42nd Street and Broadway. In the days before Prohibition, no lady was ever admitted to those sanctums in which the male tossed off a few and then chewed a coffee bean or clove to throw the little woman, who would be waiting dinner at home for him, off the scent. I had sought a certain convenience there provoked by a call of nature (no charge in those days) and, coming out, thought I would repay the hospitality of the house by treating myself to a beer (ten cents). While gazing around this beautiful wood-paneled room, which was the original setting for the famous Maxfield Parrish "King Cole" paintings (now in the St. Regis Hotel), I espied a mouth-watering buffet luncheon — sardines, pumpernickel, cottage cheese, ripe olives — a free lunch no less! Help yourself, no tipping — all for the price of one beer! It was delicious and ample, and thereafter served as my principal repast on many a dismal day.

Laurette Taylor opened at the Cort Theater with *Peg o' My Heart* four days before I opened at Haverstraw. She had an overwhelming personal success. When I got back to town I wrote her and she sent me seats for the play. The evening I went I sat next to Julia Dean. I recognized her immediately, as I had admired her the year before in *Bought and Paid For*. She seemed every inch the actress — made up — perfumed — and wearing one of those extraordinary directoire dresses that were the style then. Between the magic of Miss Taylor's performance and the magnetism of Miss Dean's presence, I felt the refreshing lift of real theater once again. When I saw Miss Taylor afterwards she told me that *Peg*

was a bigger success than they had anticipated and that its
run would delay the play she had spoken to me about for
a considerable time. This was a terrific shock. That security
ahead was gone. However, she advised me not to be discouraged by setbacks, as beginnings were always like that —
Just keep on working, she said. I wanted to say, That's what
I'd like to do, but how? But the words choked me.

My only claim to professional status as an actor came
from being a part of the theatrical unemployed. "At liberty"
was the phrase we used when we advertised in trade papers,
and one wag on reading the ad said, "Why?" Ailleen May,
the Toast of Seattle, the queen of the Lois Theater, was having just as dismal a time living very frugally at a hotel on
44th Street near Broadway. Many a night we down-and-
outers would foregather in her bed-sitting room, while smiling Florence Stewart, a character woman who had played
with Madge Kennedy in *Overnight*, would cook spaghetti.
While she cooked the rest of us were exchanging tips as to
where an engagement might be found.

All of these people were out of work — they were in varying degrees of straitened circumstances but they put on a
front that was gay and brave. I remember a story of two
desperately out-of-work vaudevillians who are hurrying
from the delicatessen with their dime's worth of food to
their wretched rooms when they are stopped by traffic and
past them goes a Rolls-Royce laden with beautiful ladies
in sables, the gentlemen immaculate in white tie and tails.
The girl vaudevillian, gazing with wonder, says to her part-
ner with a touch of wistfulness, "Oh, Bert, weren't they mar-
vellous?"

"Yes," he replies proudly, "but they can't act."

So after supper as we wandered up Broadway at night arm in arm, listening to the sheet music stands plugging away at "Alexander's Ragtime Band" on their platform pianos, we would look with a certain amount of longing at the electric lights that proclaimed the presence in this theater or that of Grace George, Nat Goodwin, or William Faversham, and console ourselves that those luminaries had traveled the same road we were traveling — had had the same disappointments, the same disillusions — but eventually they had "arrived."

Letters to my parents were a strain to compose. It was four and a half months since I had come back to New York, in which time I had worked two weeks and one day for pay and rehearsed four weeks in addition gratis. It was no consolation at all to know that none of my fellow graduates were working with the exception of Poison Ivy who, as we feared, was in the employ of Mr. Frohman.

Desperation was dogging my footsteps as I climbed and descended with nightmarish monotony those agents' stairs that held promise for some and only backaches for others, when I ran across the bright girl of our class — Dorothy Ellis — who was elated at having signed for a tour of *Green Stockings*, which Margaret Anglin had just stepped out of after playing it for two seasons. Her leading man, Stanley Dark, together with her business manager, Lodewick Vroom, were sending it out for a brief season (one-night stands) with several of Miss Anglin's company and a few replacements: Stanley Dark's wife, Eva Dennison, being the most important as she was stepping into Miss Anglin's shoes. Dorothy breathlessly urged me to hasten to the Lyceum Theater, where they were seeing people, because she didn't think they had settled on anyone for the juvenile part. I raced over — saw Dark — and was immediately engaged. Salary? Twenty-five dollars, of course!

The company was good, rehearsals professional, and my hopes and morale started to rise. There was a young actor in the cast, playing a character part, whose brother was married to Margaret Anglin. His name was Henry Hull. The brother who was married to Miss Anglin was Howard; another brother, Shelley, was, with the exception of John Barrymore, the most promising young actor in New York at that time. Shelley, too, was married — to an attractive, dark-eyed young woman, a talented ingenue who had left the stage when she married him. Her name was Josephine Hull.

Henry Hull was about my age — tall, slim — and had a rich colorful voice. We got along famously. After two-and-a-half weeks' rehearsals we opened in the middle of February in Kingston, New York, and proceeded from there to Gloversville, Williamstown, and Newark, New York (NOT New Jersey). Then into Vermont with picture-postcard winter scenery: Burlington, with ice-boat racing; Middlebury, knee-deep in snow.

The play went well, I thought, but Miss Dennison, who was dark and vivacious, seemed dissatisfied with my performance and although she never spoke to me about it I can see her now, combing her long hair and vehemently talking to her husband, Stanley Dark, and pointing at me with the comb. As heroine in the play, Miss Dennison was a maiden lady approaching forty, and when she announced her engagement in the first act I was to ejaculate "At last!" A mild laugh greeted this comment, but it didn't satisfy

Miss Dennison. So over and over again Dark would try to show me what he wanted.

"You've seen those ads," he would say, "showing the man with falling hair: Going — going — gone? Well, that's what I want: *Go-o-one* . . ." And then he would give a ghastly reading, ending up with "Do you see what I mean?" But I didn't. He was never cut out to be a director, and his daily coaching of me, I am afraid, was as unsatisfactory to him as it was to me.

Henry and I bunked together and were doing it as cheap as it could be done because both of us wanted to save some money; Henry in particular, as he hoped to get married soon. In the larger towns we played, such as Binghamton and Syracuse, there was always a MEN ONLY dump where we could doss for fifty cents a night for the two of us; and in the smaller places, by persistently ringing doorbells at the sign reading VACANCY, we could do practically as well. In these smaller places there was a certain reluctance to harboring "show folk" and it wasn't at all uncommon, on inquiring for lodging for one night only, to have the lady who opened the door grimly ask, "With the show?" — and, on our reply in the affirmative, to have the door slammed in our faces.

But on the whole this was a happy engagement. Though business was discouraging we straggled along hopefully hoping! During Holy Week, which was traditionally a bad one in the theater, we were laid off, without pay of course, at Geneva, New York. Now by a happy circumstance and through no effort on my part I was hit by an automobile in Geneva and my right hand had a slight cut that bled profusely. Apart from that I was better than new, but the driver of the car seemed very concerned and asked me what I would settle for. He was putting ideas into my head. No such thought had even occurred to me. But remembering Holy Week I said "Twenty-five dollars," and he shelled it out so quickly that I wished I had asked for more.

Geneva's weather was beautiful, the hotel O.K., and we all felt that the audiences would be larger now that Lent was over; but when we reopened Easter Monday our business was brutal, and the following Monday, in Syracuse, Dark told us we would close the next day in Oneonta. He said we were giving a splendid show but the management could not afford to lose any more money. Returning to New York our day coach buzzed with the prospect of good summer-stock jobs and the plums that were in that shimmering mist ahead — that was next season. Stanley Dark and his wife joined in and were gay, although I think they had just dropped their savings for the year on this brief, ill-fated venture.

Back in Manhattan Henry and I shared a cheap apartment. He did the cooking. Once again the agents. Once again "nothing today"; the shake of the head, the bored look at seeing you again. The Rialto was a beehive of activity but I was definitely on the outside. I salved my ego with the fact that Henry, who had real theatrical connections and had been in the "business" longer than I, despite his various entrees was still "looking" also. However, one night as we were fumbling around, trying to remember whose turn it was to put a quarter in the gas meter, Henry told me he had a job through Ada Humbert to open in a vaudeville sketch the following Monday in Philadelphia. I began looking for a temporary place to sleep, as Mrs. Heinsohn said I could have my old room back in a week. Then, on Saturday, Henry got another offer at a much better salary and decided to take it. I was with him when he phoned Miss Humbert to apprise her of his decision. She apparently said, "You're putting me in an awful hole" or words to that effect, for the next thing my startled ears recorded was his saying, "Why not take Guthrie McClintic — he's very clever, you couldn't do better. Here, I'll let you talk to him." And I was shunted to the phone. When asked if I would take the same salary as Henry, I found he was getting thirty-five dollars — and, of course, I said Yes. She then told me to be at the Irving Hotel in Philadelphia at 10:30 Monday morning to meet Miss Octavia Ellis, whose act it was. This was my first taste of being engaged without being seen.

When I met Miss Octavia Ellis that Monday morning I think it is kinder to say my feelings were mixed, but though mixed they were none of them good. She handed me a part of twenty-five sides (pages) and said we would open that afternoon. And she added that she was not at all happy about Humbert palming off an unknown on her. The act opened that afternoon all right (maybe "right" is not the word to use) at an upstairs Variety House in Philly. The show consisted of five acts: a sister act singing to the accompaniment of a piano, a dog act, a couple of Negro comedians, a comedy flicker, and "Octavia Ellis and Company." It is no excuse to say the act was awful. I was awful! No dramatic school could have prepared anybody for this one. What my predecessor was like I can't be bothered to conjure. We played five shows each day. Miss Ellis glowered at me after the first performance and put me at ease by say-

ing "You're as funny as a crutch," and after the second showing she followed it up with "Why don't you get your laffs?"
That was a hard question for me to answer. When I asked
her what I should do differently she answered "Everything"
and walked away.

Tuesday morning she summoned me to her presence and
shook with a rage that was Grecian in everything but language. She proceeded to lay me out for causing her the dis-
grace and humiliation of her entire professional career. The
house was closing her act the next night after only a half
week where she had been booked for a full one — all because
of my performance! And she added with venom that she
would see to it that I never worked again. Her spew shook
me and added no joy to the playing of the ten performances
during the two remaining days. This was theater — no, not
theater, show business — at its cheapest and dirtiest. It depressed me very much.

I returned to New York. Mrs. Heinsohn was not ready for
me yet, so I registered at a certain hostelry where the cells
cost only ten cents a night. For three nights I partook of the
hospitality of this "chez" which catered to men only. It was
something between a public toilet and what I imagine a
jail would be. There was a rumor that it was clean. You were
allowed to take nothing to your cubicle beyond what you
were wearing. Your baggage, if any, was checked in a locker
in the lobby. The noise during the night was unbelievable
and at seven in the morning all doors were opened by an
attendant and the sheets pulled from under you as a slight
hint that it was time to get moving. At eight, the water in
the public washrooms was shut off; and if you were not out
of your haven of rest by 8:30, I tremble to think of what

the consequences might have been. Three nights of this salutary economy and I was able to return to my old room at Mrs Heinsohn's. The relief of being there was so intense I could have cried.

When I was thoroughly fumigated I ventured to the Packard Exchange to apologize and explain that it had been a mistake to send me to Octavia. At the sight of me, Marie of the outer office, who had never been aware of my presence when I had come in during the preceding weeks, snapped into an alertness that might have indicated I was the Willie Sutton of 1913. Before I could open my mouth she said, "Just a minute," and disappeared. In my naïve way I thought possibly Miss Humbert wanted to apologize for the unpleasantness of the Philadelphia incident. But one look at her usually placid, school-teacherish face told me that such was not the case. It turned out I was a monster: I had deceived Henry — I had deceived her — and when she said I had ruined the career of Octavia Ellis, despite my misery I felt a strange elation. It was time someone did. . . . She ended up telling me never to come in her office again.

I walked back to 115th Street talking to myself, trying to shed my chagrin and indignation over the unfairness of Miss Humbert's attitude. When I gained the solitude of my room I began to take stock of myself. Fourteen months had passed since I had left dramatic school — in all that time I had worked only twelve weeks — had played seven different parts, four of them in stock, and not in one of them had I impressed anyone, myself included. It was ridiculous to argue the parts were not right for me. They were the run-of-the-mill juvenile parts in which several young actors had made outstanding successes. With luck these parts or their equivalent would be the best I could hope to get. Something was wrong, and I had to face the fact that it could be me. But what was it? I didn't know. I was suddenly jittery that I might always miss, like my father. I slapped myself in the face. I had to stop thinking like that — there had to be a solution — there *had* to be!

If I had owned a camera in 1911 and could have dollied it down West 44th Street from Broadway to Eighth Avenue, you would have seen just beyond the Astor Hotel on either side a series of houses with brownstone fronts and high stoops like hundreds of other side streets in New York. There was one particular row of houses, on the site of today's Morosco, Music Box and Imperial Theaters, which was known as Mrs. Martin's Theatrical Boarding-house and, although I sat on one or another of her stoops from time to time, I could never afford to stay there. On those stoops on hot summer nights would be sitting actors and actresses, many of them well known today, animatedly yet quietly discussing, arguing, predicting — most of them either rehearsing with the road company of this or that or getting ready for a season of stock. In any event all of them getting ready to desert for a season the bright lights of Broadway. Broadway . . . that was a magic word then. In theaterland there isn't its equivalent today, but to all of those on Mrs. Martin's various stoops and to all of us who could only visit there it was a hope — a goal! Just off the Main Stem, this neighborhood had the feeling of small town.

Winthrop Ames was the pioneer who changed the atmosphere of those streets into the bustling theatrical thoroughfares that they are today. It began with his building of the

Little Theater at 244 West 44th Street. That building is now known as Times Hall, and there is very little left to remind one of the exquisite theater that was. It seated with serene comfort two hundred and ninety-nine people . . . wood paneling as background for eighteenth-century tapestries lit by crystal chandeliers . . . it was a delight to behold! And the thought and the courtesy that went into it reflected the artist and gentleman who built it — Winthrop Ames. Its ample revolving stage, its switchboard, dressing rooms and Green Room, were the envy of anyone who worked there in any capacity whatsoever.

The doors were open to the public for the first time in the spring of 1912 when John Galsworthy's play, *The Pigeon,* was given its initial production in New York. In the fall of 1912 when I was being turned away from Mr. Belasco's front door, Mr. Ames dazzled the fastidious playgoers of Manhattan with his glittering presentation of Schnitzler's *The Affairs of Anatol* with a cast headed by John Barrymore, Doris Keane and Marguerite Clarke. In the spring of 1913 he produced the delightful children's play, *Snow White,* also featuring Marguerite Clarke, who, he announced, would appear in the autumn in Laurence Housman's play *Prunella.*

This, then, was the atmosphere of West 44th Street in early June 1913 which I was shortly to encounter. On one particularly grueling day, after my usual morning rebuffs, I was sitting in Bryant Park at the noon hour with my shoes off to rest those tired feet of mine that had walked fruitless miles that morning, glancing at what was left of the discarded paper in the adjacent seat. I raised my head and to my consternation saw the wavy blond hair of our class beauty, "Poison Ivy," approaching. He looked more pleased with himself than ever. It was useless to try to hide, so as casually as I could I put on my shoes, after shaking them vigorously, to give the impression that I was looking for a stone. He was very friendly and asked what I was doing. I lied that I was considering stock in Sacramento. Then he told me that he had just signed with Winthrop Ames to appear in his forthcoming production of *Prunella* and, as he was leaving, he suggested it wouldn't be a bad idea for me to go around there too, as there might be something left.

I tied my shoes, gave my clothes a hand brush, straightened my necktie and started for West 44th Street. For me it took courage even to enter the Little Theater. The scent of the live box trees on either side of its Georgian entrance seemed overwhelming, and when towering, colored George McCoy with his high silk hat and cockade, in a long black coat with silver buttons, saluted and opened the door for me I was positive it would be better if I said it was the wrong place and sought solace in a five-cent beer at May and Finn's at the far corner of 44th Street and Eighth Avenue — but I didn't. I walked up the short flight of stairs to the office. The receptionist, Miss Wilson, charming-looking and a charming girl, greeted me pleasantly — and that almost completely unnerved me. However, with the best manner I could muster, I asked to see Mr. Ames. When I told her it was about an engagement she said she was sorry but Mr. Ames was out of town. However, would I care to see Mr. Platt, who frequently saw people when Mr. Ames was away?

George Foster Platt was a distinguished director who had been associated with Mr. Ames at the New Theater. He was also distinguished-looking and a gentleman . . . the kind of a gentleman that makes you acutely aware of it and puts a tender plant like myself completely ill-at-ease. He stood up when I entered his office, motioned me to a chair facing him, and proceeded to question me as to my previous theatrical experience with all the geniality you would expect to receive if you were being booked at a police station. As my experience was not vast, I padded a little . . . he stopped writing and stared at me. He knew I was lying and I knew he knew it, but I couldn't stop talking. I wanted to go but I couldn't move. What co-ordination I had seemed to leave me. In desperation, the poor man suddenly stood up, put out his hand and with icy courtesy said, "Good afternoon, Mr. McClintic." (He didn't say "Keep in touch.") I was amazed to find I too could stand up and put my hand out to shake his, when my benumbed senses registered the fact that in so doing I had jarred the top of a very tall pen in his overly fancy inkwell, and the whole damned thing toppled over. I made an impotent effort to do something about the pool of ink that was spreading over his desk, but he cut me short with, "Please go, Mr. McClintic, I can take care of this." And he bellowed for Miss Wilson — who hastily entered one door while I made an even hastier retreat out the other.

Once in the street, however, my chagrin boiled up in a tidal wave of resentment and anger. Platt's coldly furious voice was still sounding in my ears: "Please go, Mr. McClintic, I can take care of this." Who the hell did he think he was anyway? If I'd had a brick I would have hurled it through those smug, shiny plate-glass windows and pray God I'd conk him. And why look as if I were up for a term of penal servitude just because I lied about my experience? Wouldn't it have been just as easy to say, "Don't lie, kid. I know you are nervous, but it is no crime that you haven't any experience. Relax . . ." Oh, no — not for him it wouldn't. What in the name of God was wrong with me? How could Poison Ivy get a job and I get thrown out?

This gust of anger was possibly my great co-ordinator, for somehow I clicked. I saw myself in relation to the whole formidable façade that was then the New York theater. The agencies were as outside as I was, but I wasn't going to stay outside any longer. I thought I was good. Laurette Taylor thought I was good. And I *was* good. I had allowed myself to be beaten by an outside evaluation. Worse than that, I had accepted it. Not any more . . . One hundred and seventeen pounds of distilled purpose and resolve that was me rushed towards Broadway on 44th Street, disappeared into the side entrance of the Astor Hotel, and made for the mezzanine where the stationery I used for all writing purposes was available. The printed card on each desk read: "For the special use of patrons only." While the heat was on I was going to write to Winthrop Ames.

> DEAR MR. AMES [I began, still seething, and proceeded to record the ignominy of my interview with Platt, leaving out not one iota of his hostile manner and the effect it had on me]. . . .
>
> You may not know it [I concluded], but in the profession you are referred to with a good deal of awe as "the gentleman producer of Broadway" and I have always thought underlings reflected the manners of their bosses. If Mr. Platt's attitude is a reflection of yours, I tremble for the many who will come to your door and be turned away unseen and unheard. You

have been pleased, from your ivory tower, to garner great publicity with the announcement that you would pay a bonus of Ten Thousand Dollars for the best play written by an American on an American subject. That is very fine indeed for the dramatists, be they known or unknown, but there are other young Americans knocking on your door who feel they have a place in the theater too and I am one of them. Are we to be left roaming the streets because we have no publicity value? You may not be interested but I'm telling you I am 5'10" tall, have a dark complexion and am well-spoken, from good American stock, but what is more important I have wit, intelligence, sensitivity and an unplumbed capacity for work and usefulness in the theater. More important still I have to work. I demand the right to be seen by you and not be tossed into the discard because of an unfavorable report, that very likely will never reach your eyes, of an unfortunate accident that occurred on your premises. I remain,

Yours respectfully,

GUTHRIE MCCLINTIC

When I had finished the letter, I read it and reread it. I thought it good, aggressive and coherent, but I had been purged of my anger — I could see no purpose in sending it or what good it would do other than cause resentment. There was a rumor that if you offended one manager your name was posted and no manager would touch you. I couldn't risk that, I reasoned; but the letter was good, so I sealed it. I didn't address it, and in the corner where the stamp would go I wrote the date on which it was written. Then I put it in my pocket and left the hotel. The day was still hot and it was a long walk to Morningside Heights. Once there I put my unposted letter in my trunk, along with my capital of twenty dollars, no longer in gold now, and my other worldly possessions — such as the programs of plays I had seen, my two letters from Laurette Taylor on pink paper, and some letters from home. I locked it, lay on the bed and went to sleep.

Burying the letter didn't change things. I continued to charge — and that is hardly the word — the agencies every day. At that time you had to buy tickets for the subway which you put in a choker for admittance with an attendant looking on. I used to buy a block of five and, with an ingenuity that has only been equaled by Jim the Penman, I would tear them so that they made six; and that, no doubt, together with similar hoaxes, accounts for the transit problem in New York today.

When I appeared at the agencies the routine smile had already left the receptionist's face and she would just shake her head and didn't bother to speak. My desperation was so acute that I avoided whenever possible seeing anyone I knew and spoke hardly at all. I walked back to 115th Street daily. There was usually a newspaper to be picked up along the way, and I scanned the want ads in hopes of a part-time job that would tide me over and still let me look for employment in the theater. There was a Salvation Army slogan, "A man may be down but he is never out." I was trying desperately hard to believe it. I was in my twentieth year and I wasn't ready to take the count.

Something like three weeks had passed and I was sitting on my bed one Wednesday evening about to turn in when Mrs. Heinsohn, who had been holding a soirée with the other world in her dining room, came down the hall to my door, knocked and said, "Mr. McClintic, the table wants to talk to you." It had been so long since anyone had *wanted* to talk to me that the prospect of talking to a table brightened me considerably. I brushed my hair and sallied forth.

Cousin Lulu was there, her mass of dark reddish hair jauntily untidy under an enormous hat, and her huge jowls sagging a bit as if the overabundance of dry rouge on them was weighing them down. There were just the four of us: Cousin Lulu, Mrs. Heinsohn, myself and the table. Lulu greeted me rather sourly and said in her deep Southern drawl, "Cousin Adah can't do a thing with it. It just keeps saying it wants to talk to you" — and she was indicating the table. Cousin Adah was Mrs. Heinsohn! There were no introductions and at first glance that golden oak table looked just as formidable as any of the agencies' receptionists. The lights were on and Adah Heinsohn, looking adorable as always, sat at the table with her two hands lightly upon it. Cousin Lulu had a pad and pencil. Mrs. Heinsohn's forearms began to tremble ever so slightly and then she smiled at me and asked me to slowly repeat the alphabet. I started "A . . . B . . . C . . ." and had gotten as far as "M" when the table suddenly rose up and down rather violently three times. Cousin Lulu wrote down M. Mrs. Heinsohn told me to start again "A . . ." Once again the table banged three times. Cousin Lulu, like a court reporter, recorded the next letter. I was beginning to be fascinated with the table's conversation and needed no further prompting now. Every time it banged three times and Lulu had written the letter, I would start the alphabet again. At long last it ceased banging and Mrs. Heinsohn asked if that was all it had to say and it came up and down quite positively three times.

Cousin Lulu handed me the message. Her handwriting

was almost as illegible as mine. The night was still and warm. I was possibly warmer because I had put on my flannel bathrobe to come down the hall. I was wide awake. The two women were looking at me expectantly, almost as if it were their message. I read it and read it again and you must believe me when I say it meant absolutely nothing to me. This was what Cousin Lulu had written down: MAIL THAT WHICH YOU HAVE WRITTEN. YOUR ENTIRE FUTURE DEPENDS ON IT. Lulu was at me like an M.C. in a quiz program, but the more she prodded the blanker I became. Finally she turned to Mrs. Heinsohn. "Ask the table, Adah, what he has written." Once again Mrs. Heinsohn put her hands on the table but it was no dice. The table was through talking for the evening.

Cousin Lulu had gone home disgruntled and Mrs. Heinsohn was in the bathroom as I was lying on my bed in the dark puzzling, for some instinct assured me that this message had a meaning — when suddenly there was a pinpoint of light in the dark. I jumped up, turned on the switch and felt my trunk. It was locked. The key was buttoned in the back pocket of my pants. I had only one good suit. And besides, Mrs. Heinsohn would never do a thing like that! Moreover, she couldn't have known about it. I never mentioned the incident. I unlocked the trunk, took out the unaddressed letter. It was sealed. I looked at the date written where the stamp should go. It lacked one day of being three weeks since I had written it. Nothing had happened since. A queer desperation seized me. Nothing would ever happen unless I did something.

I reached for my wax stamp book, took out a two-cent stamp and pasted it over the date, and then I opened the ink

bottle and dipped in the pen and printed:MR. WINTHROP
AMES, LITTLE THEATRE, 244 WEST 44TH STREET, N. Y. C.
I crossed out Astor Hotel on the back and printed McCLINTIC,
c/o MRS. HEINSOHN, 403 WEST 115TH STREET. I didn't open
it. I was through with thinking. It was nearly two o'clock in
the morning when I dressed and tiptoed out of the apartment
and dropped it in the mail box on Morningside Drive. Then
I walked up to 116th Street and sat on the bench there under the light. There was no use thinking about it now. It
was done.

Let's just say the day of Thursday passed and Friday
came, and on the first mail there was a note from the Ames
office saying Mr. Ames had read my letter and would like
to see me on the following Monday at 3:00 P.M. It was signed
Helen Ingersoll, secretary to Mr. Ames. Without the aid of
stimulant I appeared at the Little Theater at the appointed
time. Miss Wilson smiled as if she were seeing me for the
first time, and ushered me into Miss Ingersoll's office, where
a rather prim woman greeted me with "Mr. Ames is terribly
sorry that he cannot see you today, as he is ill, and he was
wondering if it would be possible for you to come back on
Wednesday at the same time."

I was in a state of suspended animation until Wednesday;
but on the stroke of three I was again climbing the stairs
of 244 West 44th Street. Miss Wilson's smile was even
broader, and when I confronted Miss Ingersoll there was a
hint of cordiality in her primness as she delivered the identi-
cal speech of our previous meeting, the only change being,
Could I make it Friday at the same time?

Friday it was, and the air was getting rarer when I landed
on the threshold of Helen Ingersoll's domain that day.

I somehow knew the worst had happened: Ames was dead. . . . But no — not so . . . he was still indisposed, and felt somewhat guilty at not being able to keep any of his appointments with me that week, particularly in view of my previous experience in the office. However, my letter had impressed him, and in view of its sincerity and Miss Ingersoll's report of me, he was offering me a contract to act as stage manager of his first presentation of the following season, *Her Own Money*, a new play by Mark Swan. Rehearsals of it would start the first Monday in August. I was handed the contract he had signed. It was his own, as there was no Equity then. The salary was twenty-five a week. I looked at it goggle-eyed with elation and disappointment. My mind ticked like a wireless receiving station. "Stage manager?" But I want to act. Beginners can't be choosers. No more Oliver Twists, Wallingfords, Octavia Ellises — and maybe, *maybe* an actor will miss rehearsal . . . I'll read the part in his absence — Ames will be delighted — "Pay what's his name off," he'll say, "we are keeping McClintic in this part." The vision faded, and Miss Ingersoll was looking at me waiting for me to put my name on the dotted line. After I had signed and was putting my copy in my pocket she said that Mr. Ames wished me to understand that if I didn't make good I would be dismissed. Miss Wilson's smile was broader than ever when I left the office. This was the second time I was engaged without being seen.

I went to see Laurette Taylor to tell her of my good fortune. She looked puzzled and disapproving. "Why did you do that? What good will it do you?" She was right and she was wrong, and I could have answered her but it would have been pointless.

Mrs. Heinsohn was visibly pleased and placed an enormous importance on the "manager" part of "stage manager." She knew nothing, of course, of what the job entailed. She said she was glad I found out what the table meant because it was never wrong. Now I am not a spiritualist — never have been, and cannot rightfully say I believe in it; but several times in my life and in the lives of others these unexplainable incidents have occurred. Years later when I had been out of touch with Mrs. Heinsohn for a considerable time, she telephoned me on reading the press release that I had signed Tallulah Bankhead for *Jezebel* to say, "It was too bad as Miss Bankhead would never be able to play the part." That was in June 1933. We started rehearsals in September, and after ten days Tallulah was stricken with an illness that incapacitated her for the whole season! At a dinner party at Zoë Akins's house in Hollywood in the autumn of 1930, I found myself talking to Count Hamman, an Irish Count, who was professionally known as Cheiro, probably the best known fortuneteller in the world the thirty years before that. He glanced casually at my hands and told me not to fly East as I had planned to do in a couple of weeks. But I did. The plane cracked up on a farm field in Indiana and I, luckily, came off with only a minor injury. . . . I am spreading myself ever so slightly about this, to stay those skeptics who invariably say, "Such things don't happen . . . explain it then." Well, I can't explain it, and I don't have to — because such things *do* happen; they've happened to me. One last word and I'll sit in a corner and be quiet. Mrs. Heinsohn was a normal, charming woman who had a gift, or power, or whatever you choose to call it. It sought her; she didn't seek it. She never commercialized it, and only to a very few friends would she ever demonstrate it . . . and as I take my corner I want to say, "Thank you, Adah Heinsohn!"

In writing home to tell them of my good luck for the autumn, I described Mr. Ames, whom I'd never seen, in extravagant terms that almost did him justice; and they in return, happy that at last it seemed I would no longer be a worry, wrote back that my cousins and uncles and aunts in Virginia and Pocahontas County, West Virginia, would be delighted to have me stay with them if I had nothing else to do until I began with Mr. Ames. It was only overnight from New York.

This was my first glimpse of any of my kinfolk; my first sight of land that had belonged to my great-grandfathers, back to before the French and Indian Wars. In Virginia the land was lush and beautiful. My kinfolk were plentiful and hospitable. I wasn't prepared for their thick Southern accents. I didn't think anyone could have as many cousins as I had. I was "Cousin Guthrie." I can hear them now:

"He is Cousin Ed's son. The one who is fixin' to go on the stage."

"My, my, who does he remind you of? I know: Cousin Warwick. He has the same funny squint. — Going on the stage, are you?" and then they would roar with laughter.

Two of my father's brothers had more than a passing interest for me. His youngest, my Uncle George, was a brilliant and successful lawyer. He lived in Charleston, West Virginia and, when we met, I thought I detected a curious gleam in his eye as he looked me over that seemed to indicate a termite had burrowed into the clan.

As positive but decidedly different was another brother,

Withrow — but already known to me as "Uncle Wiz." To describe him as a "character" would be a distinct understatement. He had a thriving farm at a place called Buckeye; he was a bachelor until he was well past middle age, and surrounded himself with a group of helpers, convivial spirits he had lured out of the hills of West Virginia. My cousins delighted in telling me stories of Wiz and his cohorts who, when drowned in "corn" or "apple," would cut some capers that had the mountain women laughing as they refilled their pipes or reached for another shot of likker, but on the other hand had the respectable law-abiding citizens concerned as to the effect these carryings-on would have on my grandmother. Withrow was her favorite son, and she was dedicated to bringing him in from his fields of sin. On one occasion, as Grandmother and the congregation were being exalted by the new minister, Mr. Nichols, at the evening service in the Marlinton Presbyterian Church, Uncle Wiz with a group of his pals, all high and wide, if not handsome, came galloping on horseback up to the front of the church, where they gave vent to a series of bloodcurdling screeches and then, as one man, drew their guns and fired them into the air, volley after volley until the sixshooters were empty, and with a chorus of "Yippee!" galloped off to Buckeye again. After that demonstration, it seems the pew holders inside the tabernacle found it hard to keep their minds on the sermon. The next morning Grandmother sent for Wiz. He appeared, very contrite. She patiently told him of the grief he was causing her, and tried to make him aware of how outrageous his behavior of the night before had been to the new minister, Mr. Nichols, and suggested that Uncle Wiz make amends by presenting the minister with a pair of fine carriage horses from his farm. Wiz agreed, and Grandmother straightaway told Mr. Nichols of this conversation and suggested he call on Wiz to receive his gift of penance. Needless to say the minister lost no time in getting to Buckeye. From the start, chemically, the two did not mix. Withrow definitely did not like Mr. Nichols. By way of hinting that he leave, he said he had something for him and Mr. Nichols, expectant, hastened after him but was dismayed at finding himself the recipient of a mule. He stammered something to the effect that Mrs. McClintic had led him to expect a pair of trotters. Withrow cut him short, "Mr. Nichols, if Jesus Christ could ride into Jerusalem on an ass I guess one is good enough for you. Good afternoon."

Now I met Uncle Wiz and he measured up to all I had heard. He was of middle height, not unattractive, careless in appearance, and wore a beard. When he shook my hand he said with a smile, "I don't reckon you were prepared to find such a tough nut for an uncle." The latent charm of Uncle Wiz's house, which was probably a century old, had strangely eluded him, but his own particular charm was really enhanced by that fact. In his bedroom, for instance, a tent was pitched over his bed. It was too much to suppose that this bewhiskered diamond in the rough had an effete side and was pretending he was Napoleon on the field of battle. No! Far from it: the rains had been torriential, there was a leak over the bed, the hands were working overtime on the farm and the tent was the simplest means of keeping Uncle Wiz dry.

Uncle Lock, another brother, had a son named Hunter, who was about my age but good-looking. He was in Uncle George's law office, had a car, and both feet well planted on the threshold of success. His automobile was shining sealing-wax red, and he drove it all over the countryside. I was envious of that car and his ability to drive it.

My relatives were more than hospitable and nice people as well, even though related to me. When my visit was over I returned to the shifting sands of Broadway, if not with a song in my heart certainly with a firmer conviction than ever that despite the year just passed, despite the detour of the present, my choice had been right.

VII

With "The First Gentleman"

I DIDN'T know anything about stage management when I went to the first rehearsal of *Her Own Money* at the Comedy Theater. (That it had a technique of its own one would never have known from the curriculum at the academy.) I was early for that first rehearsal — early and nervous! George Foster Platt was the director, and greeted me with a gentlemanly smile. No reference was made to his overturned inkwell nor was there any indication he had ever seen me before. But his frigid correctness and competence, far from intimidating me, strengthened my resolve that he would never again "get me." Julia Dean was the leading woman. She appeared in a different ensemble at every rehearsal, all of them the last word in fashion. She wore long earrings, used plenty of perfume as well as make-up, and in Seattle she would have been called "fast." But to me she was terrific. She was more than terrific. She was friendly and warm. At that first rehearsal, when I waited for some sign from Platt as to what I should do and none was forthcoming, I sat on the side lines watching and listening, still wondering what the hell a stage manager did. In the few "turkeys" I had been associated with since leaving school no one had ever, to my knowledge, been identified as being the stage manager. As far as I knew the curtain went up and down by itself, so I sat there listening to Broadway actors tentatively reading lines while the author, Mark Swan, sitting beside the director, would say, "I didn't mean that line to be read belligerently, but humorously, Miss Sitgreaves."

"What's humorous about it?" snapped Miss Sitgreaves in return.

"When we get further into the play you will find out," confided the author mysteriously.

Platt was content to command "Go upstage" — "Downstage" — "Dress the stage" — "Look to the left" — "Give to the right," or "Go off stage." From my perch it was impossible to know what *Her Own Money* was about.

When Mr. Platt dismissed the cast for the luncheon intermission and ordered them back an hour later, I went out with the company; and when they made for Broadway, I went the opposite direction towards Sixth Avenue and wheeled around to watch their receding rears as they turned the corner toward 42nd Street. Then I walked back to the stage door and onto the stage, picked up the script on the director's table, and started to read the play by the pilot light. I was dying to know what it was all about. I had just finished the first act when I was startled to hear someone coming along the cement corridor that led to the stage. I put the script away from me guiltily, as if I had been an invader in a boudoir and were reading private letters. The ominous footsteps turned out to be Julia Dean's.

She smiled at me as she stepped on stage. "My, you are early," she said. "I thought I would be the first back. I wanted to go over the opening scene we just did."

I murmured "Oh" and started to walk away when she stopped me with "You have never been a stage manager, have you?" I felt Broadway slipping from under me, but her voice was friendly and I answered truthfully, "No."

"Let me tell you what little I know," she said. "First you must hold the book."

"Hold the book?" said I blankly.

"Yes — the book, the script, the play," she replied with faint impatience.

"But no one has given me one," I stammered.

"Here, take mine. I will get another." Then she proceeded to tell me I should write down all the business given by the director (that is, where the actor moves on stage, when he rises, sits, or lights a cigarette, and so on), and know the exact position of all the furniture; in short, all the things the gentleman of the upset inkwell should have told me as a matter of duty this generous, glamorous leading lady was volunteering. And she warned in conclusion: " There is one more hazard in front of you. That is the moment we actors discard our parts and try to perform without them. Then you will need to develop a sixth sense to know exactly when to hand an actor a prompt, for sometimes there may be an ungodly pause while we think we are spreading magic over a situation — and you, as stage manager, may think we have forgotten our words and will throw us a line. *Don't ever do that*. Let us ask you for the prompt."

Our little interlude was stopped by the return of the company as they sauntered back one by one. But when Mr. Platt tapped his table for the rehearsal to begin I was on my job for the first time, with no thanks to him. Stage management, I found out, was never considered a road to glory but rather a rut in which, if you once got stuck, you remained until death did you part. I was young, which was unusual for a stage manager in those days, and it was through Miss Dean's attitude and friendly help that I kept my job.

During the second week of our rehearsal she once reduced me to jelly by asking me to lunch with her at the Knickerbocker Hotel; and as we were going around the corner on Broadway my neck stretched in all directions hoping to catch sight of some of my schoolmates or ex-confrères, but no such luck. I only met them when I had my shoes off!

I can't say Mr. Platt *ever* took me under his wing. He was seemingly unaware of me, but I was interested in watching him map out the business of the play. He never left his directorial chair. I did not feel he had any real communication with the actors. He gave orders. His one moment of emotion came when Miss Dean's heart was breaking at the curtain of the second act, and he added one of those directorial touches that had the cast saying "Great!" At that peak of emotion, he arranged to have a phonograph recording (apparently coming from another apartment) blare out suddenly with "Waiting for the Robert E. Lee." That tune was my theme song for the year, and whenever I hear it now it takes me back to 1913.

Beyond his icicle smirk at the first rehearsal, Platt never spoke to me except to give an order. But the cast were wonderful and helpful. There was a general feeling around the troupe that I was "bright." I slavishly recorded every bit of business given and noted every change of text. Although it was customary in those days for no salary to be paid any member of the cast or stage managers until the end of the first week of playing before an audience, I, as stage man-

ager, was paid my salary for every week during rehearsal.
No one in the theater of those days did that with the exception of Winthrop Ames. He came to a run-through once but
sat in the darkened auditorium and no one saw him.

After three and a half weeks' rehearsal the company em-
barked on the night boat for Albany, where we were to try
out for four performances at Harmanus Bleeker Hall. I
missed the boat by running an errand for the character
woman from the dock at 125th Street and North River to
Broadway and back. But I got another star for brightness by
taking a train to Albany and greeting the company when
they arrived the next morning. That errand cured me of
doing favors on duty, as the character woman never paid
me for the laxative I had bought her and afterwards berated
me for missing the boat.

I saw Mr. Ames — tall, slim, and with the faintest suggestion of a stoop — for the first time after our opening night
in Albany, but did not meet him. My own particular chore
as stage manager came off without a hitch. We opened in
New York on Labor Day and, for my first metropolitan
première, it was an awful letdown. Neither the public nor
the press cared much for Mr. Swan's little play.

When Julia Dean told me on the Wednesday of the first
week that she had accepted the starring role in another play
I knew the writing was on the wall, if not on the call board.
Two days later, on Friday night, Jed Shaw, our company
manager, told me Mr. Ames wanted me to be at the Booth
Theater at ten o'clock the next morning. That charming
theater, which he had just built, had not yet opened its doors
to the public. Ten o'clock and I was there; but as usual no
Mr. Ames. To me there was a distinctly foreign atmosphere

about the sizeable group, mostly male, who were sitting or standing about the stage when I walked on, peering around in search of the absent impresario.

Suddenly a voice quite sharp and rather high came out of the darkness of the orchestra, "Ah ya Maw Klenta?" I kept on looking when again it came. "Ya tha, ah yaw Maw Klenta?" One gentleman wearing a monocle gave me a poke with his cane and said, "I think he's speaking to you, old boy." I thanked him, and turning to the darkened auditorium said I was Guthrie McClintic. The voice from out of the dark murmured something indistinguishable and shortly there appeared beside me a dapper little man who introduced himself as Frank Vernon. He was to direct the New York production of *The Great Adventure*, Arnold Bennett's dramatization of his novel, which had been a hit in London and which Winthrop Ames was presenting as his initial attraction at the Booth. The popular American actress Janet Beecher headed the cast, playing opposite the well-known London actor Lyn Harding and an all-English supporting company.

I gathered Frank Vernon wanted me to hold the book for them at that rehearsal — in other words, act as prompter. I did. The printed word in front of me was a clue to what they were saying — unfamiliar as I was to English intonations and pronunciations — but I caught on pretty quickly. At the luncheon hour I told Vernon I had to cover the matinees at the Comedy. He asked me to come back the next day, Sunday, and as it turned out I came every day thereafter from ten o'clock in the morning to half past-five in the afternoon and worked the evenings and matinees of *Her Own Money* as well. At the end of the first week my pay check was upped to thirty-five dollars. I was sitting pretty. I could now afford to have cream with my baked apple.

During the following week Mr. Platt told me, in a manner that bordered on friendliness, that *Her Own Money* was closing, but I was being made stage manager of *The Great Adventure.*

Thus began in many ways the most broadening experience of my life up to that time. Before that engagement was over I had acquired a good deal more competence. It imposed on me a discipline that has stood me in good stead for all of my days in the theater. I listened and I watched. If George Foster Platt never left his directorial chair, Frank Vernon never lighted in his. He was so busy acting for the cast and giving deadly stereotyped readings — evidently *The Great Adventure* was to be more or less a carbon copy of Granville-Barker's enormously successful presentation in London. The principal actors had looks — they had pleasant voices; this was obviously their moment. But as I watched them rehearsing I could not help wondering, Did they know what they were doing or were they following a pattern they had accidentally fallen into? They never demurred at a direction nor raised an eyebrow at a reading. Would their road ahead be one of their own choosing? They were successful. But would they have a plus? Could they put a lump in your throat by reading Laurette Taylor's Lone Star speech? I didn't think so!

Vernon, who probably had something on the ball (I was told Knobloch and Bennett's play *Milestones* was written from an idea of his), was not a director at all; before we opened in New York he had disappeared and Platt took over; and, while he was well out of his depth, he did at least have authority. *The Great Adventure* . . . It was all of that to me! It gave me work, it gave me contacts, it gave me a little money for the first time. I fell in love. And I fell out of love. And then fell in love again. I ran across Henry Hull and we took another apartment at twenty-five dollars a month. This one belonged to Lodewick Vroom and was at 19 East 32d Street, an empty brownstone house that had only one other tenant, Frank Crowninshield and his brother in the floor below. We were on the top floor. Two bedrooms, thank God! It had dormer windows that looked down towards Madison Square. The whole neighborhood was distinctively Edwardian then. It snowed that winter; . . . church bells chimed on Sunday mornings . . . Henry was a stimulating companion and a good cook. He was getting married. . . . I was in love. . . . We were both in work. . . . I was rubbing shoulders with well-knowns and treated as if I were a human being. The chill of spirit of the last eighteen months was beginning to thaw. But I had not yet met Winthrop Ames!

He spoke to me by name during a "light" rehearsal at the Booth just before it opened. He said, "Mr. McClintic, would you please stand a little to the left. I want to see if this spotlight catches you." As I was doing what he asked I felt a surge of importance at that courteous well-spoken voice calling my name. Then he said, "Thank you."

Ames was "the Pioneer of 44th Street," with his opening of the Little Theater, and so he was on 45th Street, when he opened the Booth. It was the first theater on that thoroughfare *west* of Broadway. As we say in the theater, I "rang up its first curtain." In other words, I gave the signal for the gentleman whose job it was to raise the curtain to do so.

The Great Adventure was a real workout for me in the department of stage management. It was in four acts with two scenes in each act, and, between the scene changes and light changes and the scores of props that had to be placed in the dark during change of scenes, I, who never dream, found myself having frightening nightmares in which everything went wrong — with no one to blame but myself. I would wake up in a cold sweat. To avoid the happenings that took place in those nightmares I made elaborate plots (drawings) noting the different props used in every scene and committed them to memory exactly as one might do in learning a part, and I learned to call off the lights for each scene in the same way. I had no assistant, and by way of filling my cup to the brim I appeared briefly in the second act as a Swiss waiter with one line. It was not the type of part that was calculated to take me out of stage management. However, thank Heaven, I handled the stage smoothly and without mishap and was generally liked by the company.

That was the autumn that I began to be acquainted with the British. Though allegedly ours was a common tongue, there were idioms bandied around in the troupe that were not only alien to my untutored ears but could be interpreted with meanings other than those intended. For instance, in Providence where we were trying out, I overheard the character woman asking Lyn Harding, our leading man, "Did she get a good screw?" They were speaking of a mutual friend and I was delighted to hear him reply that she had, but I hadn't the foggiest notion that she had been asking if her friend had gotten a good *salary!* I learned to dodge in and out of the "ta's" and the "kew's" and to accept the fact that the "cash chemist" was a drugstore; that their "boxes"

were their luggage; that when they were "booking a stall"
they were buying an orchestra seat; that a derby hat was "a
bowler"; and that what we called a tux was a "dinner jacket."
I even heard the banshee wail when they opened their bedroom doors in the morning and found that the shoes they
had left outside had not been polished. (I thought they were
lucky to find their shoes were still there.) When I had seen
them wince at the word "bloody" (Eliza Doolittle in Mr.
Shaw's *Pygmalion* had not yet made it popular) and be just
as mystified at our slang as I was at theirs, I began to realize that when we emerged from that tanglewood of alien
idioms we were really the Colonel's Lady and Judy O'Grady,
or vice versa. They were warm and friendly and frequently
asked me to join them for drinks after the show — E. E. Clive,
Cyril Biddulph and sometimes Lyn Harding. The talk was
tall, and because I have large ears and can listen well, I began to hear of theaters in London: the Drury Lane, the Hay-
market, His Majesty's . . . and a new set of actors: Sir
Herbert Tree, Henry Ainley, Gerald du Maurier, Irene Van-
brugh, and a young beauty whose name was Gladys Cooper.
I made up my mind that London would be my next port of
call. In that happy winter not one of us would have believed that an assassination in Serajevo the following June
would eventually plunge the whole world into a conflict
that has not ended yet. It was the death knell to a long period of stability.

I have mentioned my memory before and I am going to
mention it again as I introduce briefly Walter Creighton to
these pages. He was a member of *The Great Adventure* cast,
playing Lord Leonard Alcar. He was striking-looking, over
six feet, very blond, slender and distinguished. I loved to

hear him talk. His father, who was dead, had been the Bishop of London, and his mother, now widowed, was pensioned and lived in Hampton Court Palace. He was a friend of Tree and Margot Asquith, the wife of the then British Prime Minister, Herbert Asquith. Creighton hobnobbed a bit in "society" in New York too, and altogether seemed to me to lead a charmed and romantic life. He returned to England when the play closed in mid-January in 1914.

Let thirty-one years elapse and in the autumn of 1944 I am accompanying and playing a minor part with Katharine Cornell in her overseas tour of *The Barretts of Wimpole Street,* which was being done for our troops. She had just finished playing seventy-two performances in Italy, opening in Santa Maria and covering the whole Southern area before going on to General Alexander's British 8th Army in Siena and then on to Mark Clark's 5th Army, first in Florence and later much nearer the front lines in Montecatini. We have flown to the E.T.O., and are now in Marseilles. I am having a noonday cocktail at the bar of the Hôtel Noailles, when I see a tall English colonel with white hair enter. I know him but I can't place him. I am certain he is not a recent acquaintance. He is alone and at the far end of the bar from me talking to the bartender. I ease over and listen. The moment I hear his voice I know who he is. I give him a gentle poke on the back. That is not the proper way to get the attention of any colonel, much less British. He turns with a startled look and I ask him if he is Walter Creighton. He is! It lacked one month of being thirty-one years since I had last laid eyes on him! With that kind of memory, I sometimes think I might have been more use to the world if I had been a detective.

Janet Beecher was my second Broadway leading woman. A few years later, when I was getting to know Winthrop Ames quite well, I was intrigued to hear him always refer to Janet and her sister, Olive Wyndham, as "ladies" — when we were casting. Not that they weren't, mind you, but the word seemed to me an intruder to the magic world of make-believe. What did it have to do with acting anyway? But he would always caution me, "I want the lady type, like Miss Beecher or Miss Wyndham."

Mr. Ames once told me that he had gone to see Laurette Taylor at the suggestion of Lee Shubert, who had just witnessed a performance of hers and thought she might be material for the Repertory Company that was then being assembled to open the New Theater. She was playing in our old stand-by, *Stolen by Gypsies*, in Kansas City. (*Yosemite*, it was called then.) This would be after her Seattle days, and just before her first Broadway appearance, which she once told me was indirectly due to Mr. Shubert. She was receiving quite a lot of publicity then because of her many run-ins with the censors on account of the sparsity of her last-act costume. The report was she was showing bare legs to just above the knees! Lee Shubert had rushed to see her first, thinking those legs might find her a place in the show that he was planning to open — his new Winter Garden Theater. He decided against it — not because of her legs, I am sure. He spoke to her at the end of the performance and asked her to come and see him when in New York. Shortly afterward *Yosemite* had folded, and she found herself on Broadway broke — two children — deserted by her husband — looking feverishly for work. The receptionist in Mr. Shubert's outer office wouldn't give her the time of day. Outraged by these continual rebuffs, she one day lost control of her good Irish temper, telling the receptionist in no uncertain terms her opinion of her. At that moment Hartley Manners arrived to see Mr. Shubert by appointment. Once inside Mr. Lee's private sanctum he said, "There's an attractive young woman outside who has the fire and spirit for that third-act scene of *The Great John Ganton*" (Manners's play which they were then casting). Shubert said, "Let's have her in" and buzzed for the receptionist who said the lady had left but she would try to get her. The office boy was sent scurrying after her, and returned triumphantly with Miss Taylor in tow. She was signed immediately; and that was the beginning of the partnership of Laurette Taylor and Hartley Manners. However, when Mr. Ames saw Miss Taylor in *Yosemite,* he recognized her quality but decided against using her in the New Theater Company because, said he, she wasn't a "lady." And, if it was a lady he was looking for, he may have been right — but an actress? Surely, that is another matter entirely. I have always thought and still do that on the great stages throughout the world actresses can do anything, be anything . . . even ladies; that is, if they are actresses.

Now I have been very rude to Janet Beecher, leaving her in the Shubert Alley outside the Booth stage door while I have digressed disgracefully, raising hell with any continuity that this narrative may possess.

Janet was a handsome, generous woman, who a few years before had created the Gibson Girl in *The Education of Mr. Pipp,* a dramatization of Charles Dana Gibson's cartoon of the same name, and had had several conspicuous successes since. Like Julia Dean she couldn't have been nicer to me. Her mother, a nice gray-haired old lady, seemed interested in me too. She was hipped on the subject of the science of numbers, of which a Mrs. Cochrane was the Madame Oom of the inner sanctum, changing every name outside Debrett for harmony and, of course, a fee. Mrs. Wyndham counted out the number of letters in my name and date of my birth and then solemnly told me that my Christian name was wrong and should have only six letters instead of the seven that it takes to spell Guthrie. Well, my first name has six letters (it is spelt G-c-o-r-g-e) but as my mother, for reasons of her own, didn't like it, it was never used. So even at the risk of flying in the face of science I stuck to Guthrie, which I had grown fond of through the years — the name I mean.

The Great Adventure was not the success in New York that had been expected. The lukewarm press cast a pall over the entire company, and they were never able to rise above it. No one seemed interested. Vernon was out, Platt had disappeared, and Mr. Ames was busy with his charming production of *Prunella* at the Little Theater, while we at the Booth crept quietly away and took to the road. We were in Boston at Christmastime 1913, and in Washington, D.C., for the New Year of 1914. Good reviews in both places neither brought in paying customers nor sparked the cast up, so the curtain fell for the last time on *The Great Adventure* in the nation's capital. The pity was that it was an amusing play, but it demanded brilliant acting and directing and it had neither. The company manager told me in parting to "take it easy" for a short time, as he was certain the office would have something for me soon.

It seemed strange being idle after six months of fairly

strenuous work. I took Edythe Latimer, a charming Englishwoman who had appeared in *The Great Adventure,* to
see one of our top-flight and too little sung-about American
actresses, Emily Stevens, give her marrow-chilling performance in a tawdry melodrama called *Today.* And Edythe, in
turn, took me to see Forbes-Robertson's beautifully spoken
and sensitive portrayal of *Hamlet.* I still wanted to act.
I believed I could. I certainly had no dim inner stirring that
I would want to direct. As a matter of fact I had never seen
any real directing then. I had seen two plays put on on
Broadway and, although I would have been too timid to say
it, neither one of them had direction. As for acting, my only
approach would be through the agencies and I still smarted
with the remembrance of Ada Humbert's ultimatum less
than a year before. I was emerging ever so slightly from the
haze of my own inferiority that the academy had imposed on
me. I decided to bide my time. If the Ames office wanted
me, I would certainly go back. I was not unmindful of the
importance of his organization. If my present fate was to
be stage management, then please, oh please, let it be at
the Little Theater.

The manager was right. I was sent for, and this time when
I went to the Little Theater I was shown into Mr. Ames's
office — and there he was, coming around his desk to shake
hands with me. After being in his employ for seven months
this was my first personal contact with the gentleman, whom
for many years I was to work for and for many more years
to know and value as a privileged friend. Although I had
seen him before I was in no way prepared for the impact
of his presence. He had an extraordinary quality of making
you feel you were necessary to him. His speech had no taint

of that accent we are pleased to call "New England." In fact there was nothing about him that suggested the Home of the Bean. His clothes were immaculate and conservative but when you gave him a second look they seemed incongruous. Winthrop Ames has said he might be descended from Portuguese-Jewish ancestry; to me he seemed a Velasquez cardinal in mufti — his long, slim hands could have served as models for El Greco; they also could have written an order for the Inquisition. I was immediately at ease when he shook my hand. The whole meeting was very matter-of-fact, but here was a gentleman who let you forget that fact. When we were both seated he said he would like me to stage-manage his forthcoming revival of Clyde Fitch's play *The Truth,* which he was presently going to put into rehearsal with himself directing and Grace George playing the leading part. Clearing my throat to squelch the sound of my pounding heart, and in a voice that sounded strangely falsetto, I said, "I would be delighted."

He went into Miss Ingersoll's domain for a moment or two and, left alone, I gazed around the gray-green walls of his office on which hung many simple gold-framed pictures of old theaters. Against the wall by the entrance door was the measuring rod which, I learned later, caused many a young actress concern when he asked her to stand against it to determine her exact height. His windows looked out over box hedges to the newly built Shubert and Broadhurst Theaters across the way on 44th Street. In the wall opposite these windows was the secret panel which he could slide open in order to watch the performances in his theater. His thick, gray carpet deadened all sound. He returned with my contract. I noticed only the salary. That was thirty-five dollars. I signed. We shook hands and I was out on 44th Street, walking towards Broadway, when I fell in with Beverly Sitgreaves (a fine actress who had played in *Her Own Money*). When I told her my news she shook her head and said, "That's a pity, Mac. Grace George is a bitch — she is a horror to work with, particularly for women; and as for stage managers, she makes their life a hell on wheels. I am sorry for you. Let me know what happens, Mac. I am at the Remington Hotel." I got back to 19 East 32nd Street thoroughly deflated, and sat there alone in the darkening afternoon brooding on what was in store for me. But, thought I, every silver lining has a dark cloud. And there was nothing for me to do but grin and bear it, anyway.

Thus I approached the first rehearsal with a certain amount of apprehension The cast bordered on being an all-star one. The names would be meaningless to most of the public today, but to the theatergoers of forty years ago they were topnotch: Zelda Sears, Isabel Irving, Ferdinand Gottschalk, and Conway Tearle.

Mr. Ames had every piece of furniture and every prop in place as on an opening night — no scenery, of course — awaiting the cast who were there on their best behavior and on the dot of 11:00 A.M. with two exceptions: Miss George and Mr. Conway Tearle. The latter, I learned from the *New York Times*, which I was buying now for a cent, was in jail — the Ludlow Street jail, where one was incarcerated for failure to cough up alimony. Mr. Tearle, you see, was a philanderer!

Mr. Ames began the rehearsal without his star or leading

man as neither of them appeared in the opening scenes. Miss George (who I was later to hear coldly reprimand an actor for not being on time with "Promptness is a courtesy even kings extend") was the first of the delinquents to arrive. Her chauffeur was having trouble with her new Pierce Arrow, she said, and she had to call a cab. She was introduced to the cast by Mr. Ames and as she was acknowledging the introductions Conway Tearle put in an appearance directly from jail, his release having been arranged by Ames, who had paid his back alimony. Now, the ladies of the troupe were dressed rather fancily for that first rehearsal, and the gentlemen ran them a close second; but Conway added a Bohemian note to the assembly by being unkempt, unshaven, unwashed, unpressed and nonchalant. It cleared the atmosphere immensely, which up to that time had been almost too polite.

Then the rehearsal started all over again. I was sitting by a director for the first time.

Mr. Ames had the business of the entire play mapped out — that is, he came to the first rehearsal knowing exactly where he wanted every actor to stand, sit, turn or pause. This represented hours of preparation on his part. But he was not one who left *anything* to the spur of the moment, as I was to be continually aware of during the coming years. Not all good directors have the same method, but whatever their approach there is none better than that of Winthrop Ames. He was quiet, courteous, concerned if the performer felt at ease or not — "Could you pass the drink with your left hand?" always followed by the questioning sound "H'm." "If you're not comfortable, please let me know" was his constant solicitation. In all my first years with him I never saw him touch an actor other than to shake hands, nor address anyone by their first name.

When Grace George made her entrance at the rehearsal of *The Truth* you forgot she was tiny and blond, wore spotlessly white gloves and was generally "well turned out." You were only conscious that here was an actress — skillful, with vivacity, tremendous pace, and an ear and aptitude for direction that I have seldom seen equaled. Her voice was light but pleasant; her speech exquisite. She was one of the quickest studies I ever met (quick at learning lines, that is) and an indefatigable worker as well. Watching her evolve a part and Ames evolve a play was the beginning of a pattern for me. While I don't go at it as they did, Miss George and Mr. Ames were a part of the theater I was hoping for: they were the first of my theater associates who implanted in me an exciting idea of the approach to a stage production. Although *The Truth* was a revival, it was being rehearsed as if it were a new play. For the first time I heard an actress (Miss George) saying to a director, "I have no feeling yet that this is *my* drawing room. Why is it? What can I do?" (And Mr. Ames would think up some business that would unmistakably stamp her as mistress of the house.) Or another player saying, "I don't feel I can say that line sitting down," or Ames saying, "Can't you say the line as you are walking across the stage? Don't be like Abe Lincoln's tugboat that had to stop altogether when it whistled."

In those days, professional scene designers had not yet crossed the producer's horizons and the Ames productions, scenically, were a brilliant reflection of his lively imagination and impeccable taste. The drawing room for *The Truth* was no exception. To this day no one has surpassed or possibly equaled the indefinable emanation of quality that stamped his productions.

And there I was, emerging from the flotsam and jetsam of the theater, sitting at his elbow across the prompt table, writing down his directions and absorbing as much as the days gave. This was the beginning of my theater doctorate — or apprenticeship — or whatever you choose to call it. It was to continue eight more years. Hours? There were none for me. There were no protective unions then to dictate whether you worked seven or sixteen hours a day. I was in the theater, it was where I longed to be. . . . I was catching up on the times I had wanted to be there. I had few diversions — no cocktail parties, no social life — just the supreme satisfaction of discovering that which I had always somehow known was there, and, to top it all, for this extraordinary enlightenment I was being paid.

What spark from a wayward ancestor turned Winthrop Ames's feet toward the theater we will never know. Graduating from Harvard in 1895, he deserted the conventional paths of his aristocratic New England forebears (the Ames clan at the end of the American Revolutionary War started manufacturing plows, and for a new, untilled country, it proved a very lucrative business indeed; during the Civil War they made ammunition for the Northern Armies; his grandfather was in Lincoln's cabinet). He spent some time abroad and began his theatrical career with the old Castle Square stock company in Boston. He proceeded a few years later to New York, where he became the head of the ill-fated but distinguished repertory experiment at the New

Theater, where for two years he set a superlative example in quality and taste for theater production in this country. When the repertory closed, the same high standard was sustained in every production he staged until his retirement in the early '30s, when he left the theater in a blaze of achievement with his really exceptional renderings of the Gilbert and Sullivan operettas.

What was the particular quality that made him memorable and apart? Certainly he never invited nor sought the kind of acclaim that David Belasco courted and got. He never had the acquisitiveness of actors or authors that distinguished Charles Frohman's career, and later that of Arthur Hopkins during his fifteen years of klieg-light glory. Yet somehow the memory of that retiring, sensitive New England gentleman remains, to those who knew him, an eduring and more potent recollection than the sum of the other two. In his approach to the theater he was a solitary figure, always seeming to be in search of a collaborator and never finding one. He was completely aware and receptive to a changing world, and had enthusiasm for it, but strangely enough remained apart from it — applauding, as it were, from the side lines. He had brilliant successes all the way from *The Affairs of Anatol* on through *The Green Goddess, Beggar on Horseback,* Galsworthy's *Old English* and *Escape* to his final magnificent productions of Gilbert and Sullivan. But apart from his achievements, which were considerable — apart from his wealth, which was also considerable — his outstanding quality and contribution was his investment in young people. I don't mean only in money. I mean in advice and interest. His wholehearted delving into problems, seeking with you a solution. This went for play-

wrights, actors and directors. Although he frequently sub-
sidized them or their ideas he never exploited them.
He shunned even taking credit for them. His satisfaction
stemmed from their making good.

Grace George was not the difficult biddy I expected. She
was the wife of William A. Brady, an astute and successful
producer. She had a wicked sense of humor, adorable dim-
ples; she liked me and I liked her — and before we opened
The Truth out of town we were on quite a friendly footing. There is a certain satisfaction to me in the knowledge
that, some thirty years later, in 1941, to be exact, I presented and directed her in *Spring Again*. She was still the
star, while a youngster named Kirk Douglas, fresh out of
the Academy, was my assistant stage manager for his initia-
tion on Broadway with one line. Aubrey Smith was her co-
star.

Ames was more formal, not forbidding . . . but encased
in what might be called New England reserve. I did not
think he disliked me but I was by no means sure he liked
me. We played five one-nighters in New England before
opening in New York, and on the train to our first stand in
Northampton, Massachusetts, Miss George wanted to pass
the time playing bridge and asked me into her drawing room
to be a fourth. I won. But when I emerged with my win-
nings I thought Mr. Ames, who didn't play bridge, seemed
disapproving. In many ways we were poles apart. On the
surface at any rate he had a conventional side that I never
had, nor could hope to assume, nor wanted to for that
matter.

We finished our five-day preliminary tour in Bridgeport
and Miss George and her husband, William A. Brady, and

Winthrop and Mrs. Ames, all drove back to New York in Brady's brand-new Pierce Arrow with great carriage lamps on each side. After the performance, as I was watching them being tucked in by the chauffeur, it all seemed very Easy Street to me; but I was also conscious of a thrill that they all knew me and spoke to me by name . . . and inside *that* car, at least *one* of them *could* act.

After three invitation performances at the Little, and very "swell" the audiences were, we opened for the critics. Their approval was gratifying. *The Truth,* which had been a failure when originally done some eight years before with Clara Bloodgood playing Miss George's part, was now a success and ran to full houses for the remainder of the season. On my own I made a beautiful prompt book for Ames with all of his directions and lighting put down in my own meticulous hand-printing together with photographed scenes from the play taken by White.

Earlier in the season, both Julia Dean and Janet Beecher had given me pictures of themselves, at my request of course, and now I made bold to ask Grace George for one; and when it arrived I felt I had won the finals. It was framed in a Tiffany silver frame with my initials on it. The next day Mr. Ames sent for me and I was glad he asked me to be seated when I came in, for his first remark was a question. "Mr. McClintic, would you like to work for me by the year?" I found my voice and said I would. My contract was a letter outlining much the same duties I had performed during the season just finishing. Ames felt that in view of my having a guarantee of forty weeks' work I should take thirty dollars a week instead of thirty-five. I didn't argue. I was leaving the actor behind, but I would find him again, I believed. And, oh, wasn't it wonderful to be in the theater and to be wanted!

Laurette Taylor finished her long run of *Peg* — 604 performances, the longest run in America up to that time — and sailed for her first trip to Europe and, incidentally, to make her debut in London. Marie Lloyd, beloved performer of the London music halls, was arrested in New York that spring for singing a song entitled "Who Paid the Rent for Mrs. Rip Van Winkle when Mr. Rip Van Winkle Went Away?" — Broadway must be kept clean at all costs. *The Truth* closed, but I was not "at liberty" for a change. Song pluggers along the Gay White Way were zestfuly singing a new number, "In the Blue Ridge Mountains of Virginia . . ." I laughed out loud: "Not for me this summer, fellas! I'm going back to home and Mother, and for the first time I can pay my own way."

VIII

Broadway 1914

My progress, which had seemed to me to be colossal in the two years I had been away, hardly occasioned the raising of an eyebrow at home. I had a job in New York and not Seattle. That was all. To my father in particular everything I had done was Greek. "I don't understand you," he would say. "You wanted to be an actor and, by the Eternal, we sent you to dramatic school to be an actor; and now, so help me, you have a job that has nothing to do with acting. Why in hell did you go to dramatic school? Answer me that." And he would wait for my explanation. "But, Father," I would say, "I am in the theater."

"In the theater," he would boom, mimicking me. "In God's name what does *that* signify? You can be an usher and be in the theater."

"But can't you see . . ." I would come back. . . .

"No, I can't," he would snap.

Nothing I could say made any impression at all. The name of Winthrop Ames conveyed less to him than that of Percy Palmleaf, who worked in the Seattle Assay Office. And — this was the last straw — "It's a strange job you have," he exploded, "when an advancement as you call it, means getting less money."

I just listened, and somehow the old irritation returned.
In the early mornings I could hear him putter around the
house, reciting to himself in funereal tones, "Tell me not
in mournful numbers life is but an empty dream . . ." over
and over again. I could not help feeling the empty dream
was me.

In the rush of my brief seven weeks at home no notice
was taken of the old Austrian Emperor Francis Joseph's ultimatum to Serbia on July 23. And when I presented myself
at the Little Theater on August 1, Europe was already slipping over the brink to war. But it was still a long way off to
me and I was eager to know what new assignment awaited
me with Winthrop Ames — W. A., as I later found he was
called by the office staff. On arriving at 244 West 44th Street,
I was shown into George Foster Platt's old office and told it
was mine (no clue as to where he had gone or why, and I
didn't ask). I was given the script of *Children of Earth*,
which turned out to be the Ten-Thousand-Dollar Prize Play,
written by Alice Brown of Boston, and told to line up some
actors for the various roles which had not been filled. Effie
Shannon was set for the leading part. When the door closed
I was pinching myself to see if it was really me. Fourteen
months before I had been reaching for bricks to smash these
windows I now looked out of. I was sitting at Platt's desk —
this time in Platt's chair. The inkwell was missing (that must
have been his personal property), and I was reading the
prize play in order that I might suggest actors for it. I felt
life was looking up at twenty-one.

Still nursing the bruises of the various snubs I had suffered at the hands of agents, I made up my mind that by and
large they were a parasitic breed living off the work of oth-

ers, and that in my new position I would never call on them except in a case of sheer necessity. At first I stuck to it, too. I later relented somewhat. I even made up with Ada Humbert. And in these days of canned amusement, agents are a necessity; but I still see anyone who writes for an interview and, of course, I don't turn my nose up at any new talent an agent wishes me to look over. As it was with Platt, I took on all appointments with actors that Ames didn't wish to handle. I kept an elaborate card index which recorded their height . . . weight . . . coloring . . . type . . . and my over-all impression of them. In no time at all I was feeling quite at ease on my new side of the desk, and what is more, liking it.

One day late in August, on arriving at the office, I was surprised to see another desk in my room and a young man I had never seen before facing me. For a moment or two I wondered if I was being eased out, but then Miss Ingersoll hurried in to introduce us. It was Samuel Eliot III — grandson of President Eliot of Harvard, the gentleman who advocated the five-foot bookshelf — and he was to be my sidekick for the winter and was going to "assist" too. This dampened my feeling of importance somewhat, but not for long. Sam was a nice fellow with a slight stutter. He had had the education I rebelled at, and he had come through unscathed. He had recently returned from a year or so abroad, principally in Germany, and was filled with admiration for their theater, which he thought the finest in the world. He had nothing but contempt for the London productions, which my English friends of the year before had told me were fifty years ahead of the New York stage. Remembering that, I asked Eliot what he thought about our local theater, and he replied he didn't know enough about it to give an opinion, but I felt he thought it poor. This attitude of deprecating the American theater reached its climax, I would think, in the early '20s, when many of our long-haired contributors to the drama (and its confusion) burst into print extolling the supremacy of the theaters and acting companies of Prague, Dresden, Warsaw, Berlin and points east. I had not yet visited those capitals, so I believed what I read. We all know that dinner away from home sometimes seems better. It may not be, but it seems, better. And that was the way it was with the long-hairs, I think.

I am grateful to Sam Eliot for introducing me to Helen Westley when the Theatre Guild was hardly a gleam in her eye. She was a vital and stimulating person then. But Sam didn't allow our theater to contaminate him, and after a short time deserted it to become a professor at Smith College. Meantime I was getting to know the other members of the Ames office: Jed Shaw, a delightful guy, who was to become Winthrop's general manager later, and Miss Ingersoll, his amanuensis. . . . His last secretary, Florence Doody, is now, happily for us, a part of our office staff today. . . . Edward Lyons was his right hand as well as general manager when I first went there. (I did not like him — I never liked him — he was too slick — too blond — too smooth.)

And now I mention one who came across the bridge from Brooklyn to be in charge of the switchboard at the Little Theater when it opened, and remained at the ever-ringing telephone there until Winthrop Ames decided to shut up shop and sit on the side lines. Then the little lady, for little she was, came to a similar position in the offices of Cornell and McClintic — newly situated in the Belasco Theater, which we were ill-advised enough to take over after the old gentleman's death — but which, Heaven be praised, we were able to shed after two years' occupancy, when we moved to new quarters over the then recently built Radio City Music Hall, where our names are still to be found in the lobby directory. The girl on the switchboard followed and reigned like a queen in the outer office until she, too, decided to call it a day and avail herself of the advantages offered by a paternal government to those who happily exist to just beyond the threescore years that Providence metes out to us. This high priestess of the switchboard was Margaret Sullivan. . . . Sully, as she was known to hundreds of actors. . . . Sully, who only had to hear a voice once over the wire to know it ever after. There used to be a slogan of the Telephone Company, "The Voice with the Smile Wins." . . . That was Sully's voice; but brother — when her Irish temper rose it shrilled with the roar of a jet plane, and its impact was equally alarming; but in the outer office, when we were casting and it was crowded with aspirants, her warm sympathy and courtesy endeared her to all of those who sat waiting. She was Irish as Paddy's Pig. She frequently resorted to a kind of be-bop talk of 1914 which, like her gold teeth, had not changed when she retired in the late forties. Year after year we got used to such quips. When the sidewalks were slippery, she never failed to warn me: "Be careful, don't fall on your astrakhan jacket!" When Miss Doody appeared one Easter Monday in a new ensemble, Sully exclaimed:

"Gee, Florence, that's swell — turn around — how much did you pay for it?"

"Forty-nine fifty," replied Florence.

"For how many?" was Sully's comment.

One morning when I arrived she came into my office with, "Mr. McClintic, after I left the bus last night on my way home a man followed me. I was so scared I said my beads backwards."

When she got married I asked her what her husband's job was and she replied that he worked for the city.

"But," I persisted, "what does he do?"

She looked at me and said, "He fans sweat off the ice."

In the autumn of 1914 our Ambassador to England, Mr. Walter Hines Page, was anything but neutral. However, over here the feeling was strong that we should keep out of war. Mr. Wilson, our President, seemed to feel that way, too, much to the dissatisfaction of Theodore Roosevelt, who was all for our declaring ourselves on the side of the Allies. Hand organs, player pianos, gramophones and hotel orchestras never tired of playing, "It's a Long Way to Tipperary . . ." and the public never seemed to tire of hearing it. In fact, it was probably the last time an unsuspecting world would ever greet war as a carnival.

Al Jolson, on the threshold of his supremacy, was layin-'em-in-the-aisles at the Winter Garden, singing "Sister Susie's Sewing Shirts for Soldiers" with the audience joining in the chorus, and there was a new motion picture theater at Broadway and 47th Street, the Strand — the first of the many cinema palaces to follow — managed by a gentleman named Rothafel, who was later better known to the American public as Roxy. At the Strand, you saw important pictures, silent of course, with stars like Theda Bara, Alice Joyce, Mary Pickford and a new comedian whose name was Charlie

Chaplin. Also news flickers were shown revealing to us shots of the British army and the French, as well as the helmeted Kaiser surrounded by his German staff. The sight of all of them brought applause, and for the Germans some boos as well.

Into the Ames office one day there came a distinguished young matron with prematurely white hair . . . lovely to look at . . . lovely to listen to . . . Mrs. August Belmont, who only a short time before, as Eleanor Robson, had been a bright star on the theatrical firmament, delighting audiences with her performances in *Salomy Jane, The Dawn of Tomorrow* and *Merely Mary Ann*. Mrs. Belmont had an idea for a benefit which was to be given for the Belgians whose homeland had been invaded by the Huns on their march to Paris. She is a lady of sound enterprise, a great organizer, and the theater lost a master mind when she married into society and transferred her allegiance to the opera. Her persuasive charm ensnared Ames and he agreed to stage it. King Albert of Belgium was the sponsor. Whose inspiration it was to have the stars participating appear briefly in parts that had made them famous, I don't know, but the result was a benefit that in this country I have never seen equaled since. On either side of the stage in great classical chairs sat two masked figures — Comedy and Tragedy. Alexandra Carlisle was Comedy, and Walter Hampden was Tragedy. Alternately they recited couplets written by Mrs. Douglas Robinson that introduced the stars, who appeared through curtains held back for the entrance by the Fairbanks twins — I don't mean the Gold Dust ones, but two lovely young girls! To any of you who have knowledge of the theater of the late '90s and the first decade of the 1900s, these names will mean something. Henry Miller appeared as Sydney Carton in *The Tale of Two Cities;* Blanche Bates as *Madame Butterfly;* Frances Starr in *The Rose of the Rancho;* William Gillette as *Sherlock Holmes;* William H. Crane as *David Harum;* Marie Doro in *The Morals of Marcus;* Francis Wilson sang a number from *Erminie;* Nazimova as Hedda Gabler; Jane Cowl in *Within the Law;* Ruth Chatterton in *Daddy Long-Legs;* old Mrs. Sol Smith as the Nurse in *Romeo and Juliet;* Holbrook Blinn as the sheriff in *Salomy Jane;* Ethel Barrymore in *Captain Jinks;* Mrs. Patrick Campbell as Mélisande; Marie Tempest as Becky Sharp; Rose Coghlan as Lady Gay Spanker in *London Assurance;* Phyllis Neilson Terry as Viola in *Twelfth Night,* and her aunt, Ellen Terry, in the Mercy speech from *The Merchant of Venice,* as a finale. Venerable Joseph Choate spoke in the entr'acte, and Madame Alda sang the Belgian National Anthem accompanied by the entire orchestra from the Met.

Eleanor Belmont so beguiled Roxy that he straightaway canceled all the picture showings at the Strand for twenty-four hours while W. A. and his staff, myself included, slaved through an all-night session to ready decor and lights for the benefit matinee. Further, Mrs. Belmont arranged with the city fathers that Broadway, proceeding south from 59th Street to 42nd Street, should be a one-way thoroughfare from 1:00 to 6:00 P.M. to facilitate the motor traffic coming to the Strand.

I was the stage manager of the whole affair, which came off smoothly, and emerged with possibly a little more kudos than I deserved. Ames, at the end, introduced me to Ellen Terry. He led me forward to her saying, "Miss Terry, you may never remember meeting this young man, but he will always remember he shook your hand." My guess is that he was right on both counts — on one I know he is. To another young ambitious in the theater, the other day, I mentioned Ellen Terry's name and was literally struck dumb to hear him ask me who she was. It's hard for me to imagine a young doctor who would not know who Pasteur . . . Osler . . . or Erdmann was; or any self-respecting musician who has never heard of Verdi . . . Heifitz . . . or Flagstad; or a budding young painter who professes to be ignorant as to the identity of Whistler . . . Goya . . . Rembrandt. In these days truly there is no business like show business!

Mrs. Belmont, as a token of her appreciation, sent me a signed photograph of herself as Merely Mary Ann and there began a friendship that has endured these forty years up until now. The success of the Belgian Benefit was so great that Ames was asked by Mrs. Whitney Warren and Mrs. Frank Gray Griswold to do another — this one for Secours Nationale, which he turned over to me to manage entirely. Though star-cluttered, it was rather a mess, I thought; but the ladies in charge seemed to think it was dandy, and I was the recipient of a silver cigarette case and a gold knife — but not because I was a Boy Scout. Moreover I was catching a fleeting glimpse of drawing rooms and a way of living which reflected a New York that was soon to disappear.

All of this was before Christmas 1914, and all of it was honorary endeavor. Now we shall turn to the endeavor I was being paid for, which was also accomplished before Christmas too. In addition to unearthing talent for the prize play, there were some changes to be made in the cast of *The Truth* that was being sent out with Miss George on tour. That I attended to, as well as conducting the rehearsals of these new people until Ames took over the last few days. He patted me on the back and said "Good work, old fellow," which seemed to me to indicate he was pleased with my job. Grace George seemed pleased too. And I was happy — completely oblivious to an adjustment, ever so slight, that was taking place, directing what talents I had into a different channel. The play opening at the Little that season was Cyril Harcourt's *A Pair of Silk Stockings*, an English importation with a cast headed by Kenneth Douglas and Mary Glynne. There was some speculation in the office as to whether the company would be able to get here, owing to the war, but they arrived intact and ready to open. Although W. A. was ostensibly impresario only, on this play, he nevertheless furnished the scenic production — and very handsome it was. I was his assistant on that. I was sent all over the town to spot furniture, fabrics, lamps and an endless number of accessories. I learned on my own to identify periods in furniture; to distinguish French pieces from English and Italian; I learned to bow to "the Louies" and shake hands with the Adamses, Hepplewhites and Chippendales — which has stood me in good stead through the years. No decorator has had to explain to me the kind of room I want. I know. At the dress rehearsal, *Silk Stockings* seemed the dreariest British effort ever, but on its opening night it perked up considerably — thanks primarily to a brilliant comedy performance by Kenneth Douglas — received splendid notices, and was one of the big hits of the season.

After that all our attention was centered on the prize play. Sam Eliot served as stage manager and among other duties that fell my way in that production was the staging of a mob scene which came at the end of Act II. Just over twenty

people were used in it and it served as a background for the
most dramatic scene in the play. To spare the principal actors, this scene or effect was rehearsed separately by me.
There was no dialogue written for these extra people, yet
obviously they had to be alive and were supposedly having
one whale of a good time at an apple blossom festival or
some such fete that used to stir the marrow of New England farm folks. My "cast" consisted of a few older out-of-
work actors, but the others were mostly around my own
age, two out of my class at dramatic school. The scene was
full of action. I went at it with great enthusiasm. I had
never had a problem like this before — neither in dramatic
school, my brief stage experience, nor in my imagination.
I watched over and over again the principals rehearsing the
scene of which it was to be a part, in order to be sure that
whatever I did did not interfere with them. I improvised
lines . . . business . . . and sub-plots. I managed to instill
in my group enthusiasm, high spirits, and a rigid adherence
as to when they were to crescendo or when to diminuendo.

After six days, the time came when it was all to be put
together. The principals and supers met for the first time.
(Ames had never allowed them to watch the scene they
were to be a part of, as he thought with so many of them
it would be disconcerting for the actors. I, together with
Bobby Ansett, the assistant props, "stood in" at my rehearsals to indicate where the absent actors would approximately be.) We rehearsed at the New Theater, which was
"dark" at the time, and it must have been filled with ghosts
for Winthrop. It was used for rehearsals primarily because
its revolving stage could take the scenery for the three
acts which we used for two weeks before we opened.

In less than a minute they could change from one scene to another.

Rushing to rehearsal on the day the supers and principals were to meet on stage, I tripped and fell down the subway stairs. I had bloody shins and sprained my right wrist and ankle. The underground looked on me as a lush, and in the crowded car I hung on the strap going uptown with my left hand until I pushed my way out at Columbus Circle. When I arrived at the theater I entered by the stage door, assembled my group in the Green Room (the New Theater had one, too) and put them "through their paces" a couple of times before they rubbed elbows with the higher-paid members of the company. I was getting sorer and lamer by the minute! And when it came time for my actors to invade the scene, I did not go out front to watch them for fear my halting gait would attract attention and maybe interrupt rehearsal, so I watched on the side lines.

For a first time they were remarkably smooth, I thought. Their scene ended the act. Suddenly Ames's voice with unaccustomed volume boomed out of the darkness of the theater. "Where's McClintic?" I hobbled out on the stage as my bunch fled to let me take full blame. "That's great work boy — great work," he said, and as he turned to a group sitting around him in the orchestra — Ed Lyons, Miss Ingersoll and others — I could hear him say, "That was very fine, wasn't it?" There was a dutiful murmur of assent as lovely blond Effie Shannon said to me, "What's happened to you? Why are you limping?" Ames echoed her question from out front and I had to stand in the center of the stage like an awkward galoot and explain how I fell down the subway stairs while the first praise I'd ever had from Winthrop Ames in front of people was forgotten in concern over my sprained ankle. I was bundled off to a doctor who found no broken bones, bandaged me up — and in no time at all I was leaping around as usual.

It seems extraordinary to me now that out of some twenty-five hundred scripts submitted that *Children of Earth* should have been the best. It was a story of New England farm folk — of parental tyranny and of an elderly spinster on the death of her father finding herself in love with her childhood sweetheart. It had moments of tenderness and a certain distinction and quality in its writing, but it was not really a good play. It might have been an interesting novel. However, W. A. gave it a wondrous production. In my mind's eye I can still see the second act with that fabulous apple orchard in full bloom through the barn doors and in the third act that misty forest at night. The lighting of these scenes was superb. Hours were spent in the theater while weary electricians were getting the right focus, volume and color of light. In his profound and inventive knowledge of stage lighting, Winthrop Ames led all other producers of his time. David Belasco, whose reputation as a genius of lighting was highly publicized, relied on his brilliant master electrician, Louis Hartman. Maude Adams, it may surprise you to know, was the other wizard of lights in that decade. Yet, in my opinion, Ames outdistanced them all. But all of this attention wasn't enough to save the prize play. The press damned it with faint praise and it went the way of all "almosts" to Cain's — that legendary graveyard for all flops in the theater. It had run five weeks.

When the prize play closed I was idle after six months activity. Nothing to do and being paid! I interviewed scores of actors for X, that unknown quantity representing W. A.'s next production. I saw plays and read plays. I suggested that Ames do a revival of Wilde's *The Importance of Being Earnest*. He was enthusiastic for a while but nothing ever happened. However, the season had been a rewarding one to me. I had been in close contact with, able to watch, many fine actors, both British and American, in rehearsal and later in performances. It opened my eyes to a lot of approaches — tricks — and techniques that are used in the creating of a part. When all is said and done, the only approach to any creative work is the imaginative one and that, unfortunately, cannot be passed on. It can be awakened, and at times a good director can pass on ideas to a technically good actor — ideas that otherwise he would not have had. All of this and a feeling of security prompted me to sign again with W. A. when he asked me, this time with a salary of fifty dollars a week. . . . What had become of the ambitious actor? I don't know. I am relating what happened. . . . My learning, if one can call it that, was entirely "picked up" by listening and watching. No director or actor ever took me aside to give me points.

Although the European war was not over by Christmas, as had been predicted, it was still something you saw on the silent screen newsreels. High-muck-a-mucks in silk hats bowing from automobiles, or immaculate uniformed generals sitting on horseback, looking for all the world to me as if they were waiting to start a game of polo . . . Broadway seemed in the doldrums. The two most important events of the year were the beginning of an obscure organization of amateurs called "the Washington Square Players" and the production of a big success called *On Trial*, written by a new

author who was going to be known as Elmer Rice. The dancing of Vernon and Irene Castle was sweeping the country
like a forest fire. And Irene had her hair bobbed, and that
fashion swept the world. From London came news of Laurette Taylor's big success there in *Peg*. Granville-Barker
brought an English troupe to New York, headed by his wife,
Lillah McCarthy, to appear in repertory. Apart from introducing Robert Edmond Jones, one of the pioneer American
scene designers, to his own country, Mr. Barker's season
was a dismal failure and resulted in another black mark for
repertory.

At the beginning of spring my English friend, Edythe
Latimer, was back in town from a road tour of *The Garden
of Allah*. With her mother and young son, she was booked to
sail back on the *Lusitania* on May 1. One day we were talking about the supernatural . . . ghost stories . . . and finally got around to spiritualism, and I told her of the message that prompted me to post my letter to Ames. She was
deeply impressed, and begged me to ask Mrs. Heinsohn if
she would see her and maybe find out if there were any
words for her from the spirit world. Adah was reluctant but
finally gave in, and Edythe and I arrived at 403 late one afternoon in early March. Without any preliminaries we journeyed into the dining room to confer with my old friend . . .
the table. Mrs. Heinsohn took her usual place and in a short
time the table became demonstrative and, what with Adah's
sympathetic urging and my doggedly keeping at the alphabet and putting down each letter as the table noisily indicated, the communication finally came through. The twilight
had deepened and when we switched on the lights this is
what I had written down. . . . Do NOT SAIL ON BIG BOAT

AS IT WILL NEVER REACH ENGLAND. There could be no doubt what this meant. Edythe's passage on the *Lusitania,* but Adah Heinsohn did not know that. Edythe had delayed her sailing to get on this ace Cunarder. It was generally spoken of as the one safe boat on the ocean, because of its speed. It could outdistance any German U-boat.

Edythe instinctively tried to ignore this message: it had taken pull to acquire the space she had; but as the days went by she began thinking that if anything *should* happen and she was saved and her mother and son lost, she would never forgive herself, remembering she had been warned. So she canceled her *Lusitania* passage and booked on the *Transylvania,* which was sailing a week later, but she had to take second-class accommodations in place of the first-class ones she had given up.

The weather of noontime on May 7, 1915, was wretchedly overcast when I called for Edythe at the Wilsonia on West 69th Street to take her to the boat which was sailing from a pier at 14th Street and North River. Her mother and son with the luggage had gone ahead with a friend. As we were driving through Times Square, there came a sound the like of which I have never heard before or since: a hundred voices in unison it seemed — hoarse shrieking newsboys crying, "*Lusitania* torpedoed . . . all on board lost!" That was not quite true, but we didn't know it at that time. I stopped the cab and bought a paper. Yes, there it was. A few hours before, as the passengers were going down to lunch, the *Lusitania* was hit by a U-boat a few miles off of Kinsale Head, Ireland, and sank within twelve minutes. The BIG BOAT did not REACH ENGLAND. It was a new kind of warfare! . . . What now?

I asked the taxi driver to take us around the corner to the Little Theater to find out if Edythe's ship would be sailing as scheduled. There was a lot of excitement at our office too, as the *Silk Stockings* company were returning to England on the *Transylvania*. Several members of the cast were there seeking the same information as ourselves. We finally received word that it would sail at five that afternoon. Everyone had checked out of their hotels and there was no desire to go down to the boat yet, so we all went over to the Iroquois Hotel on 44th Street where we had some sandwiches and a few drinks until just after three in the afternoon, when we went down to the pier.

There were no radios in those days and the news from the other side was still very skimpy. Speculation was rife as to how it could have happened, to the *Lusitania* of all boats! As we entered the dock we were handed a piece of paper which in the crush there we didn't look at until we got on board. (The sailings then had none of the secrecy or regulations that were observed in World War II; they were advertised, and visitors came on board as in normal times; and of course the "war zone," then, was only the sea within fifteen miles of the British Isles and French coast.) Once installed in our cabins we glanced at the paper that had been handed to us on the pier. It warned the passengers that they were sailing at their own risk, as the *Transylvania* was to be sunk precisely as the *Lusitania* had been. It had been sent by the German Embassy. These same warnings had been given the week before to the passengers on the *Lusitania*. The reaction to these pamphlets was more pronounced on those who were seeing their friends or relatives off than on the passengers themselves. The latter seemed to be in great spirits and joked about what they would do if they were torpedoed by a submarine.

As we stood waving to them as the boat pulled out down the North River in the yellowish, murky afternoon, we on land had none of the spirit that was sailing away with those on board. There was great rejoicing eleven days later when the morning papers announced the *Transylvania* had broken the blockade and was safe in Glasgow.

The air was tenser after the sinking of the *Lusitania*. War was closer. Many Americans had been drowned — among them the legendary mogul of the New York and London theater, Charles Frohman. Woodrow Wilson made his "too proud to fight" speech. Teddy Roosevelt advocated our joining up with the Allies immediately. Will Rogers, chewing gum and throwing his lariat, said, "The war was Teddy's fault, for when he was the Kaiser's guest after his lion-hunting safari in Africa and was standing alongside the Emperor at a military review in his honor, Roosevelt exclaimed in admiration, 'With that army you could lick the world.' And," added Rogers, "the damned fool believed him."

Although Mr. Ames had not been around the office during April or early May I thought nothing of it, so I was more than a little dismayed when Lyons told me that W. A. was sick and shutting up his office for a year and wanted me to find employment elsewhere, if I could for that time; and in the event I did, would I be agreeable to pushing my contract with him ahead a year? I was panicky for a moment. Things had been too easy, I guess; but I quickly remembered Grace George's recent announcement that in the season of 1915–1916 she would reappear in her husband's theater, the Playhouse, in a series of plays which she was pleased to call repertory. I wrote to her at once, explaining my position, and asking if there would be an opening for me in her plans for the autumn. I had an immediate reply thanking me for letting her know, and saying she would be delighted to have me stage-manage her season and play small parts when necessary. The salary would be fifty dollars a week and rehearsals would begin in August. Once again I would be holding the book!

Instead of going home I decided to stay close to New York for the two months before I started with Miss George. I was gratified at being able to send my father the money he had advanced two summers before for my round trip home. I was gratified at being able to relieve Ames of his obligation to me. I was gratified, too, at Miss George's expressed enthusiasm at having me with her. I looked forward to it.

IX

Holding the Book for the Bradys

No two people I ever knew battled more in the theater than Grace George and her husband, William A. Brady, during her repertory season of 1915–1916. Miss George was not in Winthrop's exquisite Little Theater now. She was in her own back yard at the Playhouse, where company manners were in the discard and no holds barred. Both Mr. Brady and she were of Irish extraction . . . both hot-tempered . . . both uninhibited; and every rehearsal that was honored by Mr. Brady's presence brought forth sparks and fireworks that were stimulating, illuminating and at times not without humor.

Bill Brady was a colorful, lusty figure. He had been a prizefight promoter, a newspaperman, had produced a series of hits in the theater all the way from *Way Down East* to *Little Women,* and had more charm than was right for any one man to have. When he appeared at rehearsals he wore a slouch hat pulled down over his eyes. His overcoat collar would be turned up and his hands plunged deep in his pockets. He looked not unlike a gangster about to take you for a ride. He would sit out front, cigar in his mouth, mumbling to himself while the rehearsal was in progress. This wasn't exactly conducive to putting the actors at ease. Then suddenly, out of the darkness and with the swiftness of a bullet, his voice would roar a reading of a line that an actor had just said. It was electric — it was right; it was embarrassing that it should be — but it was; the whole stage would light up. However, an actor with a true ear was hideously handicapped by this method of direction, for Brady's tone of voice was indelibly stamped upon him. You could never escape it. And as these exciting readings were hurled at you during a final dress rehearsal, it only increased the handicap.

Brady's ebullient Gaelic spirits on some of these occasions would arouse the equally Gaelic ire of that petite and dainty lady who was his wife. She was immaculate as ever in dress, had the energy of ten, and worked like a demon. Much of my knowledge of acting is due to the many months I spent as stage manager watching her rehearse day after day and watching her act night after night. I was also fortunate in having a ringside seat for every skirmish with her lesser half. On one occasion, after an agonizing all-night dress rehearsal with constant interruptions from Mr. Brady, the curtain had finally risen at dawn on the last act. Miss George and another actor had entered and started their scene when Mr. Brady's tired voice boomed from the back of the second balcony, "Is it lit?" (He was referring to a special spotlight that was used in that scene.) Miss George continued her scene, paying no attention to the interruption. (The spot was on anyway.) Once again Brady's hoarse voice croaked, "I asked 'Is it lit?'" Miss George determinedly ignored the question and pressed on with the scene, when for the third time Bill shook the rafters with his voice and in so doing must have lost his balance, for there was a sound of a body falling down several uncarpeted stairs and ending with a thud. Miss George, to avoid any further interruptions, stepped to the footlights and, looking up at the second balcony, said with some asperity, "I⊤ is lit!" She was referring to the light of course, and after that there was quiet.

Mr. Brady had great pride in his wife and he exacted from her nothing less than the best she had to give. He was always at her about her diction and her tendency to drop the end of her speeches. I remember a rehearsal when Grace had a couple of important friends out front to watch a run-through. She was going along swimmingly when Brady, seated in the second row, started on her.

"I don't get your last word, Grace," he said.

In the beginning she took it very nicely, reading the speech over again and then asking in a voice that was coated with honey, "Is that better, dear?"

"H'm," was his reply.

But as he kept after her she dropped her honeyed tones and reread with an icy overemphasis. He never stopped. He was relentless. It climaxed when at a certain line his voice firmly came over hers with "I don't get your last word," and little Grace, at the end of her tether, flared out with, "You wouldn't anyway, it's French," and went right on with her speech. Mr. Brady left the theater. They each had Irish sensitivities. They each had innate respect for the other's opinion, and they each had the capacity to hurt the other. She was a devoted wife for over fifty years and was starring in my production of *The Velvet Glove* in January 1950 when Mr. Brady died. A few months later, when she received the medal for the best diction of the year from the National Institute of Arts and Sciences, in her speech of

acceptance she gave Mr. Brady all the credit for it. I said
no two people I ever knew battled more; I should have
added, or with better results.

That was a strenuous season — five plays were presented
in seven months. . . . (Langdon Mitchell's *The New York
Idea;* Henry Arthur Jones's *The Liars;* James Fagan's *The
Earth,* and Bernard Shaw's *Major Barbara* and *Captain
Brassbound's Conversion*) and a sixth one was rehearsed
and abandoned. The high light of the engagement was the
production of *Major Barbara.* It was curiously timely, this
play about the conflict between the munition maker and his
daughter in the Salvation Army, playing it as we were against
the background of a European war in which we were not
yet involved. The production was splendid, the cast the best
I have ever seen in the play: Mary Nash, Conway Tearle,
Ernest Lawford, Charlotte Granville, Clarence Derwent and
John Cromwell. Miss George as Barbara was superb, poign-
ant, touching and witty — and Louis Calvert, as her father, very fine indeed.

Calvert had created the part in London. He was an ex-
cessively stout man and indulged his gourmet-like appetite
to such an extent that sometimes he would arrive for the
performance a little on the drowsy side. He invariably carried a large number of silver coins in his trouser-pockets
and during the performance would jingle them continuously
— I think, to keep himself awake — at any rate, it drove
Grace crazy. She had ceased speaking to him because of
his noisy clearing of his throat off stage, which she declared
"was the best example of British phlegm this side of the
Atlantic"; so, through me, she gave the order that no coins
were to be in his trouser-pockets when he was on the stage

with her. He received the command very graciously; but during the second act that night, when in the Salvation Army shelter Miss George had a close-onto-five-minutes of eloquent appeal to her father (Calvert), she was shocked and exasperated to see him leaning against a post sleeping and exuding a gentle snore. Another actor nudged him, his eyes opened, and he looked very pleased indeed to have had his forty winks. When the act was over, Miss George, as she was leaving the stage, turned to him and said with withering sarcasm, "Mr. Calvert, if I put you to sleep, what must I do to my audience?"

It seems fantastic now, remembering the intensity and total absorption of life that was contained within that Playhouse. We rehearsed almost every day from 10:30 till after 5, in addition to giving eight performances weekly. Nothing outside seemed of any importance whatsoever. . . . The gamble . . . would the play be well received? . . . The critics . . . the notices . . . the jealousies . . . the annoyances . . . the tempers flaring . . . and all of this in just one theater: a hut in a jungle of huts, the jungle that was Broadway. The war news from Europe was all but forgotten by our actors as they turned to the dramatic page to see who was mentioned first and how. But to be fair to our actors, I must add they weren't the only ones who were trying to forget the war just then.

Vignettes tumble over each other as I recall that winter. Once, just before Christmas, I saw Ethel Barrymore on Fifth Avenue at 57th Street in front of the old Vanderbilt Château, stepping out of any fellow's dream in a little fur toque and a small muff to match; to say she was lovely . . . is not enough! Her brother Jack was soon to give his superlative performance in Galsworthy's play *Justice,* which marked his departure from being a handsome and popular young actor into one who was brushed by greatness and was to have an acclaim that has been accorded to few men in our theater. Nor will I ever forget the uncompromising brilliance of Mrs. Fiske's cousin, Emily Stevens in *The Unchastened Woman* that season. This too-soon-forgotten lady was one of our greater actresses. Her *Hedda Gabler* was the finest I ever saw and her performance in *Fata Morgana* was a miracle of poignancy and delicacy. Off stage she had a pretty wit too. Once, when being accosted by a young woman outside the theater who said her mother wanted her to find out from Miss Stevens if she thought the stage was bad for a pure young girl, Emily quickly responded, "Not half so bad as a pure young girl is for the stage." Miss Stevens was not a beauty, but she was blond and fascinating, and her suicide in the late '20s robbed the theater of one of its brightest stars.

When I left the Bradys and the Playhouse in the late spring of 1916 I knew that I had had a vigorous and robust workout with two of the keenest theatrical personalities of the moment: Brady with his uncanny instinct for drama; Grace George with her unerring instinct for comedy. There were other values down on 44th at the Little Theater and that was what I was going back to, but the season just passed had been a shot in the arm for me. I had played five parts that season — none of them big, but in the two Shaw plays I had received quite good notices. However, as I looked at myself in contrast to the other young actors at that time I felt I was a misfit — too odd a personality — to continue the uphill road to being an actor, and as I had neither the time nor the financial background to try to buck that handicap, the prospect of directing seemed more logical, more attainable. And that was my frame of mind when I once again sat at my desk at the Little Theater in early June. My decision once made, I doubt that even if Laurette Taylor had approached me with a part, I would have wavered. However, I was spared that test. She didn't. I saw her once with Grace George backstage at the end of a performance of *Captain Brassbound* shortly after Miss Taylor's return from England. In my own imagination my four previous meetings with her had become a lifelong friendship. When I came face to face with her in the grimy corridor by the Playhouse's stage door, my temperature rose perceptibly. She spoke — that was all — and turned back to whoever she was talking to. I trod up those iron stairs to my dressing room. When would I stop romancing? When would I learn? Brass tacks . . . Get down to them, brother! I found myself repeating over and over again, "What is meant for me will be. I am in the theater. I am part of the theater. And when the time is right for me to emerge from my own particular part of the forest, I will." Cockeyed? But it kept my head above water!

X

Heart Trouble

In the autumn of 1916 Woodrow Wilson was re-elected by a hair's-breadth margin; "the Huns" were going hog-wild with their U-boats; German spies were rumored to be lurking in almost every other house in Manhattan, signaling to each other from the rooftops; dachshunds were distinctly unpopular, and those Teutonic brass bands that came off the *Imperator* and other German boats moored for safety at neutral Hoboken were no help to the Kaiser's cause at all as they drooled out sentimental songs from *Deutschland* in the hope of catching a few American pfennigs.

Every other play was a war melodrama. My old buddy and roommate, Henry Hull, made a hit in *The Man Who Came Back;* in theatrical parlance he had "arrived," he was in big print; I was still on the side lines but I don't remember envying him. I went to Laurette Taylor's opening night. This was her first New York appearance since her London *Peg.* Her welcome was tumultuous. Grace George sat in the stage box — I sat in the first balcony. Her supporting cast boasted several distinguished and well-known actors, but there was one name on the program I had never seen before: Lynn Fontanne. She was a young woman, tall — dark — very thin and angular. She was also English, and she riveted your attention from the moment of her first entrance. Somewhere in the middle of the second act she had a brief emotional scene and so true was she — so touching and so vivid — that on her exit she brought the house down. During the entr'acte her name was on everybody's lips. The following day all the critics echoed the verdict of the opening-nighters. A new star was in the firmament.

The play was the one Miss Taylor had spoken to me about four years before. It was called *The Harp of Life.* Her performance was beguiling and fresh but her radiance could not conceal the shoddiness of her material. As I watched her I didn't grieve that another was playing her son and not I myself. My hopes and dreams of the past had evaporated. Acting was not for me. The metamorphosis was complete.

W. A. began his season with the presentation of a pantomime called *Pierrot the Prodigal.* Once again he was the impresario; once again he inspired the décor, and once again I sat at his feet enraptured and marveling at the magic he created with light, at the beauty with which he could endow the simplest set, such as the kitchen in Pierrot's house — everything was blue, an endless variety of shades of blue: the cupboard, the stove, the table, even the flowers in the window boxes, leaves and all. It was a marvelous background for the chalk-white faces of Pierrot and his father and immediately lifted the whole thing into the realm of fantasy.

Pierrot was very special and a big hit as well. It was followed by the Ames production of an English play called *Hush.* The most that can be said for that short-lived opus is that it introduced Estelle Winwood to American audiences

— a graduate from the Liverpool Repertory Company, she made an instant hit. Knowing Estelle and watching her furnished me with further instruction in the gentle art of make-believe. She is an extraordinary artist, subtle, on a minor key, but unerring and right in all that she does. I was fascinated by her poise, her ability to stand still on the stage; she discarded all useless movement; she wasn't a "busy" actress, and her capacity to listen to other actors in a scene with her without distracting from what they were saying was magnificent. These things I had been aware of, but never before had I seen them taken out of their orbit, so to speak, and demonstrated as a surgeon might in a class of anatomy.

W. A.'s final bid for popular approval that season was his presentation of Granville-Barker's comedy, *The Morris Dance*, which was a dramatization of Robert Louis Stevenson's novel, *The Wrong Box*. Barker, himself, was to direct, and I was assigned to assist him with his casting and production. I was thrilled to be working with this top-ranking British director, who had been producer of the earliest of Shaw's successes and a distinguished author as well.

The cast was selected with Barker's approval, O.K.'d . . . scenery and rehearsals began. It turned out to be one of the most disillusioning episodes in my whole theater experience. His direction was fumbling and baffled. He had no contact whatsoever with his actors, and as if to screen the ineptness of the whole wretched effort he resorted to a series of hysterical ravings that made my old taskmaster at school, Jehlinger, seem an amateur. Of course, I did not know then that Mr. Barker was in the throes of an emotional crisis which marked the departure of his first wife, the beauteous

Lillah McCarthy, from his life to make way for the dark cloud of a second mate, who was to shut out his light from the theater. With that emotional cross to bear he was obviously not himself. His direction, through many years in London, was second to none and, although he translated some Spanish plays after his second marriage, he never really took command in the theater again — which was a great pity, for he had much to give and many years ahead of him. His Shakespearean prefaces are in my opinion the finest comments on the immortal Will that have ever been written. *The Morris Dance* was withdrawn after a three weeks' run. I had sat by Barker's side with such anticipation . . . I was empty and hollow when the chore was over.

Once again the Little Theater was closed, this time for the balance of the season, and once again there was a lull at the office. My specific occupation on these occasions was to interview all applicants for jobs, making out cards for all and sundry with plusses for those who I thought had either ability or promise. I also went scouting for talent, and on one such excursion I journeyed to the Comedy Theater which then housed the Washington Square Players. This group of ambitious potentials had started in the autumn of 1914 at what seemed a hole in the wall on East 57th Street, which they called the Bandbox Theater, and in 1916 they migrated onto the fringe of the hurly-burly of Times Square. Some of the old guard looked upon them as arty, but the press gave them plenty of space, if not always a shower of bouquets. They were the charter members of the Theatre Guild.

In the spring of 1917 they were doing a play called *Plots and Playwrights* and in it was a young actress whom the critic

of the *New York Tribune,* Heywood Broun, referred to as
"a dead-white, young American Duse." Now I had never
seen Duse, and for that matter neither had Broun at that
time, but his comment whetted my curiosity — hence my
visit to the Comedy. The young actress had dark hair (not
bobbed) and was interesting. She stayed with you after you
left the theater. Her voice was lovely; she moved with ease
and grace; there was a haunting mystic quality about her
like a shadow in a haze that at any moment might become
clear. I wrote beside her name on my program, which was
filed in the Ames office, "Interesting, monotonous, watch."
Well, I "watched" all right, and in the last thirty-three years
I have watched with something more than a paternal eye.
I married that young lady in September 1921. Her name
was Katharine Cornell. She had made her professional
debut with the Washington Square Players in December
1916, saying two lines in a play called *Bushido,* but when
I first saw her in early 1917 my interest was purely professional. Three years were to elapse before I met her.

"Assistant in Production" — that was the line of acknowledgment I had in those patrician white-and-green programs
free of advertisements which were given to all the patrons
of Winthrop Ames productions at the Little Theater along
with the after-dinner coffee, which some bright soul said
was dispensed to keep the audience awake. "Assistant in
Production" — it looked nice — it had a box to itself — but
whoever noticed it besides myself? And if they did where
would it get me? This idleness, this "making work" for myself, was not enough! Assistant — the word made strange
sounds in my ears; to my eyes, it was like bars blocking

the way . . . ? I wanted to direct — but how? Who would give me a chance? If I broke with W. A. the most I could hope for would be Assistant somewhere else. W. A. was my security. Fear or instinct, I don't know which, determined my line of inaction. I continued to "make work" for myself and be paid.

Then all of this became quite unimportant. April 6, 1917, the United States declared war on Germany. Patriotism was rampant — the draft bill wasn't effective as yet — the Government called for young men to join up. Mme. Schumann-Heink, distinguished contralto of the Metropolitan Opera (a naturalized American citizen with sons fighting on both sides), along with Marie Dressler, Blanche Bates and others, spoke eloquently — from the steps of the public library, in Times Square or on the Mall in Central Park — backing up the Government's appeal for volunteers. Thousands upon thousands responded. . . . German opera was cancelled at the Metropolitan. . . . George M. Cohan wrote "Over There" and all America was singing it. . . . Uniforms were everywhere —young girls, total strangers, would ask those without them: "Why haven't you joined up?" . . . A great spread in the newspapers said the Government was seeking candidates for an officers' training corps due to begin in the early summer at Plattsburg, New York. I decided to try to make that training corps; I can't brag that it was patriotism and I know it wasn't vanity. Anyway on one hot May afternoon I queued up with several hundred others for a physical examination. The line moved at a crawl. Inside at last, my meager frame exposed to the appraising eye of the Examiner, I was put on the scales and then told to put my clothes back on and dismissed with a jovial pat on the back and a parting shot, "We want to win this war, fella." I burned. It was obvious I wasn't the hero type, either.

Six months later I was called up by the draft board. In an unheated schoolhouse on East 51st Street, I shivered around for a considerable time in my birthday suit before they got around to examining me. After thumping everything but my head, they proceeded to have a whispered consultation, after which they asked me to sit down. Still naked, and with my teeth chattering, I listened as they told me I had a wretchedly inadequate heart — that I was taking my life in my hands every time I walked up a stair. The warning delivered, I was declared 4–F and sent on my way. So Uncle Sam had to win the war without me.

That was thirty-eight years ago. I have climbed millions of stairs since then. I have had an active and exciting life, and even passed an army physical in World War II when I went overseas with Kit. So I'm getting to the place where I don't believe they were quite right about me in 1917.

In between my brush-offs from the army, several things happened. I signed for another season with Mr. Ames, this time for seventy-five dollars a week, and made a flying visit home just in case the Government changed its mind about using me. My mother was glad I wasn't shouldering a gun, but was nevertheless very indignant at the army for refusing me. Her attitude suggested that it would serve the country right if they lost the war. Rose Glass was in uniform and going overseas with one of the first women's groups to go. Many of my old schoolmates were in khaki. I felt sort of foolish. Once again I was glad to go East. Whether I was running away or running towards, I had no idea. W. A. did another play which had a tryout in Atlantic City in the spring and was produced in Manhattan in the autumn, after I came back. It was called *From Saturday to Monday.* The only reason for doing such a play would be that it had big audience-appeal and made money. It failed on both counts. Mr. Ames was hurt by the bad notices it got. The war disturbed him, I think, more than it disturbed any other theater manager at that time. He was looking for the escapist play which he felt the soldiers and wartime audiences would like, but his instinct was not for that type of fare. He could never know what the public wanted. It was for him to be himself as an artist, and let the selective public find him. In that he differed radically from David Belasco, who did know his public and, season after season, produced one popular hit after another, none of them memorable beyond the moment . . . but in his best years D.B. was always in complete accord with his Now. Shortly after *Saturday to Monday* finished its three weeks' run, W. A. departed for overseas accompanied by Mrs. Ames, Eddie Lyons, and E. H. Sothern, on his own initiative and at his own expense, to determine what our fighting men would like and what it was possible to give them in the way of entertainment. Lena Ashwell, famous British actress of that time, had been the first in her country to conceive the idea of the theatrical profession furnishing diversion for the army. Winthrop Ames was the first in America.

While W. A. was overseas the Selwyns, a successful theatrical firm, were preparing a spring tryout of a play that Cosmo Hamilton had fashioned from his successful novel, *Scandal,* which for some unexplainable quirk of managerial ineptitude they had burdened with a new title: *She Would*

and She Did. They asked me to stage it. They had heard I
might have "something on the ball," and were interested in
giving me a tryout too. This might be the answer, I thought.
I was tremendously excited. I read the script: it was a lot of
mish-mash — but it had the stuff that popular successes are
made of. This could be what I had been hoping for. W. A.
was in the war zone and there was no one in authority at
the Little Theater who could give me permission to do it,
so I took the bull by the horns and went ahead without
clearance. I received one hundred dollars a week from the
Selwyns during the four weeks I was busy with the Hamilton play, and canceled my salary with the Ames office for
the same period (to insure a clear conscience). As was customary in those days, with this type of tryout the whole
production was on the cheap side; the scenery from the
warehouse, dresses from the wardrobe; in other words, all
secondhand. Three weeks' rehearsal . . . one week playing
in Washington, D. C.

Seated for the first time in the directorial chair, I found
myself to be on the timid and deferential side, particularly
to Cosmo Hamilton, who was a well-known popular fiction
writer. (His better-known brother was Sir Philip Gibbs.)
Timidity and deference were the two qualities I should have
abandoned entirely in dealing with the group I was coming
up against. Cosmo wore a monocle and had all the airs of
a Stuart Pretender. I had worked feverishly over this, my
first job at directing. I realized the play was diffused, ram-
bling and without focus. It desperately needed pulling together. This I felt could be done. Cosmo Hamilton and I
met for the first time at rehearsal. Every time I made a suggestion to him — either of cutting, or of transposing or re-

writing certain scenes — he would adjust his damned monocle and turn that eye upon me as if I shouldn't be living, and say: "My dear fellow, don't be absurd. It is as right as rain." I can only say it is a fallacy to believe that rain is always right. Under the burden of his presence every cliché, every overlong scene, was preserved intact. We opened in Washington — and *She Would and She Did* was plain bloody awful. The notices were bad. I got the blame. The management didn't speak to me; and Hamilton departed for New York still muttering "Right as rain." Somewhat below sea level in spirit, I was left for five days to stew in my own mess. I could have cut my throat. I'd had my chance and failed. The management had disappeared in thin air, I presume to their hideouts in New York.

It was closing on Saturday, but in desperation I made up my mind that before that final curtain fell in Washington, and with old "Right as Rain" out of the way, I was going to see how some of my discarded rehearsal suggestions, deletions and transpositions would work. The company responded enthusiastically and by Friday midnight we were ready to make the rather drastic changes that turned a four-act play in five scenes into a three-act play with three scenes. It was one of those plays it is easy to forget, and in three acts and three scenes it was just as much mish-mash and, just as easy to forget as it had been in five scenes. The virtue was that there were two scenes less of it. The characters concerned were all so high in society — and high is what I mean — that one had to hold one's nose to bear them. The big scene was in a bedroom, where the heroine carries on like one o'clock to make the guy she's tricked into marrying her do you-know-what. He repulses her with "If you and I were alone on a desert island, I would never . . ." and exits slamming the door, leaving the poor-little-rich-girl squirming around on a big double bed alone. I wired to Selwyn that I had made some changes and suggested that it might be worth his while to journey down to Washington to judge the difference. To this request I never had a reply. My work for the week had been good. The play was tighter, briefer and played better. However, when I returned to New York, the management to me was incommunicado and, unfortunately for them, they abandoned the play. It was taken over by an unknown manager less than a year later; its name was changed back to *Scandal* — and with Charles Cherry and Francine Larrimore playing the leading parts, in substantially the same cut and patched-up version that I had finally done in Washington, it ran for over two seasons. That was the first Guthrie McClintic production, and for me it was nothing but humiliation.

While W. A. was abroad, I took a matrimonial flyer. There were reasons for that impulse — but I guess there were more reasons against it. At the time it took place I was in no mood to see them and with no table to guide me I got married. This particular alliance was done with great secrecy — and was doomed to dissolve in a divorce of even greater secrecy a while later, leaving only a mild bubble of conjecture in its wake — but like all secrets of that kind it leaked. And by the time Mr. Ames returned from Europe it had leaked to him. I was viewed in a completely unfavorable light. Not only had I accepted a directing chore from an outside management while under contract to him, but I had also made a marriage that was creating "talk" — and "talk" was one thing W. A. did not like. He disapproved of the marriage. He frowned on the lady. I was in the doghouse. And I was wretched. But wretched as I was, I was delighted his return resulted in the office and the theater being a beehive of activity for a change.

XI

A Penny in My Shoe

WHILE I was squirming around at being tied outside I could at least busy myself drafting talent for W. A.'s next production. He had brought back a new play from abroad, *The Betrothal*, Maurice Maeterlinck's sequel to *The Bluebird*. It was the story of how Tyltyl got a wife: It seems some tired fairy waves a wand and a veritable army of Tyltyl's unborn children and grandchildren and great-grandchildren invade the stage — in curly, platinum wigs and swathed in delicately tinted chiffon nightdresses — to pass upon and choose, from among Tyltyl's sweethearts, the girl he is going to marry; and when that poor unsuspecting gal who is to bear the burden of conceiving many of these monsters comes in view, these unborns joyously raise their thin, piping voices chanting "It's Mother — yes — it's Mother." Ouch! It should really have put Tyltyl off matrimony, but it didn't. For my taste, this pretentious bit of sugar-coating was sheer horror. However, many people were impressed and the ladies at matinees cried their eyes out over it. The press was good and it ran for over one hundred performances. W. A.'s lighting, scenery and costumes were in every way brilliant.

The casting of it was quite a chore. Aside from the numerous other parts, I interviewed upwards of three hundred teen-age girls, everywhere from fourteen to twenty, for the coveted roles of the sweethearts, and heard, along with W. A., close to one hundred read; he finally settled for Boots Wooster, Winifred Lenihan, Gladys George, May Collins, June Walker, Flora Sheffield and Sylvia Field. They were attractive and fresh and created quite a stir at the time. It is interesting to note a few of the young ladies that didn't make the grade — that never even got to a reading. Margalo Gillmore was one, although her sister, Ruth, managed to crash the "unborns." And another reject was a vivid young actress from Australia called Francee Anderson, whom some good fairy (not Maeterlinck's) got hold of shortly after and changed that Francee to Judith; to say nothing of a husky-voiced beauty from the South whose family, it was rumored, were in politics — none other than Tallulah Bankhead.

The week before *The Betrothal* opened the pompous mood of Maeterlinck was broken one day at rehearsal by an up-roar that sounded like all hell breaking loose. Rushing into the theater lobby, I found the box office was deserted; but outside there were hundreds of people yelling, singing and weeping, milling along the streets on the tops of taxicabs — arm in arm — hats askew, shouting and laughing — office windows were opened, and wastebaskets, filled with paper, were being dumped. From every part of the air and ground there was a racket the like of which I had never heard. It took some moments to realize that the news of the armistice had just come through. Without the aid of radio, it traveled with the speed of a prairie fire on a rampage. Sound — everywhere sound. Rehearsal was over for that day. No one stopped to ask permission. The cast just rushed into the street, moving along with the crowd, singing and rejoicing too. Manhattan made a noise that day it has never equaled since . . . only to find, at sundown, that it had been a false alarm. And when the real armistice came, two days later, everybody was too tired to do it all over again. But the war was over. The world was safe for democracy.

Broadway had its moments too. Arthur Hopkins was making theatrical history at his brand-new Plymouth Theater, presenting Jack Barrymore in a series of plays — *Redemption*, *The Jest* and *Richard III*. Laurette Taylor ventured out from the security of a Hartley Manners hit called *Happiness* to do special matinees of Shakespeare — three heroines in one afternoon: Katherine in *The Taming of the Shrew*, Juliet's Balcony Scene, and Portia in *The Merchant of Venice*. She knew the plots but not the lines, and that makes a difference when you are playing Shakespeare. Julia Marlowe attended that first matinee and it was rumored her hair turned white before the performance ended. Miss Taylor herself put her own evaluation on the exhibit when the matinee was over by stepping before the curtain and saying "Shakespeare has been crucified — so have I — long live Hartley Manners!"

One Sunday night in January 1919 I went with a friend, Noel Haddon (she had created Helen of Troy in Philip Moeller's one-act play *Helena's Husband* in the original production of the Washington Square Players), to an apartment off lower Fifth Avenue where an informal meeting was in progress in which quite a few people were doing quite a

lot of talking. . . . If memory serves they were Maurice
Wertheim, Lawrence Langner, Philip Moeller, Lee Simon-
son, Helen Westley and Theresa Helburn, among others.
This was an advance get-together of the proposed Theatre Guild. Its friends and sympathizers were endeavoring
to stir up interest, canvass for money and generally keep
their idea alive. I had nothing to say so I listened, when
suddenly I felt a presence! And there in a dark corner sat
my "interesting" girl from *Plots and Playwrights,* Katharine
Cornell. She didn't see me, but as I watched her I realized
that off stage she had that mystic aura too . . . a curious
haunting luminosity. Noel talked to her just before we left,
but I didn't get to meet her. When I asked what Miss Cornell
had been doing since I had last seen her almost three years
before, Noel told me she had been playing in stock with
one of Jessie Bonstelle's companies and only a week or so
before had jumped in, at a moment's notice, to take over the
leading woman's part in a road company of *The Man Who
Came Back,* which was then playing the subway circuit. That
I didn't rush to see her in that has always been one of my
real regrets.

In the spring W. A. popped up with a routine melodrama
that had been a big success in England called *The Purple
Mask,* a period piece in more ways than one, for which
Richard Bennett was signed to star as a French Royalist at
the time of the Revolution. We opened in Atlantic City
and closed the following week in Washington, D. C. Bennett,
whose farewell appearance on the New York stage was his
brilliant playing of the Judge in my production of *Winterset* in 1935, resourceful star though he was, could not make
the sow's ear that it was his misfortune to enact in *The Pur-*

ple Mask into anything other than a sow's ear. Also he was the only person I ever heard call Winthrop Ames "Winnie" — and I may say he did it only once. W. A. didn't say anything, but he looked! The look wasn't a reprimand to Bennett — it seemed more a sudden awareness of the reaction a long line of whirling ancestors were having to such familiarity. Mr. Bennett was unhappy in his role and bowed out at the end of our two weeks' tryout. Despite that — plus the fact that its out-of-town reception was something less than lukewarm — Ames nevertheless decided to produce *The Purple Mask* in New York the following winter with a new cast. Despite the cool air that persistently clung around me at the office, I was signed again at an advance in salary (a hundred dollars a week) and a reduction in guaranteed weeks (thirty). It's a cinch I didn't write that to Father. My starting date was to be the first of the following November.

I tried meanwhile to make a success of my marriage but it was uphill going, as I was doing with an unerring instinct all the wrong things: living beyond my means, trying to look like a big shot when I was anything but . . . and then one morning in June 1919 — curiously enough, two years to the day before I would be rendered what is legally termed "a free man" — that matrimonial episode came quite naturally to an end. The parting was friendly, and the lady and I have always remained that way. But at the time of our parting I did not want to stay around New York. I did not want to go home, I did not want to answer any questions, but I definitely wanted a change of scene. Some place to go to where I could be alone and have some closed meetings about myself, with myself, and decide what to do about

Me. Out of the blue I decided to keep that rendezvous with London I had dreamed of back in the winter of 1913–1914. But that was easier decided on than done. In the first place I had no money — Well, just over three hundred dollars.

And with the war just over, space on all boats was oversold and a passport as well as a reason for going was necessary. But my mind was made up, and I began preparing as if this voyage were already an assured fact. I suppose that is the way you should always begin everything. My first setback was my inability to produce a birth certificate. The recording in our family Bible meant nothing to the State Department. I had to prove that I was born. Neither Mother's nor Father's affidavits were acceptable. It had me scratching my head, and, strange to relate, the snarl was untangled by my remembering and getting in touch with a genial distant cousin of mine in New York who was a well-known eye specialist, Dr. Clyde McDannald by name — who, with a real Southern desire to prove that blood is thicker than water, jeopardized his integrity by swearing on solemn oath that he knew that I was born in Seattle, Washington, on August 6, 1893. That did the trick. I got a passport. . . . Now I had to get a visa.

Jed Shaw of W. A.'s office staff, and a good friend of mine through the years, added prevarication to hasten my departure by writing a letter on W. A.'s stationery stating that I was going to England to engage some actors for Mr. Ames. That got me the visa.

The next trick was to procure a passage over, and there is where Margaret Collins steps into the picture. Genial, lusty, ribald "Peg" Collins, treasurer of the Booth Theater for all the time that W. A. was in control of its destiny, true daugh-

ter of the Emerald Isle, and as true a friend as anyone could
wish for, knew some wire-pullers behind the scenes that
you sometimes think only the Irish know about — and lo
and behold I had a first-class passage on the *Aquitania*,
sailing on July 26, for the colossal sum of one hundred eighty-
six dollars for an inside cabin on D deck, to be shared with
three other men. The only drawback to the whole arrangement was that I did not want a first-class cabin, nor did I
want to spend that much money. But it was that or nothing,
and since I had caused such a rumpus to get it, there was
no backing down; so I plunked over the ducats for the fare,
not without a certain amount of wincing, and I looked at the
hundred and forty-seven dollars I had left and mumbled
a prayer! That was to take care of my stay in London
and fare back as well. My excitement at the prospect of
going deadened any reason I had, and that was all to the
good.

Some friends, as a send-off, took me to see Mr. Ziegfeld's
Follies of 1919 "glorifying the American Girl" at the New
Amsterdam Theater on West 42d Street, the most beautiful
musical comedy house New York has ever had, and now
allowed to deteriorate on that one-time glittering theater
street which is, at present, an avenue surrendered to flea
circuses and double-feature pictures . . . 42d Street! The
Follies that summer was like a spark that set off a new era
for me. I'll never forget it. . . . Will Rogers with his lariat
and chewing gum, bemoaning the fact that some of the beauteous lassies in the show didn't know where their next Rolls-
Royce was coming from; the unforgettable Fanny Brice,
sounding right into the center of your heart with "Second
Hand Rose of Second Avenue" or "Rose of Washington

Square"; Joseph Urban's handsome scenic backgrounds, with reminders always somewhere on them that the lovely star and perennially young Billie Burke was Mrs. Ziegfeld. . . . But the high moment that night, for me, was when a Grecian goddess, Dolores by name, walked across the stage at the conclusion of a "production number" — Irving Berlin's song "A Pretty Girl Is Like a Melody." Clifton Webb told me that on the opening night of that *Follies,* when she appeared, elderly gentlemen whose springtime was far behind them suddenly felt the urge of early May creeping through their veins and were a trouble to their relatives and friends for quite some time afterwards. (After three years of lending extra glory to Mr. Ziegfeld's American beauties, this fabulous Englishwoman, Dolores, who had been a mannequin for Lady Duff Gordon, married and retired — and has lived happily ever after in a beautiful apartment looking over the Seine in Paris.) Thirty-six hours after that intoxicating evening, I was on board the crowded *Aquitania* about to plow through sunny seas for England.

My first sea voyage was a disappointment. I was looking forward to mountainous seas, but the ocean was as calm as Puget Sound and the *Aquitania* as steady as the West Seattle ferry on its way to Alki Point. My greatest kick was standing on deck alone at night and gazing at the endless expanse of water with the stars overhead. It had a hypnotic effect on me . . . an almost religious exaltation. It has always been the same with me.

Early on the morning of August 2, after six days at sea, I was on a train going from Southampton up to London. Being the first Saturday of my birth month it was the beginning of August Bank Holiday. But instead of the usual ex-

odus that occurs then, the town was crowded because the
Indian contingent, which had not arrived in London in time
for the Peace Parade the previous Saturday, were having a
colorful one of their own up the Mall to be reviewed by
Royalty and Top Brass. I had no place to stay and a Canadian who shared the cabin coming over saved my life that
first day by persuading his hotel, the Savoy, which was
"packed out," to put a cot in his sitting room and allowing me
to bunk there for the night. We spent the day together,
edged our way into the Mall, saw the Indians in all their
splendor, and from the distance I glimpsed the King,
George V, with his mother the Dowager Queen Alexandra
and Queen Mary, as well as the Prince of Wales. My Canadian friend and I dined at the Savoy Grill and I took him
to the closing night of *The Naughty Wife* at the Playhouse,
with a cast headed by Gladys Cooper and Charles Hawtrey.
What a beauty, Gladys Cooper! What an actor, Charles
Hawtrey!

I moved the next day to lodgings in Bloomsbury to accommodate my purse. London was exactly what I hoped
it would be. Nor was it strange. Traffic on the left side
didn't bother me and I could even count their money. On
the top of buses I explored it and all of its corners, from
Hampton Court to the Tower. I sat on Colonel Newcombe's
bench in Lincoln's Inn Field and strolled around the Roman
Bath that David Copperfield found off the Strand. Westminster Abbey . . . Piccadilly Circus . . . Hyde Park Corner . . . somewhere in between, I found what I was looking for. I began to get straightened out. The few people I
knew were warm and friendly. Although I was much alone,
I was never lonely.

I wrote Margaret Collins and touched her for two hundred dollars, which I promised to pay out of my coming year's salary. She sent it straight off and I stayed as long as I could. I haunted the theaters. I queued up for the pit several times each week — there they had rush seats at the back of the lower floor (it would be the rear of the orchestra, in America) for the equivalent of fifty cents. I thought their productions and acting had more style and manner than we had, but lacked our tempo and vitality. The most arresting young actress I saw was Meggie Albanesi, playing on a Sunday night at the Arts Theatre in a play about Napoleon. I thought she was terrific. I fell hook, line and sinker for Gerald du Maurier and his suavity and ultra-natural style of acting.

I was feeling so at ease and happy that I began hoping I could stay there forever, but misty autumn and yellowing leaves reminded me my time was almost up. One day I received a letter from Noel Haddon in New York saying "Kit Cornell" was shortly going to appear in London and might be lonesome, and suggesting that I look her up; but when the letter arrived Kit Cornell had gone to her opening date in Manchester, and when she returned to London I had left. A few weeks later she made her first and only appearance in London as Jo in *Little Women* and scored a resounding hit. . . . I should have been there.

One morning, just before I left, while I was contemplating Nelson atop the column in Trafalgar Square, one of those large British pennies rolled down and settled right in front of me. I put it in my left shoe for luck, and have worn it there ever since. I was down to eighty-five dollars when I booked passage home on the *Lapland* — steerage.

That set me back seventy-five dollars. I would arrive in Manhattan with taxi fare and no more.

Going over I had shared a cabin with three others; coming back I shared quarters with one hundred and eighty-five males. We were parked in a section of the hold, sleeping in tiers with straw for mattresses and one blanket apiece. We ate, slept, and washed in this fetid atmosphere for the eight days it took us to reach America. It was the end of October, and the sea was fairly rough, so I decided it would be in the interest of hygiene if I sat out on a sandpile at the end of the ship, which I managed to do twelve to fourteen hours a day — and acquired a windburn that made me look as if I had been hitting the high spots on the Riviera.

I arrived home in New York no longer tense but relaxed and refreshed. I was resolved to play it straight from here on: no more emotional involvements — no more crises. I was going to direct: I was going to prove myself. I was going to make good.

XII

The Table Pays Off

No LONGER were the Ames offices on 44th Street.
We were cooped up in temporary quarters at the Aeolian
Hall Building while the Little Theater was being remodeled.
A balcony was being installed; the offices were to be on top
of the building, and above that W. A. had planned for himself a very charming apartment. The offices and the apartment were reached by an automatic elevator. His offices
would be there but he never again would present a play at
the Little. It had had its place in his life, and he was going
forward. Oliver Morosco leased it when it reopened in
February 1920.

Eddie Lyons — nice guy — was conducting an inquiry on
the quiet as to where the money came from that took me
to Europe and back. Margaret Collins, Sully — in fact every
employee of Mr. Ames — were quizzed as to whether or not
they had lent me money. Peg Collins was the only one who
had, but he got nothing out of her. Why this investigation?
I'll never know. But he was out to "get" me, that's certain.
And my one-time friend, Helen Ingersoll, W. A.'s secretary,
was hand-in-glove with him! But against that, W. A. himself
was friendlier with me. It seemed as if a storm had passed
and the air was clearer.

There had been an actors' strike during the summer and

a new organization had sprung into existence called the Actors' Equity, affiliated with the American Federation of Labor. Ethel Barrymore had been one of the few top-ranking dramatic stars to side with the striking actors. She was now appearing at the Empire in Zoë Akins's play, *Déclassée,* which was a big success. Patrician and lovelier than ever, she had the heart of Manhattan beating a mile a minute. She had Alexander Woollcott on the verge of collapse as he endeavored to capture her elusive glamour in mere words on paper. Woollcott of the *New York Times!* I think most theater people valued a verbal nod from him as the greatest boon that could fall their way. Not that we scorned plaudits from Percy Hammond, Heywood Broun or Burns Mantle — far from it — but praise from Woollcott was something special. Probably we felt that way because of his intense love of the theater — his boundless enthusiasm — his appreciation — his discernment — his likes and dislikes. His reviews were no halfway affairs. He either went overboard for you, or you went under. His invectives as well as the bouquets he tossed fomented arguments, started feuds; but no one remained neutral under his barrage of words. One wit, commenting on his effusive praise of a certain actress, referred to him as "The Seidlitz Powder of Times Square" — but to be allowed space in Alec's own particular hall of fame was something. Nor was his enthusiasm confined to the theater. Some years later, when he ceased writing for our New York dailies and became the Town Crier on the radio, he went the whole gamut from extolling new books by unknown authors and soliciting contributions for Seeing Eye dogs for the blind to vituperative condemnation of the America First group. He was stricken during a broadcast and died a few hours later, early in 1942. The theater, I believe, was his true love. He referred to himself in regard to it as its "uncle." All of us lost a great friend on his death.

When I was casting Sam Behrman's play, *Brief Moment,* it seemed obvious to me that the part of Sig, a friend of the hero's whose brilliant and caustic remarks enlivened the audience, if not the hero, was written from Woollcott and cried aloud for his presence in the part. Alec no longer being connected with New York papers, I offered it to him. He snatched it as a puppy would a bone. He was excruciatingly funny in it and as "ham" as his most despised ham actors could be — but the audiences loved him. Once he said to me: "Don't try to kill the applause on my exit" — this was at a moment when I felt it hurt a scene — "I am the type that wants to stop the show." I am quoting a letter he wrote to me some four years after *Brief Moment* was no more.

December 24, 1936

DEAR GUTHRIE,

I thought that was a good show last night (Maxwell Anderson's *Wingless Victory*) — a good cast all the way through. I thought Miss Kitty took her big scene with the infallibility of Toscanini.

In fact, I feel indebted to you for three good evenings in the theater this year. Two of them were *Hamlet* (with Gielgud and Judith Anderson) and I shall be going again.

In cleaning out my desk I came upon the enclosed abortion. It seems to be the stillborn remains of a project I once had — and still have, for that matter — to do a profile of you. I forget now why I got no further. Probably I stopped on the day I went from under your management (but at a more appreciative salary) to the less tender care of Jones and Green.

However, I wish you a Merry Christmas.

A. W.

This is the enclosed "abortion" Alec mentioned:

At various times in the past twenty years, the author of this monograph on Guthrie McClintic has been swept off his underpins by a great wave of sympathy for Otto Kahn. Here was a man who was both equipped and disposed to be the most considerable Maecenas in the history of our theater, but he spent season after season in vain quest of a talent that would stay put long enough for him to endow it. More particularly did he trudge up and down Broadway looking for some producer who would play Gatti-Casazza to his munificence, someone whom he could back, as the Metropolitan and the Boston Symphony were backed, with any confidence at all that he could get a reasonable co-operation in vitality, intelligence and devotion to the task in hand.

Three years ago, when the passion to endow the drama was rather more prevalent among the local Medici than it has been of late, I amused myself by trying to select for them the right man to take charge of a nobly uncommercial theater that was then, as so often before, in contemplation. It was easy enough for me to submit a list of impresarii, all of them with flair and talent enough for their role in such an enterprise, but in the same breath I felt obliged to warn the Medici that they could not hope to work with a single one of my nominees without having to wrestle with several powerful impulses to shoot the fellow, or at least to lay him out cold with some blunt instrument. To be sure, I felt I could promise that, if matters reached the point of actual homicide, enough evidence would be forthcoming to insure an acquittal. But even so, the prospect was dismaying.

For instance, Mr. A. would bring ripe experience to the direction of an endowed theater, but he would also bring along a marked tendency to take up rehearsal

ather was a big man with a powerful, low voice (1889)

Mother was little and had a lovely speaking voice (1889)

Frank C. Bangs

I graduate from the American Academy of Dramatic Arts (1912)

Winthrop Ames seemed a Velásquez
cardinal in mufti

I become a pro as The Artful Dodger
in Oliver Twist (1912)

Alice Boughton

I was still hoping to be an actor (1914)

Haywood

Ailleen May was winsome and blond

Matzene

Julia Dean wore long earrings and used plenty of
perfume

When I was fifteen and it
was "terribly elegant" to wear
false hips & "extra bosom" (Somewhere before Seattle time) with love
to you both— Laurette Taylor

Laurette Taylor: magic hovered over her
like a halo

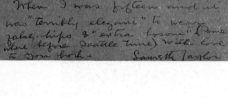

A sketch of Mrs. Leslie Carter by John
Colton, author of *The Shanghai Gesture*
(1926)

Grace George had an unerring instinct for comedy

Opening scene of *The Dover Road* (1921)

ings were going all right though I didn't know it when Charles Cherry made his entrance in *The Dover Road* (1921)

Kit and I relaxed self-consciously in the garden at Beekman Place while a camera snap
additional publicity shots for *The Barretts of Wimpole Street* (1932)

The Third Juliet (1934–1936)

In 1935 Kit introduced Maurice Evans to American audiences in *Romeo and Juliet*

edda Hopper, Judith Anderson, James Rennie and I discuss *Divided by Three* on the terrace at Beekman Place (1934)

Katharine Cornell and her father arrive for the opening of *Missouri Legend* in Buffalo (19

A sketch of me done by Alexander Koriansky during rehearsal for
The Three Sisters (1942)

Eileen Da...

A photographer catches me during the rehearsal of *The Three Sisters* (1942)

was substituting for Edmund Gwenn, but Judith Anderson and Kit played up to me
as if I were a star in *The Three Sisters* (1942)

Me and Kit (1954)

time with interminable anecdotes, and he would betray an embarrassing disposition to cast the minor feminine roles with weird females whose sole credentials were a capacity to excite the amorous fancy of Mr. A. Or consider Mr. B. He was such a touchy megalomaniac that a play of his would no sooner begin to sell out than he would feel not only that he needed no Maecenas hanging around (because hereafter, thanks to his magic touch, all his productions would sell out), but that it was a downright presumption for any mere banker to aspire to a place in the theater. Then there was Mr. C — a keen and sensitive impresario, but one likely to spend a costly part of every season in his cups. Or. Mr. D, a brilliant showman, but one given to cataleptic lapses of judgment and an indifference to any play once launched which would remind the grieving playwright of those lackadaisical matrons at the kennels who kill their progeny by rolling on them. As for Mr. E, he was a fellow of tremendous talent, but one so absorbed in matters of light and decor that the question of what play would be selected always seemed unimportant to him, and the subsequent necessity of engaging actors for it a dismal formality. As for Mr. F, his shining and conspicuous gifts could not long conceal the fact that he was a tinpot tyrant of so vile a temper that rigor mortis would set in before the end of the rehearsal period, and the play would open at last with even the neediest actor in the company hoping it would be a flop.

You might gather from these casual and hasty vignettes that the list at the time seemed unpromising, and in the interval nothing has occurred to encourage a belief that an ideal director has as yet emerged from the ranks of the younger men. If and when better times return, I suppose I could not do better than nominate Guthrie McClintic, but the chances are he will be up to his neck in projects of his own, and besides, no one who knows him in the theater could doubt for a moment that the impulse to shoot him too must arise quite often. He is an eminently resourceful director who has had much valuable experience in the past twenty years, and who adds to a brilliantly perceptive approach to any manuscript an ability, rare among directors, not only to tell the actors what he wants them to do, but to show them unmistakably.

In the supporting cast of Miss Barrymore's *Déclassée* company was a young actress known as Clare Eames (niece of the great Wagnerian soprano Emma Eames). I was lucky to count Clare among my friends. Resembling the most aristocratic matrons of Ancient Rome, her mind was clear and sharp, and her ambition limitless. Her criticism could be caustic but it was valued, and her praise even more so. She was the first person of my age with whom I ever discussed the theater — seriously, that is, not in terms of being a star or a success, but of adjustment, of ideals, of ultimate goals. Don't misunderstand me. I think every mother's child of us wants success but some of us are tainted with wanting satisfaction as well! Clare was dynamic, without fear of any kind. She heard "wild harps" playing and that was what she was gunning for . . . Ridiculous many times, but with the ridiculousness that was touched with greatness . . . After an argument with her you knew you were alive and, incidentally, the theater as well. As an actress she was uneven, but at her best — as she was when she acted Prossie in *Candida*, the first time Kit played it — she was magnificent. She later played in London where the distinguished critic James Agate referred to her as a modern

Rachel (who I trust you all know was a great French actress of the early nineteenth century). Clare married Sidney Howard and was at his side in all of his early writing years. They had separated when she died in England in 1930. Their only child, Jennifer, is married to Sam Goldwyn's son.

There was another actress, too, who drifted across my circle of awareness that autumn who has been a valued friend, a severe critic, and a shrewd appraiser of all I have tried to do. She was just about to make a big hit in *The Famous Mrs. Fair.* I forget the shenanigans I pulled to get into the Henry Miller Theater one Sunday night to see that dress rehearsal, starring Miller and Blanche Bates, but I was there; and in my memory its two brilliant actors have to surrender first place to the girl who played their daughter. She was lovely and blond and very, very moving. Her name was Margalo Gillmore.

Meanwhile, in W. A.'s precinct, Leo Ditrichstein had been engaged to take over Bennett's role in *The Purple Mask.* This gentleman hailed from Vienna — wore a monocle — had an accent — clicked his heels — kissed ladies' hands — and had the brand of charm that Americans called "Continental." However, he was always on his toes in the theater — a hard worker — and enjoyed a certain popularity. I had literally nothing to do beyond attending to a few extra touches on the scenery. The play opened in Hartford on Christmas night and it was obvious from the moment that Ditrichstein entered that it would serve as an excellent vehicle for him. There is a moment in the third act when the heroine, alone in her bedroom — the doors barricaded — the stage flooded with the bluest of blue-moon lights — hears the sounds of a horse approaching bearing a lonely rider. It stops beneath her window. You can imagine her terror as she cowers in a corner when she further hears the lonely rider climbing up towards her room, on a vine apparently, and getting closer and closer. Then his shadow is silhouetted in the moonlight against the curtains of the French windows. His taps on the window are apparently a signal she recognizes. She runs, opens it, and is enveloped in his embrace — Purple Mask and all. Up to this point the scene went wonderfully at the Hartford opening. But suddenly I heard the sound of climbing again, unmistakable and persistent. It struck me as funny. I leaned over to W. A., who was sitting beside me, and whispered, "I think his horse is coming up too." Unfortunately a woman sitting directly behind us heard me and started to laugh, and the laughter spread. W. A. got up abruptly and left the theater and went around to the stage door. I followed. When the curtain was down, he bawled the living daylights out of me and it was in hearing of the entire company. I felt it would have been more to the point if he had directed it at Ditrichstein's stage manager, who had bitched the effect. Later that evening at supper he had the justice to apologize to me before many of the company who had heard the original outburst. As I was stammering some kind of acknowledgment, Ditrichstein interrupted with a jocularity that possibly I misunderstood, saying, "Why do you keep him around?" Ames looked at him a moment and said, "Because he is a great guy in an emergency."

Exactly a week later, when Ditrichstein was playing in Newark, W. A. and I slipped out during the second act to have a drink in a bar opposite the Broad Street Theater. He said casually that he had heard my marriage was on the rocks and, when I replied "That's true," he said he was glad, as it had always worried him. The conversation veered back to *The Purple Mask,* which he felt was ready for its Manhattan opening, and after a bit it came back to me. "You mustn't go on being my assistant," he said. "I will never let you direct for me. You see I have found out that the only fun I have in the theater is when I direct the plays I produce. You must branch out for yourself." "I want to," I answered, "but I want it to be right. I don't want another experience like *Scandal.* I have been meaning to talk to you about it. My instinct on that was O.K. but I feel certain now that I took the brunt of the Selwyn failure." He replied, "I think you probably did, but that isn't the end of your life." There was quite a pause while I finished my drink. Then he spoke very quietly. "I'll tell you what I'll do. . . . If you find a play that you like — a play which will be inexpensive to do — I'll put up the money for it and let you present it and direct it. . . . And, if it is a success, you pay me back my investment . . . and if it isn't, we'll forget about it — but you'll be on your own then."

We were sitting in an ordinary cheap joint — it was tired and stale from its New Year's Eve the night before — only one other couple was there at the time — the bartender was dozing behind the bar — W. A.'s expression hadn't changed. For a long minute I wondered if he had really said what I believed I'd heard him say. I finally found my voice and said, "Thank you." He paid the check and we went back to the theater. It was New Year's night, 1920. It was over a year before he mentioned it again.

❀ ❀ ❀

Mr. Ditrichstein opened the following week in New York at the Booth. Both himself and the play scored a success, but I think W. A. was a bit ashamed of it because the house-board read "LEE SHUBERT PRESENTS *The Purple Mask*" — with no mention of W. A.'s name anywhere, even for the staging of it. With that chore finished he packed himself, his wife and his first-born, Judy by name (not yet five months old), off to Santa Barbara for the winter. Meanwhile I was busy on the telephone telling various play agents that I was in the market for a play. They were courteous and said they would "keep me in mind." I waited and waited and waited, and not a damn script appeared. Of course in 1920 it was infinitely more difficult for a young unknown to acquire a script than it is today. There were many established, responsible and solvent managements then and, naturally, they had the top of the barrel. An unknown author or rejected manuscript seemed my only hope. For no reason I can think of I didn't mention Ames's offer to anyone and, as I found out later, neither did he.

Out in Santa Barbara he had fallen in love with the California sunshine, the beauty of the country, and for the moment was obsessed with the idea of establishing a repertory there with a dramatic school attached, doing Greek plays in the open and the classics in the theater and opera in the summer — making it an American equivalent of Reinhardt's Salzburg. He wired me to join him out there and, in February 1920, the day before a great snowstorm hit Manhattan and crippled it for six weeks, I set forth on my first visit to California. I lived at his house. It was during my time there that we ceased to be employer and employee but friends. He was Winthrop. I was Guthrie. I found the baby adorable and even Lucy warmed to me. We listed over two hundred and fifty plays in all languages. At night he would read aloud, translating freely French classics, while I responded with auditions of Shaw, Galsworthy, Shakespeare, and others. We discussed actors who might be interested and available, the school and its type of instruction; it was a heady project, but when he returned East to the harsh reality of Broadway the whole scheme was abandoned. And that was a pity.

On my way back to New York I detoured by Seattle for a short visit. Harold was gone but Rose was there still teaching, busy as a pack of bird dogs, and telling me with her usual enthusiasm about her present crop of promising pupils. My mother and father were well and glad to see me, but I couldn't awaken a spark of interest in them concerning my hopes for the future of W. A.'s offer. They were only pleased that I was doing well. Maybe it was my fault. I don't know. I still don't.

At the Little, no play had been unearthed for me to do, but I made up my mind that I wasn't going to be idle, sitting on the side lines waiting for that script. I wanted some actual experience in directing. I wanted to find out how much I knew, or thought I knew, was practical. For instance, I had been feeling that dialogue could overlap, as it does in reality — that the grouping of furniture in a stage drawing-room could have a greater reality without every piece facing front, and at the same time be more fluid and easier to act on, and around; that it was possible to say a line with one's back to the audience — these and many more that were theories to me I wanted to test. A good stock company I decided would be my solution, if they felt I was a good risk. When I told W. A. he was enthusiastic about the idea and I approached my old hate, Ada Humbert, with whom I had become friendly in the intervening years. She immediately sent me to Jessie Bonstelle. I was interviewed. She liked me, and I was promptly engaged to direct and act as well with her Detroit company for the summer. My salary was seventy-five dollars a week. I was to furnish my own costumes, wigs, and so on and put on a new play every week — seventeen in all. That would be a workout all right!

Miss Bonstelle was an extraordinary woman, tremendously competent as an actress and the finest of stock managers. She had no taste or even common sense about an untried script, but she had one of the keenest noses for acting talent I have ever encountered. She was operating two companies that summer, Detroit and Buffalo, and playing alternate weeks herself in both towns. One day just before leaving New York Miss Bonstelle asked me to come to Brady's office over the Playhouse to meet the Detroit company. They were unknown to me, but as it turned out later there was some promising talent for me to work with. The late Frank Morgan was the leading man; Walter Abel, the juvenile; a keen, dark-eyed young woman, Maude Howell by name, played general business and was assistant stage manager; and the leading woman was Katharine Cornell. She gave me a warm smile when we were introduced in the reception room, and when Miss Bonstelle asked us to go into Mr. Brady's private office I lagged behind and watched the company as they filed in. I was fascinated with Kit. I couldn't take my eyes away from her. I watched her as she moved with slow, easy grace across the hall of the outer office, and suddenly I thought: That's my wife . . . isn't it funny she doesn't know it, but I am going to marry her. I couldn't say I was in love with her then, but I knew I was going to marry her. My intuition was tipping me off to future events in my life but with no inkling as to how they would come about. This sensation, premonition — or whatever you choose to call it — took hold of me and I couldn't shake it off.

Before I left New York to join the Bonstelle company I had again signed with W. A. — this time for a weekly one hundred and twenty-five dollars, fifty-two weeks a year! On arriving in Detroit I was making for a boardinghouse out on Woodward Avenue where Frank Morgan and his wife Alma and myself were going to dig in for the season when I was intrigued by a large sign that read MEET FRIEDBERG AND WEAR DIAMONDS. I wondered, Would I be so lucky? However, I rolled up my sleeves to face a good hot summer at the Old Garrick Theater. Kit did not appear in our first two bills. Neither did I. Miss Bonstelle opened the season. Life was strenuous but exciting. We played ten performances each week: Sunday nights and three matinees. The company rehearsed every day except Thursday morning, which was given to them for "study," while I, as director, hustled around the town trying to dig up props and furnishings for the next week's production, offering in return for the loan of a sofa or a desk a pair of passes to the show and a line of acknowledgment on the program. Miss Bonstelle gave me a free hand even in casting. I burned the midnight oil — played parts — experimented and sensed values. . . . And audiences liked me; and, more important, the company did, too, and worked like Trojans along with me.

In stock the working scripts were facsimiles of the prompt books used in the New York productions with all business recorded thereon. I was constantly endeavoring to improve what had been done before. It was a grueling, thankless job, but I kept at it — and on the whole I think Detroit had a very superior type of stock that summer. Our business was uniformly good. When the season was over I felt I could work with actors, gain and hold their respect, and all in all had acquired a new security — the security of knowing my job.

Kit's first appearance was in the third week's bill in a tryout of a new play by Austin Strong, whose *Three Wise Fools* had been a success under the aegis of John Golden two seasons before. Golden had more than a paternal eye on the one we were doing. In Detroit it was called *Heaven* and in New York, two years later, *Seventh Heaven.* I thought it was a lot of hooey! The heroine, as we played it, was a prostitute who had a wicked sister who lived off her earnings and terrorized her with a big whip into hustling for them, and at the end of the second act, when our heroine had fallen in love with a street cleaner who was about to join the taxi army that saved Paris in 1914, and her bad sister was trying to push her into the arms of a dissolute man of title (played in Detroit by me), our heroine rebels and beats the hide off her sister with the horsewhip that sister had previously used on her. That moment was terrific. The audience ate it up. I think that particular incident was responsible for the play's ultimate success. Everyone has, I'm sure, at one time or another wanted to do violence to an oppressor. Well, *Seventh Heaven* did that for you. Our heroine beats the daylights out of her sister as the curtain falls at the end of the second act, and presto — the Mr. and Mrs. in the audience have been released of a subconscious desire without interference of the law.

Kit gave a stirring performance as the put-upon prostitute, and Helen Menken made a big hit in it when John Golden presented it in New York in the autumn of 1922. Mr. Golden, whose reputation as a producer of "clean plays" was second to none, could not possibly have his heroine a prostitute, so he cleaned her up for Manhattan by making her a nice little pickpocket, thereby leaving no blot on his reputation.

Working with Kit every day was increasing my bewilderment over my lack of any of the emotions I felt I should feel for the girl I was convinced was going to be my future wife. I was getting to know her though, to appreciate her warm generosity, to respect her discipline and capacity for work, to be aware of her acute shyness and diffidence. And around her was an eerie sensation of distillation of spirit — something you find away from the haunts of man, deep in a forest . . . or in the middle of the ocean at the dead of night. Her appearance, too, was unusual, in no way suggestive of her Anglo-Saxon background. Dark hair . . . dark eyes, far apart . . . in a heart-shaped face. . . . Not pretty, but possessing beauty. Of one thing I was convinced — she definitely belonged on the stage — there her extraordinary individual qualities seemed to crystalize. It seems ridiculous that I should let anyone else edge in on this platform at the moment, but I am going to step down to allow Bernard Shaw a word. This letter I am about to quote was written soon after her first performance in *Candida* (December 1924).

DEAR KATHARINE CORNELL:

I don't think I was ever so astonished by a picture as I was by your photograph. Your success as Candida and something blonde and expansive about your name had

created an ideal suburban British Candida in my imagination. Fancy my feelings on seeing the photograph
of a gorgeous dark lady from the cradle of the human race . . . wherever that was . . . Ceylon . . .
Sumatra . . . Hilo . . . or the southernmost corner of
the Garden of Eden.

· If you look like that it doesn't matter a rap if you can
act or not. Can you? Yours, breath bereaved,

BERNARD SHAW

And he wrote that from only seeing a photograph. . . . I
was face to face with the original!

One night at the Statler Hotel, where Kit and I had gone
for a bit of dancing and relaxing, we were on the dance
floor when the bolt of lightning hit me . . . the earthquake
came . . . the tidal wave engulfed me. . . . I knew I was
in love! In love with Kit Cornell! This was different from
anything I had ever felt before. This I recognized as the
"for better, for worse" variety. I have been walking on air,
lo, these many years now. After that revelation I worked
harder than ever and shirked nothing but my sleep.

While I would never say we flaunted our feelings, nevertheless it would be idle to deny that it didn't require a Sherlock Holmes to discover that we were "interested" in each
other. Some four or five weeks before the season was over
Miss Bonstelle, who had just come back from Buffalo to
reappear with her Detroit company, apparently had heard
some of the romantic rumors that were in the air about us,
for she summoned me to her dressing room one evening and
said, "What's happened to Kit?" I asked her to explain. She
continued, "She's losing her popularity. Letha Walters [who
was "second woman"] gets a bigger hand on her entrance

than Kit does." (My mind went immediately back to Ailleen May and Laurette Taylor in Seattle.) "Do you know what's happened? I hear she is interested in some man and it is taking her mind off her work. Do you know who it is?" Since she was pleased to talk by insinuation I gave her no satisfaction. Kit and I grew more intense as each day passed, quite oblivious to the narrowing-eyed coolness that was emanating from Miss Jessie. I did not realize at the time the spot she was in. She felt in some way responsible to Dr. Cornell (Kit's father) in allowing this emotional upheaval to take place and that, coupled with her own deep affection for Kit and her desire to protect her and shield her from what I represented in her mind, made it awfully tough going for her. Although I was blissfully unaware of it at the time, I was certainly not what you called a "catch" for anybody!

Kit was not appearing in our closing bill and journeyed immediately to Cobourg, Ontario, to have a brief visit with her Aunt Lydia, who has a residence there. With Kit gone the world seemed vacant. I realized completely how serious my feelings towards her were and also my intentions, but there were a lot of corners to turn before this dream could become a fact. When the season was ended and I was taxiing to Detroit's New York Central Station to take the train for Manhattan, I passed that sign I had seen every day that summer and I consoled myself that although I had not met Friedberg I had met my fate.

XIII

A Benedict

BACK in New York, hotter than Hades — how we ever lived without air-conditioning I'll never know, but the legitimate theater seemed to thrive on heat then; summer was the heydey of the Ziegfeld *Follies* — W. A. was waiting for me. He was enthusiastic about a new play he had just bought (a first one from the pen of the then dean of London dramatic critics, the sixty-four-year-old William Archer). Archer, whose textbooks on playmaking were in every library — Archer, whose translations of Ibsen, steep going though they were, were the first to appear in the English language and served every great star that appeared in them, from Janet Aichurch and Mrs. Patrick Campbell to Nazimova, Mrs. Fiske, and Ethel Barrymore, to say nothing of Richard Mansfield — Archer, who seemed to have stepped directly out of Victorian England — who, at the age of sixty-six, rescued a drowning man somewhere off Dover and whose only concern, when he was standing dripping in all of his clothes, was to find that some dreamboat had pinched his umbrella while he was saving the man's life — Archer, who was hesitant (in case it offended) to use the word "concubine" in the presence of Mr. Arliss's leading lady . . . He exemplified everything that was fine in British character.

No one had been cast when I was tapped for suggestions. Archer wanted for the Rajah in his play a big man over six feet, and built proportionately, English preferably. The theatrical market seemed to be out of that type at the moment. George Tyler, who for many years had managed the career of that admirable actor, George Arliss, had just presented him in a play by Booth Tarkington called *Poldekin* which had been received — play and star — with distinct animosity by press and public alike. A disgruntled Tyler, without consulting Arliss, had put an ad in the Sunday papers that read something like this: "Mr. George Tyler, producer of flops, presents that well-known ham actor George Arliss in a wheeze on Americanism called *Poldekin* by the notorious hack-writer Booth Tarkington." The ad created a lot of talk, but not a lot of business. Whatever Mr. Tyler's intentions were, Mr. Arliss took a very dim view of the whole incident. His reaction I had gleaned from the grapevine. While Arliss and his almost too meticulous method of acting were miles away from the sinister Rajah that Archer had in mind, I nevertheless felt that he could be a wholly intriguing villain, *if* he could be had. On the q.t. I found out his play was going to close and that he was not averse to changing managements. This idea and information I passed along to W. A., who became enthusiastic about the prospect and talked Archer into accepting it, and Arliss was sent the play. He liked it and the part of the Rajah, and signed immediately. My next job was to find a leading woman.

W. A. said he had spoken to Olive Wyndham about it but indicated he would like, if possible, to get a "newer face" — a "young Ethel Barrymore." I immediately suggested Kit. It was not a great part but I thought she would be charming in it and I arranged a meeting for them. I lived several hundred years waiting outside his office while that interview was taking place. When it was over and Kit had left, Ames came into my office shaking his head. I knew it was thumbs down for her. He felt she had no emotional power and when I, quivering with indignation, asked "Has Miss Wyndham?" he quietly ended our talk with, "After all, Miss Wyndham *is* a *lady*. . . ." She played the part. I clammed up, a habit I wish I could resurrect. It would have been silly to mention that Kit was in the *Social Register* (and anyway I fixed that, for when she married me she was dropped). W. A.'s lady complex came over him at the oddest times — like a sudden attack of hay fever with each sneeze saying "Must find a LADY . . ."

A good cast was lined up and our four weeks of rehearsals were most interesting. George Arliss had an uncanny sense of his own limitations, a precise knowledge of what he could and of what he could not do. And the extreme tact with which he persuaded Archer to rewrite here and there so the dialogue would be in the vein that he could deliver best and with the greatest effect would have done credit to a diplomat. He was a star in star business, and as such turned in glittering performances that delighted and commanded a large public. He was stimulating to work with. He had a keen mind and a great sense of humor. *The Green Goddess* opened at the Walnut Theater in Philadelphia, and three weeks later came to the Booth, where it ran for over a year and later played for two seasons to capacity business on the road. Afterwards it was done as a silent motion picture, and when he deserted the theater for talking pictures in the early '30s he did it again, this time as a talkie. From

The Green Goddess time on, he appeared in the theater only in productions that were done by W. A. Both, *Old English* and *The Merchant of Venice*, were successes. His Shylock was criticized in New York, but between Manhattan and the road it ran for over a year.

On the opening night of *The Green Goddess*, when Mr. Arliss finally acknowledged his ovation, he made as punny a speech as I ever heard, starting with "This success does not surprise me for when you have a good Archer with good Ames you can't miss." Ronald Colman was in *The Green Goddess* at its Philadelphia debut in a short part for a short while. He was given his notice, and when I remember what we got in his place I'll never know why! I had to do the "dirty": he was one of three promising fellows I had to give the sack to. With Colman I was acting for Ames. But when I bounced Clifton Webb, I was entirely on my own — Well, almost! But in the dropping of Joshua Logan from the cast of *Parnell* I have to take all the credit. (He was acting then.) It is very obvious these boys have blossomed since, and I am happy to report my relations with them are extremely cordial.

Kit returned to town toward the end of the first week in September and on the evening of the eighth of September, 1920 — a date I'll never forget — I took her dancing on the roof of the Pennsylvania Hotel (Statler now); during one of the encores, we went out on the balcony overlooking the city and North River, and there, to the accompaniment of the orchestra's rendering of "Whispering," I revealed to her my assets — which were none; my hopes — which were many; my entanglement, which was serious but not insurmountable; and then asked her if she would marry me when I was free and clear of all encumbrances — and she, without so much as a pause, said yes. I kissed her and whisked her hastily back onto the dance floor again for I feared I might just float off the roof.

The joyous period that usually follows the announcement of one's impending nuptials was in our case singularly absent, inasmuch as there were no showers, no stag dinners, no congratulations; and of the reaction of our respective families, it would be an understatement to say they were negative, particularly on Kit's side of the fence. Dr. Cornell (her mother had died several years before), I was told, burst into tears and bemoaned the fact that he had lived to see the day when a child of his could even contemplate such a fate as Me. But against all admonition and threats and revelations concerning Me (and they were something — in fact when I heard some of them I almost became shocked) — in the face of it all she stuck to her guns: that when the law gave the green-light signal she was going to marry Me.

My family, on the other hand, on being informed by letter, were neutral to the point of being apathetic. They weren't surprised at my intended's being an actress but wondered if I knew anything about her "family." Naturally, I couldn't go into that: Dr. Cornell didn't give a rap about my background. He knew about Me, and was wondering how much time he would draw if he used his gun. W. A., when I told him the news, said with a poker face, "You will have plenty of time to think it over before you are free to marry." And there he said a mouthful, for my first marriage was one that had to be dissolved with the greatest of secrecy, not only on account of the lady involved but on account of an omission that was made at the time of the ceremony. That provided homework for me for quite a long while.

And here is where William Barnes and his charming wife, Maude, step on the scene. She had taught Kit English at Mrs. Merrill's school in Mamaroneck a few years before. William Barnes was owner of the Albany *Journal* and a more fearsome person it would be hard to imagine, although in his wife's presence he was as gentle as a lamb. A hangover from another era, he had been the boss of the Republican party and was the one who spiked Teddy Roosevelt's nomination in the 1912 convention. At the time I met him, he was still mighty powerful in the Empire State and the Republican party as well. Maude was very fond of Kit and we saw quite a lot of her and William during the feverish winter of 1920–1921. When she heard of the matrimonial handicap I had to hurdle before I would be free to take Kit for wife, she suggested that her better half might be of some help in making that state of Elysium possible. And accordingly I went to see the fearsome Mr. Barnes in his lair — I mean office. That rather dour geniality that he exuded when Kit and I journeyed out to Westchester for lunch with them on a Sunday was entirely absent when I faced him across his desk. When I explained in detail my predicament he heaved a sigh that sounded like the beginning of a tornado, and with his sagging jowls shaking — and in a voice that would have done credit to Siegfried's dragon — boomed, "You have been a God-damn' fool." And, after a pause in which I saw my life as being ended, he added, "I will mull this over and if I have any suggestions to offer I will let you know." Without ceremony I stumbled out of his office.

A short time later he summoned me back to his presence

and told me that on the following Sunday he wanted me to pack a suitcase with clothes I did not need (that in itself presented a problem as I had but two suits to my name) and take a train to an upstate county in New York. There I would be met by John Doe, who would take me to his house where I was to rent a room for six months in order to establish residence. I need never go back there, he said, but I must hang up my clothes and leave the suitcase to give the appearance of residence. I was at the time managing with unique skating on thin ice to live just over my income of one hundred and twenty-five dollars a week and any added drain brought the doors of the workhouse or penitentiary closer, but I canvassed a not-so-fashionable-then Third Avenue for a wicker suitcase and some secondhand clothes, journeyed upstate, paid six months' rent in advance, hung up my clothes, and came back to Manhattan a resident of, I think, Greene County. That particular episode set me back two hundred and twenty dollars. But I felt the path was being cleared for me to get out of the forest. I had made the first move towards freedom. All I had to do now was to sit tight and await orders.

Meanwhile I was still hounding agents for plays with the same avid intensity that I had looked for a job eight years before. And for a time with as little success. But I did find a sympathetic ear — that of Myra Furst. She represented the well-known British firm of Curtis Brown, who at that time handled many of England's best-known authors and playwrights. Myra listened to my story and promised that, if anything she considered good were available, she would guarantee that I saw it straight off.

Early in February of '21, W. A. and family took off again

for Santa Barbara for another stay there; but before he left
he said, as if I had been loafing, "Why haven't you found
that play?" He had hardly time to reach the coast when
Miss Furst breathlessly burst in on me saying she had my
play. It had been written by A. A. Milne whose London success *Mr. Pim Passes By* had been done by the Theatre Guild
the year before. This play that she was giving me to read
had not been produced anywhere as yet, but a London production was rumored to be coming up. The Guild had seen
the script and the Board had decided against it. And I was
the next to see it. She wanted an immediate answer. It was
called *The Dover Road*. She had barely left the office before
I warned Sully, "No phone calls — no interruptions," and
started to read the script. I finished it in less than two hours'
time, called up Kit and asked if she would let me read it
aloud to her later that night. "Yes," she said and I did. She
liked it and I liked it even better after reading it the second
time and aloud. It had great charm, was whimsical but not
embarrassingly so, and very funny. From the point of view
of budget it was any producer's dream — one set, six speaking parts and four nonspeaking servants. I felt that W. A.
could not complain of cost.

The next day I phoned Myra Furst that I wanted to buy
it, and went down the hall to Eddie Lyons's office and
told him of the play and asked him for a check for five hundred dollars to pay the advance. With all the sanctimony
of Uriah Heep he said W. A. had never mentioned backing a play for me to him. "When did he make this offer to
you?" he queried. "What ever induced him? Strange he
didn't tell me" — and ended up with the snide conclusion
that "There must be something wrong with the play if the

Guild turned it down, for they're an up-and-coming organization." But he said he would get in touch with Mr. Ames and let me know. I should have communicated with Winthrop myself straight off but I had no desire to intrude on his holiday and it had never occurred to me that Lyons, his general manager, wouldn't know about it. Myra sent around the contracts, but no check arrived from W. A. Lyons had heard nothing, he said. A week passed and as far as I was concerned I felt both foolish and intense. W. A. certainly had not been giving me a run-around, but somewhere there was a dog in the manger. Still no word — said Lyons. So I betook me up to the Astor Hotel and on their telegram blanks wired W. A. myself. I was taking no chances in sending one from the office. I briefly stated the particulars of the play and the necessity of having my check for the advance royalty immediately.

The next morning I had a reply that read DELIGHTED. ASK LYONS FOR $500. REGARDS. WINTHROP AMES. Armed with the telegram I knocked on that gentleman's door and handed him the wire.

He only said, "Isn't it funny he never answered me?"

I kept a dead pan and said "Yes." But I harbored dark suspicions, nevertheless, that he had never got in touch with W. A. at all. I waited until he handed me the check. I sent it off pronto along with the contracts to Myra, who in turn had to send them to the English office for Milne's signature. I held my breath for the two and a half weeks it took for my contract to be returned to me. . . . Miracle of miracles — *I owned a play*.

Kit, meanwhile in the early spring, had signed to play a small part in a new play, *Nice People*, by Rachel Crothers, which Sam Harris, a beloved and a great producer, was putting on with Francine Larrimore as star. And in her support were Kit and Tallulah. It opened the Klaw Theater, later called the Avon, and was a success running through the summer and into the autumn. My divorce was due to come up in the early summer and Kit, despite her father's increasingly antagonistic attitude, was going to marry me anyway. We started thinking about a place to live. Alma Morgan, Frank's wife, had told us the summer before in Detroit of a street east of First Avenue where she had lived as a child. It was called Beekman Place. It was only two blocks long and backed onto East River. Kit and I wandered over there one day — the location was fascinating — the river seemed intimate and the traffic on it, together with the view of the Queensboro Bridge, gave the Island of Manhattan a new excitement for us. There were only brownstone houses there then, most of them entirely occupied by the owners, and those that were not had no vacancies. We were disappointed, but there was nothing we could do and at the moment there wasn't a great hurry. Then some time in May an advertisement appeared in the Sunday *Times* that read:

For Rent — 3 floors and a garden on Beekman Place — number 23. Unobstructed view of the river.

We went that afternoon and there were indeed three floors and there was a garden and there was an unobstructed view of the river. Mrs. Schmid, who owned this five-storied house, planned on living in the top two floors. She wanted to rent these lower three immediately, but finally agreed that if I took them then she would have no objection to my subleasing them for the summer, which luckily I was able to do;

and as I was signing the lease I suddenly said I would like
to have a clause inserted to the effect that if the property
were ever for sale I would have the first chance of buying
it. As my capital at that moment was barely enough to pur-
chase the plain gold band that was to be used in the forthcoming ceremony, I would never know what happy sprite
prompted me to have that clause inserted. But it was, and
I signed it, and we had a place to live in for the next three
years — that is if I made enough to pay the rent — one hundred and fifty dollars a month, I think it was.

I was reading *The Dover Road* aloud about twice a week
— in fact, any time I could harness a willing ear; and every
time I read it I liked it more. W. A. returned from California
and I gave it to him to read. When he handed it back to
me a few days later, his only comment was "It's a nice little
play." He also told me he had given it to George Arliss to
look over but gave no indication of what that worthy soul
had thought. He further expanded that inasmuch as I had
it on a year's option I needn't hurry to get it on, as it was
tough finding theaters that were available at the moment.
Moreover, it might be done in London first and it would
profit me to know how it had gone there. But I cast it in my
mind's eye nevertheless. Arliss, I thought, would be ideal
for the star part; but he was, happily for W. A., not available.
Also I thought of Kit for the leading girl . . . but two ladies
from Scotland were going to change all that.

Kit and I sometimes went on a Sunday for a picnic on a
deserted estate in Connecticut, and always part of the ritual
was that after luncheon I would read to her. On one occasion
I took with me another play that Myra Furst had sent me,
one which was a big hit in London and had been bought by

an American management and by some fluke was free again. It was *A Bill of Divorcement,* by Clemence Dane. I read it aloud and both of us were terribly moved, and Kit voiced her conviction that she could play the girl, Sydney. Her success in London in *Little Women* cut no ice at all with New York managers, and her slick performance in *Nice People* suggested second parts, if anything, so her conviction was just that and no more, not even a hope. W. A., I knew, would never endow me with two plays, nor had I any right to expect it. But I thought he should read it, so on the following day I handed it to him. He read it at one sitting, was enthusiastic, and immediately cabled for the rights; but the reply came back that it had just been sold to a British actor named Allan Pollock. That was that. And for Kit a happy fate was stacking her cards. For I doubt at that time Winthrop would ever have entrusted her with the part of Sydney.

Maybe two weeks passed when one morning Kit phoned me that she had a message from Ada Humbert saying that Charles Dillingham wanted her for a part in *A Bill of Divorcement.* I went with her to Miss Humbert's office. It seems that Dillingham was in receipt of a cable from Allan Pollock advising him to engage Katharine Cornell for the part of Sydney. Dillingham, through Miss Humbert, was offering her two hundred and fifty dollars a week. She would have played it for free — the opportunity was so great! The part she was convinced she could play was hers. Let's say, it was hers if she made good. Neither of us doubted that she would! But to get it without an effort — out of the air, so to speak . . . What was the story behind it? Briefly this:

Allan Pollock was a Scotchman who wore his kilt with a swagger that was the envy of his regiment. He was seriously wounded in World War I. Part of his convalescence consisted of his getting used to the reconstruction job that had been done on his face and insides as well. It left him, not unnaturally, terribly depressed. He felt his life was over, that he no longer had a career to look forward to. Before the war he had been a personable and up-and-coming actor on Broadway. A group of his friends from the Players' Club, headed by A.E. Thomas, banded together, bought *A Bill of Divorcement* practically at the moment that Ames was angling for it, persuaded Dillingham to take over the management of it while they supplied the backing, and then presented it to Pollock as a "getting well" present. He was most concerned about the girl who would enact Sydney. None of the suggestions he had in London appealed to him at all, when out of the blue two elderly ladies from his home in Scotland journeyed up to London to see the play their local hero was going to act in New York. Afterwards, while having a bite of supper with Allan in his flat, they were expressing their enthusiasm at the prospect when one of them suddenly said, "You know all the time I was watching the play I kept thinking how wonderful the girl who played Jo in *Little Women* would be as Sydney." Allan, who had seen that performance of Kit's, snapped into immediate attention but could not remember her name. So he phoned an old friend of his, Leslie Faber, who had played in *Little Women* with Kit, got her name and sent a cable off to Dillingham that night. That was the way it came about.

Despite the upward trend our lives appeared to be taking

I was becoming tenser by the minute. So many things could spoil it! My divorce was, in my mind, by no means certain. For reasons that are too tiresome to relate, it was decided that I should be the plaintiff in the action, but the lady who was defendant refused to accept service because she felt divorce was unnecessary, and it would be in all the papers, and that would be unpleasant. No amount of reassurance had any effect. A mutual friend of ours came to the rescue by tapping her with the papers one afternoon when he was having a cocktail with her. On one side a beautiful friendship was broken, and on the other it was cemented.

I had no idea how long one waited after that but wait I did, forever it seemed, with nothing happening. We saw William and Maude Barnes quite frequently but that little problem of mine was never mentioned. In one of my blackest fits of depression at the lack of any action on my matrimonial front the phone rang and Barnes's sepulchral voice barked that on a specified night I was to embark along with my witness on the Albany night boat, where I would be met by a car that would take me to another town where my divorce trial would be coming up. In case you remember a previous occasion, I must say *this* time I made the boat. I was met by my lawyer, whisked away by motor to a courthouse in a nearby town where a murder trial was in progress. I was deposited in the judge's chambers and there, during a recess of the trial, in the space of less than five minutes, I was once again "a free man." I was warned that three months must elapse in New York State before I would be eligible to marry again. My lawyer seemed very happy for William Barnes and said he would wire him at once. I was very happy for me and phoned Kit immediately. Another gauze was lifted . . . the future . . . our future at least was not just a mirage after all.

The summer passed . . . our spirits were high . . . we set our wedding day. Since Kit's father would in no way condone the marriage, we were planning on a civil ceremony when her Aunt Lydia in Cobourg decided that there was an onus attached to her only niece's being married away from her family by a justice of the peace, and planned a simple wedding to be performed at her house; and thither we went, Kit preceding me by a few days. We were married on a Thursday. The Saturday before she closed in *Nice People*, and the day following our marriage she began rehearsing *A Bill of Divorcement*.

Janet Beecher's mother, Mrs. Wyndham, told my fortune the week before I left for Cobourg by reading tea leaves and discovered I would cross water before I returned to New York City. As I was being examined by the Canadian Customs, somewhere before we came to Hamilton, I thought how preposterous that prediction was. Almost the first thing that Kit said on meeting me at the station in Cobourg was that she had arranged that we would return to the States that afternoon by ferry across Lake Ontario, a journey of some five or six hours, to Rochester, New York, where we would pick up the Century when it came through just after midnight. I seem to invite "messages," but there must have been times when they were not right.

Lydia, Kit's aunt, was as gracious as she was lovely. Her Uncle Douglas and his wife were cordial, and Dr. Cornell, with superhuman control, managed not to be hostile. The Cornells were Episcopalians but, as I was divorced, no Episcopal minister would officiate at the ceremony, so a

Methodist clergyman was drafted. He arrived in a funereal black Prince Albert and was wearing a slightly rusty silk hat. He explained the ceremony to me . . . asked to see the ring . . . told me to transfer it from my right to left vest pocket so it would be easily accessible when needed . . . and as a parting tip said, "When I say 'Amen,' you salute the bride." Now I am a person that at times takes everything literally, and that was one of my literal days, and when I, who was half numb anyway, asked, "Why?" he looked at me in amazement and with a condescending smile said, "Should I say *kiss* the bride?" I didn't say "Why?" that time. He did not tell me, however, that cue to "salute" came three times in the service, and when on the first "Amen" I started to salute, *sotto voce* he snarled, "Not now." And the second Amen found me again saluting when again he snarled. When the cue came up for the third time I remained passive and received from the gentleman of the cloth an ever so dainty kick in the ankle and an almost tonal admonition, "Salute!" I did, and we were Mr. and Mrs. I remember giving the minister ten dollars in gold, and as he took my hand in both of his to wish us happiness with great fervor I was conscious that Dr. Cornell's gaze was upon me. I sneaked a look around and I was right. There was nothing at that moment that even indicated that we would ever be friends. Luncheon, as far as I was concerned, was a little on the hysterical side, and I was glad when we were away and crossing Lake Ontario. I was a benedict for keeps now! I felt like the Count of Monte Cristo when he declaimed "The world is mine." If that was not quite true, at least a big part of it was by my side.

When we reached Kit's apartment the next morning we

found a package there which, on being opened, revealed a lovely pair of Adam candlesticks. They had arrived a few days before. With them was a note that read:

DEAR MISS CORNELL:

We join in sending you these candlesticks to betoken a little of the affectionate regard we have for Mr. McClintic, and with the hope that they may light many happy evenings for you both.

We hope you will let us be your friends as we have, for so many years, been his.

THE STAFF OF THE OFFICE OF WINTHROP AMES
September 1921

And the signatures that followed began with W. A.'s, and ended with Margaret Sullivan's.

XIV

The *Bill*

BASIL DEAN, who staged the original production
of *A Bill of Divorcement* in London (which we subsequently
referred to always as "the *Bill*"), was in charge of the New
York rehearsals as well. His reputation as a top-ranking English director had preceded him, and Kit went to the first
rehearsal the day after we were married excited and with
high anticipation. When she came back to the apartment
around six o'clock in the evening she was a little bit puzzled
and the rehearsal had been disappointing. Disappointing
because Dean seemed intent on making a carbon-copy re-
production of the London company's performance, as cockeyed a theory as has ever been used in productions following an original. There has been no good play since the
beginning of time that hasn't been able to survive and
even be improved by any number of other interpretations.
A Bill of Divorcement was a good play and three very
different type of actresses made great hits in it — Meggie
Albanesi in London, Kit in New York, and Katharine Hep-
burn in pictures.

Kit had survived that first day of facetious remarks at
rehearsal that are invariably showered on any bride by casual

acquaintances. I, too, had been all but smothered with a barrage of wit at W. A.'s office. Kit was puzzled primarily that she was told her next rehearsal call would be the following Monday, but delighted we could take advantage of a friend's offer of a shack on a deserted island off Norwalk, Connecticut, for a brief two days' honeymoon. The two days' interlude we later found out were due to Dean's efforts to get Kit out of the cast. Pollock, however, held firm in the face of Dean's objections, his argument being that he had seen Kit in *Little Women* and that performance convinced him she would be good as Sydney. He won out. And that took courage and belief to do. The success of any play means a great deal to the star, but in this instance I think it meant a great deal more than usual as it was Allan's first appearance on the stage in seven years — thanks to the war — and the play's getting over would contribute to his physical and mental well-being in addition to padding his bank balance. I saw no rehearsals. It seems odd to think of that now, after the many years Kit and I have worked together. Of course we talked it over endlessly at home. Dean was not sympathetic nor helpful to work with. Kit was so concerned about herself in relation to the part that she did not take time off to bemoan Dean's lack of co-operation. She said he was constantly at her about her walk. "Must you walk like Sir Henry Irving?" he was flinging at her, in between trying to impregnate her with Meggie Albanesi's readings. I never saw Irving but I will say if he walked like Kit then he walked real nice.

When it opened in Philadelphia it was received politely but without any great enthusiasm. Janet Beecher replaced the woman who played Kit's mother, and much of the time

that should have been given to polishing the play was surrendered to getting Miss Beecher ready to open before their
two weeks were over in Philly. Charles Waldron, who later
would play Kit's father in *The Barretts of Wimpole Street*
for many years, was also in the cast. Kit's performance was
exciting to watch as it grew during those two weeks. All
of those latent qualities that few were aware of were shining through now. It was lovely — tender and gay by turns —
and played with an emotional restraint that tore your heart
out. Although my contribution was nothing more than
holding her close I was bursting with pride. But . . . New
York was ahead! Tomorrow or almost!

We hoped to move into our new home on Beekman Place
on Kit's return from Philadelphia October 9, but it wasn't
ready, so we parked at the Hotel Chatham until it was. The
day of the opening, Monday the tenth, was cloudy and towards evening it began to rain. Among the many supersti-
tions in the theater there is one that if an actor or a bit of
scenery gets a bit of storm on it at an opening it brings
luck to the whole venture. I did not know that one at the
time. Kit was quiet and in full control of herself. She had
no maid so she went to the theater in the afternoon to lay
out her one costume and make-up. There had been quite a
rumpus among some of the better-known actors as to where
they should dress; but Kit, who had the central part in the
play, raised no squawk at all at being put on the third floor.
She barely touched her dinner and I took her to the theater
early. I sat with her in her dressing room for a while, then
I wished her luck and kissed her and walked around the
block several times before going into the theater.

It was playing at the George M. Cohan on the east side

of Broadway between 43rd and 42nd Streets, and it was a "dressy" première. Many of "gentleman" Charles Dillingham's regular opening-nighters were in evidence, as well as a few friends of ours — Frances Wollcott, Laura Elliot, Maude and William Barnes and Eleanor Belmont. As the lights dimmed just before the curtain rose on the first act I dug my nails into the palms of my hands and said a prayer. I possibly had more nerves than Kit. Certainly hers were less in evidence. I thought it went well, but all first-night audiences bewilder me. They always have. They still do. I had been through many opening nights with W. A. and Grace George, but there my concern for their smooth operation was paramount. In this one my concern was personal. Kit's performance was a lovely and touching one of a girl who discovers her father, whom she had believed was insane because of shell shock from World War I, is really the victim of an inherited insanity — and, on realizing this fact, renounces the marriage she was contemplating with an eligible young man rather than pass on the taint and remains as companion to her father, who has been released from the asylum. Kit's slender, dark beauty, her lithe movement, her careless hair (long then), the haunting sound of her voice, and the extraordinary flash of terror in her dark eyes when she first learned there was madness in her family — all of these remain with me still.

In 1921 and in all my previous time in the theater it was customary to take curtain calls after every act, and in a three-act play the big ovation, if there was one, came after the second act. After the second act of the opening night of the *Bill* there were many curtain calls, and Kit took one alone — her first — and I thought her applause was genuine and solid. When the play was over many people came backstage, apparently enthusiastic. I remember one man in particular, whom I had never seen before, whose appreciation seemed more serious and tempered with anxious concern. His name was Carl Van Vechten. Now on that fateful October night — strange as it may seem to the theatergoers of today — there were five openings to share the critics. Helen Hayes, who had made a big hit three seasons before with William Gillette in *Dear Brutus,* was being starred for the first time in Booth Tarkington's play, *The Wren.* The Theatre Guild, already an established producing unit, were presenting Arthur Richman's *Ambush* in which another young actress was to give a good acount of herself — Florence Eldridge. Of the other two, one was an art group and the other a musical. At these five openings I have no idea which critics went where, but at the *Bill* only three of the first-line critics appeared — Charles Darnton, Alan Dale and Welch of the *Evening-Telegram.*

At the Chatham early the next day, even before we had our breakfast, a bellboy brought us the morning papers. There were many more to pour through in those days — the *American,* the *News,* the *World, Times, Tribune, Herald, Sun, Telegraph,* to say nothing of the downtown papers such as the *Wall Street Journal* and the *Journal of Commerce.* And each one of the first eight in the morning had critics of importance whose reviews were heeded by their various followings. But not one of them probably was as widely read as Woollcott of the *Times.* I turned to that one first, as Kit lay quietly beside me. Woollcott reviewed Helen Hayes. My eyes raced down the other columns. *Ambush* came second. The *Bill* was fourth. It was a tepid, not unpleasant notice that said nothing at all beyond imparting a feeling of oblivion for all concerned. Like a bat in hell I tore through the rest of them. All the same! Then I opened the *American* . . . Ah . . . Dale had been there — and when I finished reading his first paragraph I concluded it would have been just as well if he had not been. He wasted a lot of printer's ink in spoofing the play. He was kind to Allan, but when he got to Kit he had run out of adjectives. The best he could say was "Miss Cornell performed flippantly as a flapper." Outside, the day was cloudy and dark. Inside, it was cloudier and darker. The phone rang. It was Allan Pollock. His Scotch temper was sizzling. My Irish one was torrid and when we had purged ourselves of what we thought of those guys who had reviewed the play we felt a great deal better and were virtually laughing when the second tidal wave of the afternoon reviews caught us — not so unaware this time. I waded through the *Evening World, Telegram, Sun, Mail, Globe, Post* and *Journal.* It was very discouraging. The same timid, lukewarm comment from the second-string press, and of the two "firsts" the notice of Darnton of the *World* was an echo of Alan Dale's. On the other hand, Welch of the *Telegram* (unfortunately little read) was very good, and beautiful for Kit. I read that particular part over and over again. But when we got to the theater that night, despite the artificial gaiety that reigns backstage when the critical drubbing has been brutal, the front of the house was draped in funeral crepe. Mr. Dillingham was not around to give the actors a pat on the back. His manager looked very sad and faintly accusing, as if in some way the company had been responsible for this very apparent debacle. The second-night house was rustling with paper (passes, in case enlightenment is needed); the receipts in gold standard currency were just over two hundred dollars. The cast played magnificently, as if they were the biggest success in town, but the handwriting was on the wall. The theater which Dillingham had under a four weeks' guarantee was released.

But away from the temple of woe that was Dillingham's headquarters the underground was at work and life was stirring. It seems the anxious enthusiast of the opening night, Carl Van Vechten, phoned Woollcott that the *Bill* needed help, the kind of help that only he could inspire, and needed it at once. Moreover it was deserving it. Depressed by his theatergoing of the past few weeks, Alec attended the sparsely filled Wednesday matinee. He was impressed. Always seeing himself as a kind of Paul Revere, warning the countryside of the fare their esthetic souls should partake, he, figuratively speaking, got on his horse and advised all the critics that the *Bill* was a Must — an immediate Must — and that their next Sunday's dramatic page should carry their reviews of it otherwise it would perish. He must have sounded off pretty generally, for after the Wednesday-night performance Tallulah, with her characteristic generosity of spirit, climbed the stairs to Kit's dressing room to tell her that Woollcott's Sunday notice was going to be splendid. The following night a slim, intense, young Englishman, whose star was shortly going to rocket in no uncertain fashion, came back and introduced himself to Kit to tell her, as only he could, that he had not thought he could like anyone in the part of Sydney after seeing Meggie Albanesi but that Kit, in her own way, was equally admirable. His name was Noel Coward. . . . A short time before, at the Ames office,

I had met him for the first time and we had had quite a fervent powwow about the theater in general and a play of his in particular called *The Rat Trap* which I had just read. His enthusiasm was contagious. I liked him immediately. . . . That night, too, a card was sent in to Kit addressed in W. A.'s familiar handwriting that read: "I think you're damn swell. My homage to you."

Our spirits were better, but whether the *Bill* would be able to continue seemed to lie in the laps of the critics. Friday evening the *Mail* and the *Globe* contained brilliant notices for both play and Kit by Burns Mantle and Kenneth Macgowan. Still no business! Sunday came — and the *Bill* and Kit were all but smothered with an avalanche of superlatives. The critics had gone, had seen, and were conquered. Our phone was constantly ringing. Friends who had remained cautiously quiet after the opening were now filled with congratulations and wondered if it would be possible for Kit to get them "four seats for a week from Friday — we will pay for them, of course," they ended as Kit said she would. And I was sending for other editions and cutting out the notices to mail to my family and to Kit's family and a host of friends. The next night at the Cohan theater the management discovered that the corpse they were about to dump into potter's field was breathing; in fact showing signs of becoming lively. From the gross of two hundred dollars of the previous Tuesday receipts jumped to over twelve hundred dollars and the advance buying had been strong all day. Dillingham was now faced with the problem of getting another theater, since he had released the Cohan the day after the opening.

I went around to the Booth Theater to tell the good news

to our friend Maude Howell, who had been with us in stock and who was now George Arliss's stage manager. As I walked on the stage, before the performance, there was Arliss made up like a plush horse for his first entrance in *The Green Goddess*. He looked at me for a moment, narrowing his eyes, his faint squint more in evidence than ever, as if trying to recall where he had seen me before — then, adjusting his monocle, he turned to Maude and said, "Who is that young man?" and before she, poor bewildered dear, had a chance to reply he turned back to me and with malicious charm said, "Of course, it's Miss Cornell's husband!" And that's what I still am! I left the Booth stage door that night a marked man — I was the husband of a well-known actress.

As the week progressed, seats for the *Bill* were becoming increasingly hard to get, and by Friday night there were standees. The good news was that the management had secured the Times Square Theater on 42nd Street and they were moving there when the time was up at the Cohan. Kit was being interviewed, photographed, receiving fan letters and flowers, and when I would call for her after the theater to take her home she would introduce me to various groups of admiring acquaintances who would overwhelm me with affable vehemence as they said, "Aren't you proud of this little girl?" The enthusiasm that is inspired by being a success has always left me a little cold, and with the wrong kind of articulateness. It did then. After counting ten I mumbled something sick-making, and then lapsed into a loud quietness; and they, I am sure, were thinking, Poor child, to be married to *that!* . . . "Well, good-by my dear. You were wonderful — marvelous. And good night, *Mr. Cornell*. You should be very proud." . . . It still happens. It struck me funny then. It strikes me funny now.

Kit's play was a hit, and she was hailed as a star of to-morrow. I was her newly acquired side-kick. But what would I turn out to be? No doubt to make me feel good, a friend of mine told me another friend of mine had said of our marriage: "What in the world did she ever want to marry *him* for? All he has ever done is to buy lampshades for Ames." Well, it was enlightening to know how friends re-garded you. I did buy some lampshades for Ames, and they were damn nice ones too; and I bought some Jacobean fur-niture for our dining room at Beekman Place and charged it to Ames, although he didn't know it, and I prayed that the Almighty would see me through. The furniture from Kit's apartment had taken care of our bedroom and the liv-ing room floor. The only furnishings I possessed were per-sonal, my dinner clothes and the other suit for the clothes closet.

On Sunday, October 23, a sunny, sparkling autumn day, we moved into 23 Beekman Place. Frank and Laura Gill-more lived at the opposite corner, at Number 20. Margalo told me she was peeking out of the window of their house as we were taking our bags out of the taxi to cross our thresh-old as tenants for the first time. We had both our names on the door. And there were rumors that our next-door neigh-bor construed that to be open hanky-panky. Our telephone number was Plaza 1800. The Colony Club was Rhinelander 1800. Frequently, much too frequently, Colony Club mem-bers would call our number (there were no dial telephones then) late at night, in the early morning, with never an apology, just a curt "Will you please get off the line?" Finally, exasperated when Mrs. B.B.C. called one rainy evening and asked for the cab starter, I waited a second and with a disguised voice came back on the line to receive her order to send a cab immediately to her apartment on Park Avenue, as she had to make a train. "Right away," I answered and hung up. Five minutes later she called again, anxious this time to know if I had sent the cab. "Yes," I answered, "but I will send another." Two more times she called, the last time frantic. She had missed her train and it was all my fault. She was going to have me fired, she said, and with as sweet a voice as I could muster I replied, "Who the hell do you think you are talking to, you old bag?" The explosion was something herculean. I searched the papers the next day but there was no item saying that she had had a stroke. The nuisance became so great that I finally had the number changed. It became Plaza 123. (Four digits weren't necessary then.) The 23s were adding up. A momentous one was just ahead!

XV

The Road to Dover

NOVEMBER came — Pauline Lord literally shook Manhattan with her psychic performance of *Anna Christie* on November 2. Another step up for Eugene O'Neill . . . Another feather in Arthur Hopkins's hat . . . The magazine notices were beginning to appear about the *Bill*. Kit was on the up-and-up, all right! Her reviews were splendid! Rachel Crothers, who had a row of recent successes to her credit, decided to let her newest play serve as the debut of her agent, Mary Kirkpatrick, into the ranks of producers. It was called *Every Day*, and Tallulah Bankhead had the leading role. It opened at the Bijou (45th Street west of Broadway) on the night of November 16. Talu's beauty and spirit had more comment from the press than the play, which came off rather badly.

As for me, the theater situation remained unchanged: no theater — and I was sitting tapping my feet on the side lines like an actor in the outer office, waiting for a nod from the receptionist to proceed into the management's inner sanctum. I was hugging *The Dover Road* close — mapping out the business, planning the set, thinking of actors to play in it — wondering when a theater would be available. Cards, fortunetellers, astrologers, offered me no enlightenment.

The day after Thanksgiving I was summoned into W. A.'s private office, where he told me if I could be ready to open my production in New York within four weeks' time he could secure the Bijou Theater for its showing, as Miss Crothers's play was a dud and Miss Kirkpatrick, who had leased the theater for eight weeks, was now looking for someone to take part of her remaining time off her hands. "You will have to make up your mind in an hour or so," he continued. "Don't feel you have to grab this. I know the time is short; but if you could be ready, the Christmas season would be a good time to open, otherwise you might have to wait until early spring before there is another break."

I was thinking a mile a minute. I walked over to his window and looked out at the Broadhurst and Shubert Theaters across the street. I saw my weeks of frustration at an end. I saw an answer for my parents' sacrifice. I saw vindication for me and for Kit in having married me. I saw, too, my name on a houseboard. I turned back to W. A. and said, "Yes, I will be ready."

"You are sure?" he cautioned.

"Positive," I replied and I was back in my own office phoning Kit the exciting news. No time to waste! Jumping Jehoshaphat, no time at all! That was a Friday. A week from the following Sunday, December 4 to be exact, I began my rehearsals. In those eight days I had arranged about scenery, without benefit of a designer then, engaged the cast and interviewed scores of actors. The better known ones were giving me a wide berth despite the fact they knew W. A.'s money was behind my venture. I was an unknown quantity both as a producer and a director. Why take a chance? I talked my head off one night, used every atom of persuasion I had, to induce H. B. Warner, a very popular star at the time, to play the central role of Mr. Latimer; but Warner, with devastating charm, told me for special matinees he would love to do it but for an evening bill, no — it hadn't a chance. He had another play he preferred, called *Danger,* by old Right as Rain Hamilton (which ran all of eight weeks). On the average of eighteen hours a day I interviewed actors before the charming and popular English leading man, Charles Cherry, consented to play the role that Warner had refused. Fortunately the cast was small — only six speaking parts — and I was lucky in finding admirable types, although they were all of them virtually as unknown as myself. Winifred Lenihan, graduate from W. A.'s *Betrothal,* was my leading woman.

This time at the director's table, although my concern could not have been greater, my timidity was gone. I was my own boss, accountable only to me, and I doubt if there could have been a tougher taskmaster. I had read the play aloud so many times and my listeners had proved to be so many advance audiences for me that I knew where every laugh was; and, believe me, that's a very valuable thing to know in an untried comedy. I knew what the situations demanded. Every movement on the stage I had seen in my mind's eye, rehearsed by myself, at Beekman Place; and, furthermore, I could demonstrate its workability to any actor. "If you don't feel comfortable, say so," I would caution as I gave a piece of business (echoing the courtesy I had lifted from W. A.). My actors were keen and responsive and our daily sessions were exhilarating. We rehearsed morning, night and noon. I was so intent on my job that I had no moment of misgiving, no feeling I could be wrong. I was directing a play that I had chosen, with a cast selected by me and scenery of my own planning. I was completely absorbed — there was nothing else in the world that mattered. Kit came to some of the rehearsals. No one else! . . . My friend in the Booth box office, Peg Collins, one day took me aside to warn me that Eddie Lyons was after my scalp. She knew he had whispered to W. A. that he thought it was very odd that I had not asked him to any of the rehearsals or sought his advice about scenery or cast. Typical of Eddie! . . . Certainly I wanted no strain in my relations with Ames now. I immediately sought him out and explained that I had thought of nothing but the work I was in the midst of, and that I purposely hadn't asked him to rehearsals or consulted him because I felt that this was to be a test of me. I had to sink or swim by the result. He might have reminded me that, as he was financing the test, he might quite naturally have some concern about his investment. But he didn't. He accepted my explanation with reserve. I did not see him again until the day after my opening.

I was satisfied, in fact elated, as my rehearsals proceeded and decided we would be ready to open on the Friday before Christmas — that was the twenty-third. (Another 23!) But ominous clouds gathered over my hopes when I reviewed the openings that were against me. . . . Thursday night, the twenty-second, H. B. Warner in *Danger.* . . . Friday night, the twenty-third, William A. Brady was presenting an all-star revival of *Trilby.* . . . Saturday night, Norman Trevor, a well-known leading man, was opening in a new play. . . . Beginning Monday, the twenty-sixth, the week was entirely filled: Faversham's revival of *The Squaw Man*

. . . Leo Ditrichstein in a new play . . . Olga Petrova in a concoction written by herself. Two big London successes with imposing casts were in that week too: *Bulldog Drummond* and *Captain Applejack.* I was confronted with the fact that I had no more chance than the proverbial snowball in Hades of garnering any first-string critics to review my opus against that formidable opposition. Remembering the opening press of Kit's play and with the advice of nothing but a pack of cards I decided to have my première on the afternoon of Friday the twenty-third. Carefully making my handwriting as legible as possible I wrote to every dramatic critic in New York explaining the reasons for my move and expressing the hope it would be possible for them to attend. I emphasized that I couldn't say they would like my endeavor but, if they didn't, I preferred to take the count from the gentlemen of the first line. W. A's publicity man was against my sending it, but fools plunge in! I licked the stamps on every one of those letters and put them in the mail box myself. I could only wait and see.

On the nights of December 21 and 22 I had two previews with invited audiences — some actors, but mostly nurses and bank clerks. The set was charming — the acting suave and distinguished — the audience seemed enthusiastic. After the final one I had gone backstage and given my brief notes to the company, plus a spiritual slap-on-the-back for the next afternoon's opening. We were all feeling elated.

When I came out into 45th Street the theaters had shed their audiences and were dark. Walking toward Shubert Alley, I found myself behind three well-known figures of the street: my nemesis, Eddie Lyons; Ed Giroux, general manager for Oliver Morosco, and Luke Phelps, who occupied a similar position with Arthur Hopkins. They all knew me and, with the exception of Lyons, occasionally gave me a grunt of recognition. I had no desire to encounter them then, so I stayed in the background. Walking behind them in the dim light I suddenly felt an uninitiated little boy again. These mundane silhouettes represented responsible theater figures . . . two great men consulted them and abided by their decisions — Winthrop Ames and Arthur Hopkins. Who was I? What was I? What they thought I was, my eaves-dropping told me.

"I told W. A. it would be awful, but he wouldn't listen," Lyons was saying.

Luke Phelps was more concerned about the booking at the poor Bijou Theater. "I wonder what they will get to follow it?"

"Stinks," opined Giroux.

Dear God, could it be possible this was to be the verdict on my years of preparation — my months of waiting — my weeks of rehearsal? I stopped in my tracks and retreated towards Broadway. Walking down through Times Square in the bright lights, with the crowd jostling me, I reflected these three managerial entities could be right. I thought *The Dover Road* was good. I thought the actors believed in it. The two preview audiences gave every indication of liking it, but I had to admit that was what I wanted to believe so maybe I was kidding myself. Certainly every play that has opened on the Great White Way has had behind it someone who believed in it. Maybe I was the one and only one who had faith in Mr. Milne's little play. I had a sharp pain in the center of my brain. I did not mention the incident to Kit, and after a brief supper in the kitchen we went to bed; and as I was trying to lie still and quiet I could already see the scathing reviews.

The next day was cloudy and drizzling. I got a cab and started for the theater. (Kit was coming later.) At First Avenue the longest funeral procession I ever saw — how long I don't know, but it seemed to me over one hundred horse-drawn hacks — was leisurely plodding up First Avenue toward the Queensborough bridge to whatever happy hunting ground lies on the other side of the East River. The taxi driver was all for breaking through. Others did. I can't say that I was stopped by respect for the departed or even courtesy on my part. Just plain superstition held me back. My doom would be sealed if I did anything other than wait. And wait I did, with the driver, I am sure, thinking I was a nut. Arriving at the theater, I dispensed some gifts I was giving the actors as a token of my appreciation for their hard rehearsals and co-operation — flasks filled with Scotch for the gentlemen, and vanity cases for the ladies. I had a few telegrams. I read them without knowing what they said or who sent them. I sat on the bare stage and looked out at the dark, empty theater that would hold the key to my fate that afternoon. . . . I could not forget the three predictions of the night before. I was too restless to stay still. I went out on the street. A nice steady rain was falling. I ran into Jed Shaw, whom W. A. had allotted me as a company manager, and as nice a fellow as I ever knew but deaf as a post. I asked him if Lyons had said anything to him about my play. He smiled and nodded "yes." But I don't think he heard me. I don't know why I asked.

Matinee time came. I stood on the sidewalk by the stage door and watched the audience arrive. I saw George Arliss

and his Mrs., W. A. and Lucy, Kit and Laura Elliot, and
there were others, too, who brought the total gross of the
opening performance up to five hundred and eighty-four
dollars. When the last of the opening audience arrived I
went into the theater and stood in the back. The curtain
rose. I had lit the scene beautifully, in the best of the Ames
tradition. That afternoon I thought it looked dim and drab,
about as unsuitable for the lightest of comedies as anything
imaginable. The actors' pace seemed funereal. Moreover,
I couldn't hear them. The audience turned out to be as
croupy a bunch as ever were assembled under one roof.
If there was any laughter, I didn't hear it. But I stuck it out.
At the end of the first act I fled down the alley to the stage
door, took a generous swig of my bootleg hootch, then presented myself to the cast and told them it was going well.
To my amazement they seemed to think so too. I talked to
the electrician about the lights. He assured me they were
on the same marks they had been on the two previews and
dress rehearsal. I took another swig and went back to my
spot to stand. As far as I was conscious, the performance
never gained momentum. Occasionally I heard some laughter that seemed hollow and far away, and at the end there
was applause. I ran backstage, got into the furthermost corner and faced the back wall. I could hear the actors greeting their friends and voices swelling and disappearing. But
those, too, had a distant, faraway feeling. I felt the whole
thing had been a fiasco. And I was trying desperately hard
to pull my face together and myself as well so that I could
put up a good front. Kit finally found me and seemed quite
happy. She said many people had been back to congratulate
me but nobody seemed to know where I had disappeared to.

W. A. hadn't come back! Kit jubilantly told me she heard one customer say, "This will either be a big success or a flop!"

We went home for dinner. W. A. phoned there. His voice was encased in a veneer of reserve that only meant to me a total lack of enthusiasm. He thought I had done a competent job, but had no idea what the press would be like. Dear God! In my misery I had forgotten about them! He said every first-line critic had been there. After delivering Kit to her theater I returned to the scene of the crime. There was almost nobody in the streets. It was raining harder. I went into the Booth; Arliss, who had seen the matinee, conspicuously avoided me. I felt I had already committed Broadway's unforgivable sin — produced a "turkey." I was to be avoided as if I had leprosy. My second audience was pitifully small, but appreciative. I stood on the sidewalk at the end to hear any comments that might be thrown about. It was still raining. Cabs were scarce. Suddenly an authoritative voice behind me said, "Get me a cab, bud" and an opulent-looking gent slipped me a quarter. I settled for that as a comment, kept the quarter and got him a cab. Then I got one for myself and went to pick Kit up. As we started homeward the morning *American* was just out. I was all for buying it. Kit stopped me and said: "No, we are reading them all at the same time in bed in the morning at home." So that was what we did.

We had a Japanese manservant that winter who answered to the name of Hara and looked like a Nipponese wrestler. All smiles, he brought up our breakfast and a great stack of the morning papers. Nerving myself to read the first one was not unlike steeling oneself for a dip in an icy pool.

The first one I read, naturally, was Alexander Woollcott of the *New York Times*. My benumbed senses began to tingle again when I realized it was what is called "a rave." All that I had thought *The Dover Road* was, in all the months before the opening, he concurred with. This is what I read:

Stray visitors to the high many-windowed room which looks out over the Thames from Barrie's home in Adelphi Terrace are like as not to find there, tucked away in the settle by the fireplace, a sunny, twinkling young Englishman, who looks rather like a leading juvenile and writes and smokes rather like Barrie himself. His name is A. A. Milne, and surely he had been smoking away at Barrie's own pipe the afternoon that he first thought of the smiling comedy which, after much musing, emerged on pieces of white paper as the delightful play called *The Dover Road*.

London has not seen it yet, but it was brought to New York yesterday afternoon under the happiest auspices imaginable. All those who would like to sit down before the best piece Mr. Milne has written for the theater, indeed, all those who would like to see one of the best examples of fine-textured high comedy that has come out of England in the last ten years, will find it now — and for some time to come, we hope — at the Bijou in West Forty-fifth Street.

A scrupulous effort to report next day ad seriatim on all the things of which the gentle, tranquil laughter of *The Dover Road* is made would be a little too much like trying to bring home to America from the French Alps one of those gay, feather-light soufflés of which the cooks up there know the secret. But perhaps some suggestion is feasible.

Suppose, then, that a charming young girl, bent on running away with some other woman's husband, could be halted with him in the first flight, could be kept cooped up with him in the same house for a week, chaperoned but permitted to see him at odd times — such painfully odd times, for instance, as breakfast, when he has a cold and hasn't shaved yet. Suppose this more gradual familiarity were to be administered judiciously throughout the week. At the end of it would she be willing to continue the flight? And even if she were, would he be?

It is the quaint Mr. Latimer's fancy to play Providence in just this fashion at his lovely, secluded house a little way off the road that leads to Dover — which, as you know, leads in turn to Calais, and then to the Riviera and bliss as advertised in novels. How he entraps and holds two such impulsive couples and what comes of it — all this is set forth deftly, winningly, happily in the new piece at the Bijou.

Fortunately, it has been wisely cast and, furthermore, it has been staged — marvel of marvels — with some taste and sense. Here is Charles Cherry more comfortably cast as Mr. Latimer than he has been for many a season. Also Winifred Lenihan and Reginald Mason playing most skilfully as the first of the victims of his benevolence to be introduced. And yet the two who come nearest to understanding and realizing just what Milne had in mind are, we imagine, George Riddell as the brooding butler and Lyonel Watts as young Nicholas, another reluctant home destroyer. Difficult as it may seem to burst into sudden applause for anyone named Lyonel, it is inevitable in the case of a comedian as felicitous as this Mr. Watts. His is such a young performance — in fact, a Roland Young performance.

Another newcomer and a welcome one, is the Guthrie McClintic who makes his first appearance as a producer with *The Dover Road*. Luckily for him, he was able to start with a play by the author of *Mr. Pim* which happened to be better than *Mr. Pim*. But he has risen to the occasion, and as the American theater's poverty is most conspicuous in the matter of directors, his advent takes on the nature of an occasion. More power to Mr. McClintic, then — more power and a Merry Christmas.

When I finished reading it aloud, Kit started to cry and sobbed and cried for the rest of the morning. Every time the phone rang and someone said "Isn't it wonderful about Guthrie?" she would start sobbing all over again and say, "Yes, isn't it?" I leaped from paper to paper absorbing every review like a thirsty camel in the desert. They were all good with the exception of Alan Dale — that was the notice that Kit had stopped me from buying the night before! His was a stinker! But one bad notice out of nine morning papers made it unanimous as far as I was concerned. I suddenly wanted to get to the office to see W. A. and talk to him — buy the afternoon papers — get extra copies of the morning reviews — see the actors at the matinee.

I dressed as if I were going to a fire, and as I entered the office I literally fell over Arliss, who was on his way out. He extended his hand and said, "Congratulations. I didn't like your play when I read it. I didn't like it when I saw it yesterday, but I am glad to say I seem to be in the minority." Winthrop, who was accompanying Arliss to the elevator, said, "You've had a wonderful press, boy." I went into my office. Saturday before Christmas the place was deserted. Having put Arliss in the automatic elevator, Winthrop came back to sit with me and said he was delighted with the notices — he had the afternoon ones cut out and produced them from his pocket and gave them to me. They were unanimous in their approval, without one dissenting voice.

He said he could not be sure that it would immediately catch on, but he was going to see that it had every chance. As he was talking, Jed Shaw passed my door. Ames called to him: "How are things at the Bijou? Any 'life'?" Jed smiled and shook his head. W. A. turned quickly to me: "Don't be discouraged," he said. "It may take a week or ten days before we know anything." Dear deaf Jed chimed in, having heard none of this: "Never saw anything like it. The ticket brokers have bought up the entire lower floor for sixteen weeks. The phone never stops ringing over there, and there is a line at the box office that goes to Broadway." As soon as I decently could, I was at the Bijou, and sure enough there was a line. . . . I wanted Kit to see it. I was afraid it wouldn't be there again. It might melt like snow in the sun. . . . I could look at that houseboard with pride: GUTHRIE McCLINTIC PRESENTS THE DOVER ROAD BY A. A. MILNE — DIRECTED BY MR. McCLINTIC. The colored doorman, cleaning the slush in front of the theater, smiled at me. The stage-door man stood up when I went backstage. The actors were jubilant and I was jubilanter. This, then, was my putting up the flag. Nine-and-a-half years out of dramatic school. Nobody — not even the table — could have foreseen such an end. The end? What am I talking about? It was the beginning. I had only climbed the first hill. . . . That afternoon, I mailed an entire set of notices home . . . Special Delivery!

XVI

Red Hair out of Shanghai

CHRISTMAS was merry that year — unreal and merry. I was trying hard to explore the sensation of landing squarely on my two feet on Broadway. One day a dramatic-school buddy stopped me in Times Square and asked how it felt to be a success. I suppose it's a silly question, but I had no answer. I had always romanticized that when you had good fortune you felt a certain elevation and apartness. None of these magical sensations descended on me. I found myself to be the same guy as the week before or the year before. I was glad there were those who thought I possessed some of the qualities I believed I had. I had learned my job; I had worked hard and it was paying off. It had happened to others before me and it would continue to happen.

I, too, found myself being photographed and interviewed. The first of many bits of fiction that were to be bandied about concerning Kit and myself in the press was a newspaper item that was printed from coast to coast in varying versions, that *The Dover Road* had been a wedding present from W. A. Nothing could have been further from the truth. A few weeks after the opening, a friend of mine said to Winthrop, "Aren't you proud of Guthrie? Isn't it wonderful what he has done?" To which W. A. replied, "I think that young man has heard more than enough about himself."

He was right. I had. But it was pleasant and therapeutic.

Apart from bolstering my ego, *The Dover Road* was a financial success as well. When the curtain rose on the production that rainy Friday afternoon it had cost seventy-five hundred dollars. In less than two weeks that sum had been paid back and we were in the black. Soon I was delivering to the receiving teller at the Harriman National Bank (it was one of the banks that did not reopen after the famous holiday of '33) checks of five thousand dollars — or more — which represented my weekly profit. It did not take long for me to wipe out old debts, and to pay for the furniture I had purchased on W. A.'s credit. All in all, even at the time, it seemed as if it were too good to be true. Married on September 8 — Kit a big hit on the tenth of October — *my* auspicious debut December 23 — and now our bureau drawers were beginning to fill up with legal tender. And all the while there was a pleasant blare of publicity around both of us. Kit was becomingly modest and I made vain attempts to emulate her. Plays were being sent her and offers for a year ahead were being tossed at her feet.

The most persistent of these professional wooers was Al Woods. He wanted to sign her on a five-year contract and make her a star the following season. She was not easily tempted, but her refusals meant nothing to Al. He continued to deluge her with plays, until there were times we suspected it was his way of getting them read for free with an opinion thrown in. She surprised him in the autumn of 1923 by accepting a small part (it was the leading woman's part, but small) in support of Lowell Sherman in a play called *Casa-*

nova, and surprised him even further by romping away with all of the notices. She had become by then what was commonly called "the critics' pet." And eighteen months later, in early 1925, when *Vanity Fair* had all of the New York critics vote on the actress they thought would be the leading one of the next ten years, Kit's name was the only one on every ballot.

In the spring of 1925, under Wood's management for the second time, she created Iris March in Michael Arlen's dramatization of his sensational best-seller *The Green Hat,* a vehicle that her luminous performance kept on the boards for three seasons and that ultimately elevated her to stardom. I directed that opus at her insistence and much against my will. I opposed her doing it. But she was right and I was wrong. I believe her legion of admirers that have supported her through many years of glittering successes — in Shakespeare, Shaw and Chekhov — had its beginning in the audiences that flocked to see her as Iris March. Starting with *The Green Hat* I have, with two exceptions, directed every play she has appeared in since.

It also marked the beginning of a series of hits I produced for Al Woods. Al Herman Woods, the high priest of the Eltinge Theater, whose offices there reminded one of the reception room in a honky-tonk . . . but in them you would run across anyone from Mayor Walker and Michael Arlen to Sacha Guitry and Yvonne Printemps . . . Al was a graduate from the melodramatic hits of previous years — *Bertha the Sewing-Machine Girl* and *Nellie the Beautiful Cloak Model.* His greeting to the world — king and commoner alike — was "Hello sweetheart." It is reported that, when he met King George V of England at the time he produced *Friendly*

Enemies in London during the First World War, a groan of dismay arose from bystanders as he said, "Hello sweetheart, have a cigar." His Majesty laughed and took one.

Al was a striking-looking fellow, above medium height, with a splendid head that reminded me of Beethoven's. One eye was walled. He always wore silk shirts and although they were changed twice a day they always looked as if he had slept in them. His passport was in his inside pocket and on every boat Europe-bound he had a reservation, just in case. A diamond in the rough, he had a great instinct for melo-drama and a Hebraic sense of quality. His boundless en-thusiasm launched more than one successful career. We became great pals. Others he addressed as "Sweetheart" but me he called "Gunthrie." I could never cure him of it — always "Gunthrie." Why, I would never know. His hearing was good and he had no speech impediment. "Gunthrie," he would say, "here's a script I wancha to read. The heroine is a beautiful gal. It would be a great part for Kit. You see she marries this so-and-so and he thinks she has had a lover and she has but she doesn't want him to know it and by keeping it from him it drives him nuts. Say! Lowell Sher-man might be great for the guy. Anyway he says to her, 'You so-and-so, you've been two-timing me.' And she says, 'Don't talk that way to me you so-and-so.' It's terrific! But you read it, Gunthrie. If *you* do it, it will make a lot of money." And he would hand me a script. Sometimes they were awful, sometimes not.

A few of the hits, apart from *The Green Hat,* in which he and I were associated were *Scarlet Pages* with Elsie Fergu-son and Claire Luce (not the Ambassadress); *The Trial of Mary Dugan* in London and on the Pacific Coast; *Crime* in

New York and London; *Jealousy* in both places, but the most colorful of them all was *The Shanghai Gesture*.

This tender idyll concerned the madam of a whorehouse in Shanghai (of all places), who was quaintly dubbed "Mother Goddam." It was a lusty, gusty melodrama about a Manchu princess who, years before the play began, had been seduced by a fleshpot from dear old Britain who was "in tea" out in China. She was deserted by him when she was with child, and sold into a life of shame — where, incidentally, she did very well. After her babe was born she knocked off work for a few hours and deftly substituted her little bastard for the Englishman's legitimate daughter (damn clever, these Chinese), then prepared to wait some twenty years for a toothsome revenge. As it happened, just about then her one-time lover, a big shot now, returns to Shanghai with his family. He sees Mother Goddam riding in her spectacular Rolls-Royce and once again he heaves with an illicit desire for this fascinating Oriental he had once cast aside, not realizing, of course, who she is. This is Mother Goddam's long-awaited opportunity. She gives an elaborate dinner to which all the great of Shanghai are invited and there before them all she unmasks her ex-lover and sells the legitimate daughter (his) to Chinese junkmen. (Junks are boats in China, and these poor girls are held for the carnal delight of the coolies who can pay — such had been Mother Goddam's fate twenty years before.) But, alas, she was hoist by her own petard, as her own little bastard, despite her sheltered life and European education, grew up to be just that. In the final scene of the play she discovers her offspring in her house of illicit delight (incognito of course) in the embrace of a Japanese roué; finds her more than a little bit nasty as she is coming out of an opium jag. Horrified, Mother Goddam decides to destroy this rotten stalk and chokes her daughter to death. If you think this sounds a bit unreal or funny, remind me to tell you the story of *Medea* sometime. *The Shanghai Gesture,* when it was finally done in New York, was a taut and exciting melodrama.

It was written by John Colton (who had co-authored the dramatization called *Rain* of ,Maugham's *Miss Thompson*) for Mrs. Leslie Carter. That lady was a lively and unique Victorian out of Louisville, Kentucky, who first attained prominence by marrying one of the social eligibles in Chicago in the late '70s, and in the '80s attained notoriety as the center of a sensational divorce case (her own), and cashed in on it in the '90s by crashing the theater as a star for Mr. Belasco portraying such lurid ladies as *Zaza* and *Dubarry* in the equally lurid plays of the same names.

Her debut in the theater followed her divorce case, and as far as I know she is the only woman who has ever successfully capitalized on a scandal. For the better part of ten years she was the biggest drawing card in the American theater. She had yards of red hair, and whatever part she played it was always in evidence. When she was handed to me to direct, her association with Mr. Belasco had been at an end for twenty years. Her appearances in the interim had been infrequent and mostly unsuccessful.

I was opposed to her playing Mother Goddam as I thought she was too old-fashioned in her method of acting and too old as well (she was somewhere in her sixties then) but she had bought the play from the author and it was available only with her enacting the central character. So she was in, and I was assured that with my reputed magic abracadabra she would take on new life and be a sensation.

When I first called on her in her New York apartment she greeted me effusively. The lights were low, the air was blue with incense, and Mrs. Carter startlingly effective in a yellow Chinese mandarin coat and trousers. Her flaming braided coronet coiffure, through the haze, looked as if it might have been her own. She seemed delighted with me and the prospect of my directing her and when I explained my approach to a script and how I began my rehearsals she clapped her hands and said I was what she had been dreaming about — someone to take the place of "Mr. Dave," as she referred to her beloved Belasco, someone who would understand her and see that she regained her rightful place in the theater. She had animation, magnetism and a faded charm. I am afraid I fell, for the time being, to her vintage blandishments, and saw myself as her deliverer, bringing her out of the tanglewood of her theatrics of twenty years before. But when I started rehearsing I found she not only was deeply rooted in her tanglewood but had no intention of stirring out of it.

I had developed a method of rehearsal which was considered unusual at that time. That is to say, I began my rehearsals with my company sitting around a table and reading their parts. I still do it. I usually keep them at it for seven days. The actors get to know each other and, what is more important, they get to know the play and what, as a director, I expect of them. I think of myself as a sort of advance audience, and I try to instill in them the kind of performance that will make me react as I did when I first read and was captivated by the play. At the initial rehearsal I never interrupt the actors as they read. I have my stage manager time it and, when the reading is over, I dismiss them until the following day. After the company has dispersed I frequently wonder, in secret, whatever prompted me to undertake that particular production but with a spartan upper lip I press on.

At the second rehearsal I begin to establish the mood and tempo of the play, scene by scene. I endeavor to make the actors indicate their performance without ever giving them a reading. If I indulge in histrionics, in other words enact a scene, which I invariably do, I paraphrase the episode I am attempting to illuminate but never read an exact line. These actors around the table I have chosen because I believe they are right for and can play the parts they are reading. My job is, as far as possible, to meld them into a harmonious whole. Therefore I want to allow them freedom to create in their own way, with me wielding the baton. After a week of this breaking down of the play I put the actors on their feet. A diagram is drawn on the floor indicating the entrances and exits; furniture is placed, and they are told where and when they move. This way of beginning rehearsals had proved effective and it is still the way I start on a play.

But Mrs. Leslie Carter would have none of it. New methods were not for her. She sat at the head of the table, where I placed her, dressed as always in a long mandarin robe with a very tailored hat jauntily perched on what, under the pitiless glare of rehearsal lights, I became sure was a monstrous red wig. Petulant and eyeing the company with suspicion, as if there might be some among them whose talent would show her up, she was constantly missing her cues, misplacing her glasses and alibiing herself with "I didn't look at this act last night, honey." Then squinting hard at her script she would continue, "I have written something down here. I can't read it. Come here, honey, and see if you can figure it out." And when I would lean over her shoulder in an endeavor to decipher her scrawl she would whisper, "Honey, I don't know what I am doing until I am on my feet."

"Well, get on your feet, I don't mind," said I out loud.

"But I want everybody on their feet."

"When I am ready," was my comeback.

"You had better be careful or I'll take your pants down and give you a good paddling," was her playful rejoinder.

Over and over again she would complain, "I can't study until I know where I am going to stand on the stage." But this could not have worried her much for that was the one and only thing she did know. When she got on her feet I found out she was a star of the school whose one spot on the stage was upstage center and the only time she deserted it was when she obliquely turned to make an exit.

There were rumors that in her Belasco heyday Mr. Dave used to wheedle her into an effective opening-night performance by the judicious use of a whip — in other words beating the daylights out of her. And it wasn't hard for me to believe. There were times — many of them — when I would have loved to administer the same treatment but somehow it seemed brutal to strike an old woman, so I abstained.

In the early days of rehearsal I would put on a phony front of deference and she followed suit, never heeding a word I had to say but offering lip service at all times. She would greet me warmly when I arrived at rehearsal and lead me off into the dressing-room corridor, where she would tell me very *sotto voce* that Mr. Buckler, the leading man, was upstaging her. "You must protect me," she coaxed. By "protection" she meant that he should act facing upstage so that at all times she would be facing front. And growing cosier she would take my right hand and place it over her enormous left breast. Once, when I couldn't suppress a smile at this gesture of camaraderie she, with arch insinuation said, "What are you smiling at, you lascivious devil you?" Although I tried not to I laughed out loud and that particular road to mutual understanding was abandoned.

She knew at that moment I was probably the most talked-of and highly regarded young director of the day so she attempted to evade my "new nonsense" in the way of directing by resorting to guile. When I complained about her not knowing her lines she said, "I do. I just keep my part in my hand because I always did that with Mr. Dave." Then to really butter me up she asked me to address her as Mrs. C., adding that the only other person she had granted that intimate boon to was Mr. Dave. "My mother couldn't understand it," she confided. " 'Dolly,' she'd say — that was Mother's name for me — 'Dolly,' she'd say, 'how can you bear to have him always calling you Mrs. C.?' But he always did; even in the middle of the night he would say 'Mrs. C.!' " Then she would dig me in the ribs and laugh. I was happy to know they worked at night but I never felt the urge to call her "Mrs. C."

Rehearsals became increasingly difficult. Not only was Mrs. Carter ignoring with deliberate forgetfulness any suggestions I had for her but she began to interfere with the other actors in those brief moments when she was not on the stage. She remembered nothing, not even something she had raised hell to impose the day before. With precious hours passing and no progress being made the entire production became to me a catastrophic nightmare. I felt this raddled red-wigged remnant of yesterday would be the end of me. My growing reputation as a director would go up in smoke. I couldn't sleep. I was harassed, irritable and increasingly bad-tempered.

On one particularly trying afternoon, after endless arguments, alibis and evasions, when we were rehearsing the second act dinner scene where, before a group of the Shanghai diplomatic set, Mother Goddam reveals her identity to her ex-British lover, she was in the middle of her "I survive" speech, lamentably faltering through, when she suddenly stopped and spoke to me across the footlights. "I don't think this table is at the right angle. The audience can't see me" — and she started to walk off the stage.

I suddenly saw red. "Damn it," I yelled, "I am tired of your excuses, I am tired of tables being wrong, people being wrong, business being wrong, when the only thing that's wrong is you. I am tired of you. I refuse any longer to waste my time or my talent on your remembered ineptitudes. Either you go back to your place at the table now and stumble through as best you can, or I am walking out. Then we will see if you can even survive to open. *Don't answer me back*," I climaxed as she looked as though she were going to speak. "Either continue the scene or I'm through." All of this was at the top of my lungs.

The theater walls vibrated. Mrs. Carter's companion rushed out of the theater to Woods's office upstairs.

There was a ghastly but eloquent silence on the stage and suddenly, with a burst of vitality she had never shown before, she returned to the table and started the scene again. She didn't know her lines but she kept on talking, sticking to her key word "I survive." Although she was addressing her ex-lover, she was pouring out a poisonous spew that I felt was directed at me. It was shattering. When she was finished the cast was stirred. I was stirred. (I guess I was stirred anyway.) Woods had come in during this, fetched by the companion. He came running down the aisle.

"What's the matter, Gunthrie? I thought that was good."

"Did you?" I thundered. "Well, if I have to achieve such effects by kicking an old woman around I am damned if I am going to continue. I feel ashamed and dirty. You can take your —— show and shove it. I am going home!" And I started up the aisle.

"Gunthrie, wait a minute! Gunthrie!" Then, "Stop him, Max!" (That was his secretary.) "Leslie, come down here."

Mrs. Carter, hobbling down from the stage with her ankles turning as she did so, held my hand and said, "Honey, you mustn't be like that any more or I'll take your pants down [yes, she was at it again] and give you a good paddling."

I was being pampered because I was top dog and had been difficult. It was like a bad dream. I was sick of the whole thing.

Later, when I was quieting down alone with Al and a jigger of bourbon in his office, I begged him to release me from my agreement to do the play, but he was adamant in his refusal and said that if she did not take direction or failed to know her lines *after* the opening night we could replace

her, but, as she had the run of the play contract and it was
further stipulated that no change of text could be made
without her consent, it was imperative that she open and it
was equally imperative for me to remain at the helm. So I
went on with it.

Each succeeding day of rehearsal was just one more of
frustration and despair for me. Mrs. Carter's final shot was
when she told me she would not make up or dress for the
dress rehearsal. She explained it was a superstition engen-
dered in her from her beginning days with Mr. Dave in the
'80s. He never, she said, required her to dress for the dress
rehearsal, and she had never done it since then, and, furthermore, she wasn't going to begin now. I had a slow burn
and reported this ultimatum to Woods, who had a fast burn
and immediately ordered her costumes to be delivered to
the theater on the afternoon of the dress rehearsal and said
if she refused to wear them he would consider her contract
broken and cancel her opening. The bare possibility of this
was like a ray of sunshine to me. Her costumes arrived at
the theater and were unpacked by my stage manager and
hung up.

However, Mrs. Carter anticipated Woods's game and sent
her two maids to the theater to await the costumes' arrival,
and after they were hung up proceeded to rip out every
seam, so on the night of dress rehearsal she produced her
dresses with the undone seams and won her point. She did
not dress for the dress rehearsal. Neither did she make up.
With Freddy Jones's scenery looking unbelievably handsome, with all the actors looking slick and right and Mary
Duncan radiantly attractive, Mrs. Carter made her entrance
without make-up or costume under brilliant stage lighting

looking just a little bit older than Grandma Moses but not as nice.

The rehearsal started at eight in the evening, but what with Mrs. Carter's teetering, tottering, and continually fumbling for her lines we finished the second act at 7:30 the following morning, a Sunday. There were two more acts to go! Every one was dead. I told Al to call the remainder of the dress rehearsals off, as we would never get the big production into the Newark Theater in time to open the following night. Although Al was desperate, distressed and in despair, he had nothing on me. He had not been in on the rehearsals or suffered Mrs. Carter as I had.

He decided to make one last effort to save her from making what we felt would be an incredible exhibition of herself, and incidently to save his investment. Al and I went to her dressing room. She was tensed for a fight. She looked ghastly. Woods pleaded with her to relinquish the part as he thought it was too strenuous for her and she would never know the lines. She was immovable. Come hell and high water, she was going to open.

"You'll only make a fool of yourself," said Al in desperation.

"Why?"

"Because you're too god-damn' old! People will laugh at the idea of anyone wanting to go to bed with you."

That was the only moment I ever had a pang of sympathy for her. Her face remained expressionless, but her frame seemed to shrink and her hands convulsively clasped and reclasped each other. There was a moment's silence and then Mrs. Carter spoke in a tired, strained voice. "I don't recognize your right to speak to me in such a manner. I wore no make-up tonight — my clothes weren't ready — "

"That's a lie!" started Al, but she went right on.

"My clothes weren't ready and even if they had been I wouldn't have worn them. I never dressed for Mr. Dave and I never will for anyone else."

"It's your funeral," said Al. And we left her.

If Woods was ruthless she went him one better in her agonizing, inescapable resolve to force herself on a public that didn't want to see her. She was possessed with a blinding, grasping, insane conceit. She was still trying to prove to Mr. Dave, who wouldn't touch her with a ten-foot pole, that she could "come back."

My sole endeavor while rehearsing *The Shanghai Gesture* was to soften its many hectic theatrical moments and highlight its passages of emotion and revenge. I had imagined for Mother Goddam an unostentatious entrance in the first act, stealing in through a secret panel in her reception hall to surprise two very important personages, who were arranging for a few moments of forgetfulness (to put it sweetly) in her opulent house of ill fame.

When I told Mrs. Carter of this she beat her mighty bosom as though it were a drum and snorted, "Not for Mrs. Carter." (She always spoke of herself in the third person.) "Mr. Dave would never do that to Mrs. Carter."

It would have been so pleasant to have struck her then, but with superhuman control I let her have her way — but I kept saying to myself, You better be good.

On her opening night in Newark her entrance was as she desired it. You heard her voice off stage, making sounds that she was pleased to think were Chinese; all available extras, made up like Chinese, tore across the stage as if pursued by the devil and, hurrying around the set, came running across the center arch again, after which Mrs. Carter appeared — for the first time in her professional life in a black wig — looking about as oriental as a Helen Hokinson lady at a gala ball at the Waldorf. From that moment on it was as bizarre an evening as I have ever experienced inside a play-house. Although she had almost no acquaintance with her lines she strutted and stormed and almost never stopped talking, which made it not only impossible to prompt her but left the cast wondering if it were a different play she was doing that night.

In the second act scene, where Mother Goddam sold the white girl (the Englishman's daughter) to the Chinese junkmen, she had a speech with which to goad them into raising their bid: "Look at her, Mr. Shu Ki. This is a white girl, not a yellow one. What am I bid? Think of your hairy chest against her lovely young breasts. Think of your ugly mouth against her soft red lips. What am I bid, Mr. Shu Ki? What am I bid?" On this stanza Mrs. Carter became so hope-lessly entangled in her lines that the speech came out as a most incredible obscenity. At this I ran out of the theater and proceeded to cross the Square to the entrance of the Hudson Tubes, which I used as a point of vantage in case the Jersey police patrol were stopping by to take those concerned with *The Shanghai Gesture* to the clink. They didn't, and when I thought it was reasonably safe I went back. The final curtain fell just before one o'clock. The only things right that night were Mary Duncan's performance as the degenerate daughter, Poppy, and Freddy Jones III's scenery.

Despite the disconcertingly good notices she received from the Newark critics the following morning, Al and I knew she would never be able to play the part, first because she was too decrepit and, secondly, because no self-respecting actor could or would play with her or endure her shenanigans. For example, there was in the cast a young actor who had a brief scene with her in the last act. He was quite good but she did not like him, and at the opening performance every time he spoke a line, instead of replying she would mutter in a low voice, "Get off the stage." He went manfully on until finally she ran at him and frightened the poor devil into a hasty exit. Reprimand her, you say! But that was only one of a score or more offenses that she had inherited from the palmy days of Mr. Dave, when her drawing power was potent and her word law. And another thing that that chaotic opening revealed to us, apart from the necessity of replacing the star, was that the play was in dire need of cutting, transpositions and scene consolidations. That opening night was literally the first time I ever saw the entire play run through. All of these changes had to be accomplished within the two weeks following, because there was virtually no ticket sale at all and Al had decided to close it the following week in Atlantic City. So I rolled up my sleeves and steeled myself for a fight — not a loud McClintic-style encounter but a temperate kid-glove affair that to me was sheer torture — all of this because Mrs. Carter had to O.K. the changes as well.

When she arrived at the next rehearsal she was feeling her oats enough to be an hour late, quite puffed up about her notices and muttering constantly to her smiling self. "What did you say, Mrs. Carter?" I inquired. And with as much malice as the face could hold and keep the semblance of a smile she replied, "He who laughs last . . ." and stopped.

"Yes?" said I.

"Laughs longest," she concluded.

But, poor woman, she didn't know! All the laughs were not in yet!

I proceeded with the rehearsal. The author had disappeared. Rumor had it he was on a binge. Who could blame him? For the next fortnight I functioned partly as a play doctor and partly as a diplomatist. Mrs. Carter became more amenable. I think she was frightened and she felt, for the first time, the animosity of the company. Also someone must have told her that despite the salvos of the press she wasn't "getting over." She would O.K. cuts and promptly forget them — not on purpose but because she couldn't remember. Her first success for Mr. Belasco had been in the melodrama called *The Heart of Maryland,* in which she saved the hero's life by hanging on the clapper of the bell, thereby stopping it from ringing. In the last act of *The Shanghai Gesture* there was a scene on "the green stairway of the ANGRY DRAGONS" in which Mother Goddam strangled her daughter after frantically pursuing her up three flights of stairs. With her hands on the girl's throat she holds her against the rail of the top balcony; the rail breaks, and daughter comes hurtling through the air as the curtain falls. In theory this was effective melodrama. When she seized her daughter's throat, the girl struggled and together they disappeared off stage, where a dummy the exact replica of her daughter was put into Mrs. Carter's grasp. She reappeared with her hands about the throat of this inert form, and that was what went hurtling through the air.

This was her favorite scene. She told me that every one of her sucesses in the past had contained a scene of physical violence. As a matter of fact I thought her only moment of effectiveness was in the staircase scene. I was amazed at the way her weak ankles supported her in that run up the stairs. On the opening night she gebitched that moment plenty. Instead of pushing the dummy against the balcony rail and letting it break, she picked it up and flung it. In its downward descent the poor prop's head caught on the prong of a great lamp and came off. And we all thanked God the curtain was almost down. But that wasn't the end of the play. The scene reverts to Mother Goddam's bedroom, where she enters dragging the girl's body and has approximately twenty minutes of old-fashioned emoting while she arranges a Chinese going-away party. This, too, was one of Mrs. Carter's favorite scenes. This, too, had to be deleted in its entirety. This, too, had to be O.K.'d by Mrs. Carter. This, too, had to be managed by me.

When I took Mrs. Carter aside and told her the play was thirty minutes too long she was evasive as always. "It would not be if I could get a run on my part," she grumbled. "You think I don't know my lines, but I do. I know them perfectly in the bedroom — isn't that true?" she asked her companion, who was assenting with a positive nod of the head. Mrs. Carter tops her with "You see! But when I hear those awful actors you surrounded me with, I admit I don't know what I am doing. No one would. Honey, you and Mr. Woods have let me down terribly" — and she snatched my handkerchief from the breast pocket of my jacket to wipe away a couple of tears she had managed to squeeze out. Then she used it to blow her nose. "Oh, honey, I am sorry. I have ruined your beautiful handkerchief. What you must have paid for it," she muttered as she examined the monogram. "I will have it washed," and she put it in her bag. I never saw it again.

"Mrs. Carter," I persisted, "you must listen to me." And I explained to her how, if she seized her daughter on the first landing and the girl escaped her and ran to go downstairs, tripped and fell the whole way down, seemingly breaking her neck in the fall, it would be just as hair-raising as what had been originally planned. Moreover it would bar any accidents such as happened on the opening night. And by her coming down the stairs to her dead daughter, she could take her best speech from the final scene, speak it there, and the play would be over. It would save at least twenty minutes of playing time, and the precious minutes it took to change the scene. As a matter of fact it could be done that night. A strange look was on her face.

"You mean . . . Mary Duncan will fall down the stairs?"

"Yes," I replied.

"But she might hurt herself."

"I don't think so," said I. "I can show her how to do it so she won't hurt herself."

"But she might — hm — Very well, let's try it." And she looked happy as we returned to the stage. The staircase was always set against the back wall. I explained to Mary what I had planned. She seemed faintly alarmed and wanted me to do the fall for her. I obliged. It was very effective. Several of the cast thought I must have been injured. I did it again. Then Mary did it. It worked! I rushed upholsterers over to pad the stairs, and we played it that night and every night thereafter during its long run. Over twenty minutes had been saved! Every day we rehearsed. Every day a new cut. Mrs. Carter was still disastrously shaky in her lines. Her performance in no way improved. Nor did the business.

We closed as scheduled in Atlantic City — but the script was in order.

Mrs. Carter was out. She threatened suit. She had a run-of-the-play contract, but as she never knew her lines she didn't have a leg to stand on. When she realized that, she dropped the suit. Later I heard an arrangement was made by and with John Colton whereby she received a good part of his royalties each week to salve her injured feelings and that left us free to find a new Mother Goddam — which we did straight off in the person of that first-rate actress, Florence Reed, who learned the part in ten days and opened at the Martin Beck Theater in February, 1926, after two weeks' rehearsal. As she was many years younger than Mrs. Carter, several of the leading actors were changed to match her age. Florence was a joy to rehearse — eager and responsive to everything I could give her. She made the unostentatious entrance I had planned for Mrs. Carter, and, furthermore, made a big hit for herself and continued playing Mother Goddam for the better part of three seasons.

What did *The Shanghai Gesture* contribute to me? First, it may not have advanced me artistically but it did establish me as a director of hits. Second, I learned that to turn what could easily have been a failure into a smash-hit you had to be ruthless; personal feelings could not be allowed to obscure either your vision or your path. Third, that it is next to impossible to teach an old dog (maybe that's not the right word) new tricks. Mrs. Carter was in no way related to the time in which she was then living. She was vainly trying to breathe life into a theatrical figure (herself) that had been nonexistent for almost a quarter of a century — a figure that was synthetic to begin with and once her era had passed was irrevocably doomed. Despite the many agonizing moments she gave me, I was glad of the experience. I learned about women from her.

No — that's not true: my composite woman is made up of many. But I must mention another lady who, although ten years younger, achieved her stardom around the same time that Mrs. Carter first had hers. I am referring to the first victim of my interviewing sprees out in Seattle — Blanche Bates. She was born into the theater. Her mother, Annie Bates, was a star in California in the 1850s and Edwin Booth was her leading man. Blanche Bates, also, had been a Belasco star. For seventeen years she had created such famous roles as Madame Butterfly in the play from which the opera was taken; Cho-Cho-San in *The Darling of the Gods,* and *The Girl of the Golden West.* Then she left the Belasco management, married George Creel, produced two children and returned to the stage to co-star with Henry Miller in *The Famous Mrs. Fair* and *The Changelings.* Her career had been unique in that during her thirty years of stardom she never had a failure. I sought her out to create the star role in *Mrs. Partridge Presents,* which I was doing in December 1924. As I had no business manager in those days, the sordid question of money had to be arranged by me. I was apprehensive as to what her demands might be, so, not without quaking, I approached her regarding terms.

"What had you thought of paying me?" she parried.

"I haven't thought," I replied. "I am trying to find out what you expect and then I will go into a closed conference with myself and see if I can afford you."

There was a long pause — long enough to drive a Mack

truck through. Then, with her clear, dark eyes meeting mine and in her low, beautifully modulated voice she said: "Look here. You are a young man who is going to do things. I am an old star about to retire. I have money. I don't need to work and I am not going to hold you up. Suppose we say I'll take two hundred dollars a week expense money and one quarter of the profits, if there are any."

I stammered something to the effect that it was a bargain, and that if, after she had slept on it, she still wanted to go through with it, it was a deal.

The following day she signed. I have a distinct feeling of pride when I look at that voluminous scrapbook in the office and see an old ad that reads: GUTHRIE MCCLINTIC PRESENTS BLANCHE BATES . . .

She was also an old-timer out of the same era as Mrs. Carter, but what a difference! Miss Bates was real theater — age hadn't withered nor custom staled her attitude or enthusiasm. With the exception of her leading man she was entirely surrounded by young players. John Emery made his stage debut in *Mrs. Partridge Presents;* Ruth Gordon made one of her earlier hits; Sylvia Field and Eliot Cabot made up the foursome that played most of their scenes with her. There was never a moment when any one of them was made to feel any less important to the play than she. She always played for the next fellow's line. That is the test by which I determine the true generous spirit of the artist in the theater. Playing for the next fellow's line is the simple honesty of reading which makes the reply following inevitable. Most fine players are honest in their work today, but there have been many that are fine players too whose impulse, instinctive or otherwise, is to "kill" the next fellow's lines.

Blanche had enormous vitality. She was as receptive of direction as a beginner, courteous and prompt, and had a magnificent sense of humor. During our first week of rehearsal when we were still sitting around a table, Ruth Gordon returned after the luncheon recess some twenty minutes late. She was profuse in her apologies. As we sat down to resume, Miss Bates deserted her usual place at the table and sat beside Ruth.

"Why are you sitting there?" I asked.

"I thought it might give me courage," was her reply.

On our opening night in New York, when Ruth made her exit in the first act and all but stopped the show with her applause, Blanche followed her off, gave her a quick embrace and said, "Thanks for saving the act."

Mrs. Partridge Presents opened at the Belmont Theater in January 1925 and ran until June. Burns Mantle included it among his ten best plays that season. Miss Bates retired shortly after the run ended, but not on what the fourth of her profits in that venture netted her. Dear Blanche Bates! Her interest in the theater never deserted her. In her house in San Francisco she entertained all of us — and that means everyone who was lucky enough to play that glorious city. She came to our opening nights. She brought a party. Her enthusiasm was contagious, and back at her house on Divisidera Street we would have supper with Blanche sitting at the head of her table in a rocking chair (the first time I ever had dinner at her house I thought I was fried when, with a roar of laughter, she reeled backwards in that rocker). After supper there would be bridge and theater talk: the theater of yesterday, the theater of today, the theater of tomorrow . . . The changes she had seen . . . The changes

I was seeing back in the '20s when I first knew her . . . The actors' pictures I had looked at as a kid out in Seattle . . . The Edwardian New York I glimpsed when I first came East, fifteen years before . . . the war years . . . And here we were in the '20s with radio and talking pictures about to descend on the amusement world.

The "Mad '20s" . . . ! The women with their boyish hairbobs, their boyish-form bras, with their waistlines an inch or two above their knees and a meager ruffle for a skirt. Mr. Darrow and the Monkey Trial . . . The Charleston . . . Texas Guinan and her "Hello sucker . . ." Aimee Semple MacPherson saving souls singing, "Yes, Sir, He's My Jesus" (to the tune of "Yes, Sir, She's My Baby") . . . Warren Gamaliel Harding with his sinister Boswells, Nan Britton and Gaston Means . . . Calvin Coolidge who didn't smile (can you blame him? Thanks to Mr. Volstead people were being poisoned by bootleg hootch, speakeasies flourishing on every side street, and a brand-new type of outlaw was being born to replace the bad men of the West — neurotic city slickers toting machine guns and attacking from bullet-proof cars. And this tidal wave of lawlessness was the result of the dictatorship of reform. Why should Mr. Coolidge smile?) . . . "Yes, We Have No Bananas!" . . . That young man with a horn — let's call him Bix — was blazing new trails. . . . The applecart was overturned, all right. A new wind was blowing, I guess. . . . This was the pattern of a decade that today is referred to as the period of "The Lost Generation." But I was working hard, and Kit was working hard, and none of the people we knew or worked with, or rubbed shoulders with, seem to me to have been a part of those '20s I read about now.

That was the time when two young people sneaked into our lives in very humble capacities — but who now rule Kit and myself with rods of iron. I am referring to Gertrude Macy, who is Kit's manager, and Stanley Gilkey, who is mine. Also, around about then, Laurette Taylor and I came together again. This time I was asking nothing, wanting nothing. We met on an equal footing, so to speak, and from then on we were fast friends. In her later years she played infrequently, but her too few appearances behind the footlights were always hailed as an event — her greatest success since *Peg* being her never-to-be-forgotten performance in Tennessee Williams's *The Glass Menagerie*. When Kit and I were in England in December 1946 we spent a week end with the Oliviers at their country place, Notley Abbey. We had just finished breakfast on that Monday morning and were all immersed in our own separate papers. I had gone through every column of the then skimpy *Times* of London, from the Personals on the first page to the Court Circular and Obituaries on the last, when at the bottom of the last column I read these lines: "Miss Laurette Taylor, who played *Peg o' My Heart* with great success in London in 1914–1915, died yesterday in her New York apartment." . . . Laurette once told me of a rehearsal of hers in which a well-known director spoke his piece by saying, "This is your scene, Miss Taylor, and I feel you should have the center of the stage for it," to which she replied with that sparkling hesitancy that so often characterized her utterance, "You know, Mr. ——, this may seem odd to you, but I have always thought that wherever I was — *that* was the center of the stage." And she was right. When her final curtain fell she was center stage, and that is where she will always be!

XVII

From Beekman Place to Moscow

THE THIRTY-ONE days of January 1922 ticked jubilantly by while I was getting acclimated to a successful me.
I bought another play, with my own money this time; a good
one, too, called *A Square Peg*, by an American author,
Lewis Beach; and it was a *succès d'estime* of the following
season while I, as my own angel, was several thousands in
the red. The groundhog saw his shadow on February 2, and
the audiences for *The Dover Road* continued capacity and
enthusiastic. I had beautiful letters from many people concerning it. A certain satisfaction trickled through my veins
when I received a congratulatory wire from my nemesis at
the Academy, Charles Jehlinger. A. A. Milne penned a
warming letter of appreciation and Clare Eames an eloquent
one about my production. Clare and Sidney Howard came
frequently to our house. They were going to be married in
the late spring. Sidney wrote a short story called *A Likeness
of Elizabeth*, in which he described in detail the two rooms
on our second floor. When he sent a copy of the book *Three
Flights Up* around to us, his inscription read "To Kit and
Guthrie, With many and grateful thanks for a setting —
among other things. Sidney." Those lovely Victorian rooms,
with their beautiful mirrors in gilt and white enamel going

up to the high curley-cued ceiling, over white marble man-
telpieces against white walls, with red Italian brocade curtains at either end and the lovely curved arches connecting
the two rooms, had an indefinable charm. Big bay windows
were at the back overlooking a tiny garden and East River,
and when dusk was falling you could close your eyes and
imagine it was the Thames — and Blackwell's Island (Wel-
fare today), St. Thomas's Hospital. Why one should have
troubled to is beyond me, for it was beautiful anyway.

Austin Strong, who always saw himself as Cupid in regard to Kit and myself, because of our having met at the time
his play, *Seventh Heaven,* was done in stock in Detroit,
would bring his beautiful wife, Mary, in for a bite of supper after the theater. Theresa Helburn, who had taught
Kit at Mrs. Merrill's School, would drop by with Philip
Moeller and talk about plans for The Theatre Guild, which
was in its first flush of success. Laura Elliot brought Aaron
Copland, who excited us by playing his "Music for Theater."
W. A. was a frequent visitor too. We were beginning to get
matey with Margalo Gillmore and her family, who lived
across the way at Number 20. Every Sunday night we had
a buffet supper. The house, or at least our part of it, was
being filled with our sounds, our friends and our thoughts.
We were falling in love with it. Here we had gained recognition for the first time. So it was something of a shock when,
in mid-March, the owner told me they had a prospective
buyer; and did I wish to take advantage of the option in my
lease which gave me first call if it were for sale? We could
not see ourselves away from it. It was a part of us. Kit and
I went into a huddle, and finally an arrangement was made
whereby old Mrs. Schmid, the owner, would continue to

occupy the top two floors until the mortgage was paid off. Pinching myself to make sure the whole transaction was real, I signed a check for $12,500, which was half the purchase price, agreed to pay the remainder in three years, and — presto! I owned a house in New York. As I looked around those walls with a new proprietary air, little did I realize that thirty-one years would elapse before we would say good-by to "23." Thirty-one years — some of which time it seemed the only constant in the New York theater world. . . . Depression came — important managements disappeared — some died. The Theatre Guild built a theater and after many years of occupancy abandoned it — new managements sprang up — the Shuberts, Bill Brady and Gilbert Miller were the only ones of the old guard that were still around when we emerged from the war years. And Kit and I were still at Beekman Place.

Every room was filled with memories — mostly happy, mostly theater. I wish there were some magic dial which would turn time back and I could hear once again, on the piano that Deems Taylor selected for us, George Gershwin playing his newly composed "Rhapsody in Blue" or "The Man I Love" with Kit whistling the obligato. Or Noel Coward playing and singing his latest songs and strumming back through the years while we sit rapt at his feet till he comes to my favorite, "Parisian Pierrot." And Ethel Waters singing till the wee small hours her favorites for Kit's father, Dr. Cornell. Yes, "Doc" Cornell, as he was called in the profession, was a frequent guest at Beekman Place. It was in the second year of our marriage that Peter (as I called him) and I became great friends. He was as genial a companion as one could ask for. His sense of humor was keen, and his

timing in recounting an amusing incident convinced me that
if he had ever been stage-struck he would have become one
of our better comedians. When I was hospitalized for a
hernia his only comment was "Guthrie must've got it from
lifting his voice." In his own apartment in Buffalo he was a
merry and lavish host, as many an actor on our various try-
outs there can verify.

Beekman Place was our home but also it served on numerous occasions as a kind of studio. Many a beginning rehearsal
was held there. Sitting around the dining-room table, the first
group of players ever to appear under the management of
Katharine Cornell gave their initial reading of *The Barretts of
Wimpole Street.* When we finished reading that day I think
five of us would have declared anyone crazy if we had been
told that fourteen years later we, the same five (Brian
Aherne, Brenda Forbes, Kit, myself and Gert Macy) would
be playing *The Barretts* in Italy, France and Holland for
American soldiers knee-deep in mud in the middle of World
War II. But they would have been right. It was overseas
that I heard a remark from a G.I. to his buddy in a black-
out at the end of a performance of *The Barretts* that I would
love some time to use as a quote if we ever revive it again.
This G.I., elated that he had persuaded his friend to attend
the performance, said, "Didn't I tell you it's better than a
whorehouse?"

The Barretts had been turned down by twenty-eight managements in New York when Kit bought it for me to produce. It turned out to be one of the outstanding successes
of the twentieth century, and the firm foundation on which
Miss Cornell's management was founded. Although she was
against doing it in the beginning, I persuaded her to play the

part of Elizabeth Barrett and I further persuaded her to become her own manager. I did it for several reasons. Actress managers are something of a rarity in this country. Therefore the publicity angle was good. It provided her with complete freedom of movement and choice of plays and cast, and, as she was and is what is known in the box office as a "hot ticket," I felt there was no harm in obeying the old adage "While the sun shines make hay." Her reign as an actress-manager is the longest in the American theater. I feel like a proud father.

I have only to close my eyes to hear a group of unknown youngsters — Sam Levene, James Stewart, Myron McCormick, Millard Mitchell and Eddie Acuff, to be exact — making one's pulse beat just a little faster as they read Sidney Howard's *Yellow Jack* at a first rehearsal. I tingle now when I remember Gielgud's electric first reading of *Hamlet,* which sparked Judith Anderson, who played the queen, into a breathtaking performance of the closet scene, at Number 23's table, leaving the rest of us proud and humble at being a part of it. Or the quiet wonder of Kit's reading "the shawl speech" from *Candida,* with Raymond Massey, when we were preparing that magnificent revival for the Army and Navy Relief in May 1942 — or Kit as Masha, whistling Tschaikowsky's "Sympathy," while Anton Chekhov's *Three Sisters* was beginning to come vibrantly alive during the eight days of breaking it in at Beekman Place.

We liked rehearsing at 23 because of the informal nature of our early rehearsals. It seemed more *gemütlich* than the stage of a theater, which, today, the dictatorship of the Unions have made forbidding — forbidding in atmosphere, forbidding in price demand, added to which is the annoy-

ance of the one inadequate light bulb overhead. At Beekman Place, with the dining table extended to its full length
and generously supplied with cigarettes, ash trays and ice
water, we could read, relaxed and quiet — without the interruption of the chit-chat that frequently emanates from the
front of a theater. And when we would pause between acts,
there was the garden to stretch your legs in and the East
River to contemplate in case you wanted to end it all, or
a cup of tea and a biscuit in case you needed sustenance.

It was while Kit was playing *The Doctor's Dilemma* in
San Francisco, in early December 1941, that Ruth Gordon
(whose several expert and sensitive portrayals have distinguished my productions) urged me to reread *The Three Sisters* with the thought of her doing Masha. I did and immediately became obsessed with the idea of Kit doing it, playing Masha herself, with Ruth doing Natasha. I read it aloud
to Kit and she grew enthusiastic too. I phoned Ruth of our
scheme and suggested the switch in parts, and she was agreeable and excited about the whole venture. No sooner was
it announced than Moscow-born Valentina and her Russian
husband, George Schlee, phoned me that it was imperative
I see a friend of theirs, Alexander Koriansky (Sascha, they
called him) and they were so right!

Valentina, blond and lovely, whose appearance is the best
advertisement her exquisite clothes could have, asks in that
piquant accent which over thirty years of residence here has
not eradicated, "Who will do translation, Guthrie?" (No
articles ever occurred in her English conversations.)

"I haven't decided," I reply.

"There isn't good one," she continues. "You must get
Koriansky. Sascha is fine artist — best critic in Moscow be-

fore Revolution. He knew Chekhov and all Moscow Art Players. You must get Sascha."

The upshot was I got Sascha. I hadn't talked to him five minutes before I knew he was my man — slight of build, short and bald, with keen blue eyes, great sensitivity and a sly sense of humor — I felt, as you do with people you are immediately in sympathy with, as if I had known him all my life. We worked together daily for over six months. He would read to me from his original Russian text. I had a secretary take down in shorthand his English as he read it. I would stop him on every speech.

"That meaning isn't clear. Exactly what does Vershinin mean? Does he mean thus-and-so?"

"No," would come Sascha's positive protest.

"Well, then make it clear. How can I direct an actor when the speech is obscure?"

Back and forth we would go until I was satisfied and he was satisfied that I knew Chekhov's intent. Day by day, week by week, this process went on, until finally we emerged with a script in the most "sayable" English I have ever encountered in *The Three Sisters*.

When I asked Alec Woollcott what he thought of the translation, after he had praised the cast and performance at a final rehearsal, he replied, "I never thought about it. I wasn't conscious of its being a translation, so it must have been good."

While Sascha and I were slugging away at getting Chekhov into English, my spare time was consumed in rounding up a cast. In case you have forgotten it, *The Three Sisters* is a play representing the upper middle class of Russia at the turn of the century, a play about a family — a brother and three sisters, and their friends and their in-laws and family retainers — whose whole life has been tied up with the army, in which their father had been a popular and respected officer. A family of breeding and birth, whose lives seem to have stopped with his death and the removal of the army post from the suburban town in which they live. But they are marooned there by their lack of money and their conventions. Their dream is to return to Moscow where they were born, where there is life! Moscow is a symbol, as well as a city — but they never get there! Not circumstances but character defeats them. Of the three sisters, Masha, who is married to a dullish older man, falls in love with Colonel Vershinin, a dashing officer of forty-two years. He has been in her father's regiment and is passing through with his battalion.

We had hoped it would be possible for Alfred Lunt to play Vershinin and Lynn Fontanne to do Olga; but, alas, they were not free, and we had to look elsewhere. Luck was with us in that Judith Anderson *was* free — *and* enthusiastic. That took care of Olga. Gertrude Musgrove was Irina, the third sister. And Ruth Gordon was cast from the start as the controversial Natasha, who marries the brother, Andrei. But who for Vershinin, the part Stanislavski created with the Moscow Art Theater? It was wartime, and that limited us too. Four months were consumed in search of a leading man. . . . Meanwhile the remainder of the cast was signed up; many of them were important and high-salaried actors. They were uniquely right for their parts, and therefore we could not consider abandoning the production because we might not get the ideal Vershinin. And furthermore, the play was in no sense a star play: all the parts were equally good. . . . So we continued looking — and patted ourselves on the back at long last when we were able to secure Dennis King.

Casting *The Sisters* was no bed of roses. There was the part of brother Andrei. Chekhov describes him in the text as being stout. I combed my card indexes; interviewed a great number who had written and suggested themselves for the part and even had some of them read to me, a thing I rarely do because I feel any sensitive person reading a part is so apprehensive and nervous — everything seems staked on this one shot — that they seldom do justice to themselves, whereas when they are put together with other actors at a first rehearsal, all reading around a table, all of them are nervous together. So rather than "read" them I almost invariably cast by having a talk with those actors whose work I don't already know, and I endeavor to sense their qualities in regard to the part I am seeing them about. If I feel they are right I let them read the play, then talk to them further about the part — what I would like my reactions to be if they played it; and from their responses, I make my decision. As for Andrei, no stout young man that I knew or heard read satisfied me at all. And despite the fact that Chekhov was no longer living, and, therefore, there could be no objection if I cast against his description, still I had no intention of riding roughshod over it. I consulted Koriansky. He enlightened me considerably. It seems Chekhov had described Andrei as being stout because the only actor whom he thought right to play it with the Moscow Players was a fattish man, and inasmuch as the play was written expressly for that company he covered himself from any criticism of his choice by describing the man he wrote it for. Some years later, when the original Andrei had left the Moscow troupe and a slender man had replaced him, any references to the avoirdupois of the brother were deleted from the script. My concern regarding this particular part was nullified. I had already Eric Dressler, who seemed to me quite right, in mind. He was engaged at once and gave a very fine performance indeed.

For the part of Chebutykin, an old friend of the family, I had wanted Dudley Digges and although he seemed excited at the time I talked to him about it, when it came to his signing a contract he reneged, saying he had a previous commitment. I think he was really wary of putting his head in Chekhov's noose, so to speak. Instead he played safe by appearing in an importation from England which ran one week. For the part Digges turned down we were especially fortunate in getting that delightful person and expert actor Edmund Gwenn. When I think of that cast I swell with pride. Katharine Cornell, Judith Anderson, Ruth Gordon, Edmund Gwenn, Dennis King, Alexander Knox, Mackay Morris, Tom Powers, Gertrude Musgrove, Alice Belmore-Cliff and Eric Dressler, among others. And in the background Walter Craig (Tony Dexter now in movies) played the guitar and sang Russian songs in his fine baritone voice, while Kirk Douglas, about to go into the United States Navy, made his second appearance on Broadway carrying on a samovar, and Jan Sterling was one of those who waited on the guests at the birthday luncheon in the first scene.

The rehearsals were exhilarating and stimulating. With the exception of Teddy Gwenn and Dennis King, every person in the cast had been under my direction not once but several times. A few had played with Kit before. They were harmonious, receptive and all imbued with a respect and regard for the play. As we read round the table we were gradually able to assimilate all the sounds that Chekhov so persistently highlights his play with: Masha's whistling — the tinkle of the guitar — the officers' singing — the knock from the floor below — the sleighbells in the night — the fire alarms — the extraordinary love scene between Masha and Vershinin, in which no words are spoken and they indulge in the most delicate exchange of emotion which is conveyed by a phrase of music passed between them from the famous love duet of the opera *Eugène Onégin* — it lays bare the very essence of their secret passion and longing. And then the unforgettable march, which is played at the end by a military band as Vershinin's battalion is leaving . . . All of this, together with the secondary dialogue, which was the conversation indicated by the Moscow Art prompt script. It occurred in the background mostly in the first two scenes. In our production these dialogues were written by Sascha and myself, in line with the play, of course, the exact words of which were never heard by the audiences but which gave life, vibration and richness to the performance as a whole. At our last run-through at Beekman Place I think the consensus was we were wonderful. We had made the heart of this touching, elusive play beat! . . . We thought.

We were eager to get to the Maxine Elliott Theater, which I had procured for the remaining twenty days of rehearsal. There I had all my props, all my furniture and the dressing rooms were available to the ladies so they could don their substitute long skirts of the period — 1900. On that first day at the Elliott excitement was at a high pitch. The feminine contingent had their long dresses on; the soldiers adjusted their swords and belts; the theater was dark (that is, no attraction was playing there), so there could be no interruption; the furniture that was going to be used was on the stage to be sat on, lolled on, perched on; every prop was there — and luxury of luxuries, there would be three weeks for the actors to experiment and get used to it all before an audience saw them. I might add this was made possible by the cuts Miss Anderson, Miss Gordon and Miss Cornell took in their salaries until the production was paid back. All the business of the play I had mapped out weeks before — diagrammed it on my script. I was so familiar with it that I didn't have to consult it. I knew the play as well as I could ever know it, and perhaps better than anyone else in this land of the free. It moved me profoundly.

And yet when that first rehearsal at the Maxine Elliott was over I thought I could never pull it off. Somewhere there was a leak and all that we had acquired around the table had drained away. Kit sensed my frustration and left me to myself. When I got home I went directly to my study on the fourth floor to brood. I went over and over the day's disillusionments. "This is a great play," I said to myself. "You have as fine a cast as you could ever hope for it. They are all enthusiastic. It was magic yesterday. Today it was dead. Why? What's happened? Nothing! Nothing has happened. What the hell is the matter with you? Get back in that theater tomorrow and don't try to make time. Take the first ten minutes of the first act and do no more. Do it over and over again until it starts to kindle and then, like a fire, it will spread through the play. The actors are with you. They want just that. Your anxiousness in trying to get a finished performance in seven hours is ridiculous." Kit left me severely alone. She was having her own thoughts on the floor below. I played the phonograph record of the last-act march. Somewhere Sascha had found the one that was used in the original production in Moscow. Between kicking myself and listening over and over again to that record I recaptured my spirit.

The next day I had the drive of ten. The cast was marvelous, humble, working in an endeavor to create something rare and elusive. I acted my head off — paraphrased scene after scene, draped myself on sofas, poised halfway upstairs and made a turn to illustrate what I had seen in my mind's eye. If the actor felt I was right he would do it. If not, he would voice his objection. But on both sides we were valid. On both sides we had respect for the other person. Gradually things began to take shape and meaning, and after days of strenuous rehearsal we found excitement once again. Alec Woollcott came twice to rehearsals. At the dress rehearsal Sascha brought Dr. Rumansky, an elderly Russian who had been the original manager of the Moscow Art Theater. When the rehearsal was over, in Kit's dressing room, he showered us with praise. We opened in Washington, D. C., with every seat sold for the entire engagement a week before we arrived there. In the opening-night audience was Eleanor Roosevelt with Mr. and Mrs. Harry Hopkins, the Soviet Ambassador, Maxim Litvinov, and his English wife, Ivy Low. They, too, came back to Kit's dressing-room with warm enthusiasm. We were applauded by the audiences and applauded by the press. On our way to New York we gave a Sunday performance for the G.I.s in training at Fort Meade. It was five above zero and there was no heat in the improvised theater in which we played. The ladies of the com-

pany wore their fur coats over their costumes on the stage.
Teddy Gwenn caught a cold. . . . It was the last play one
would imagine G.I.s would respond to. . . . They cheered
at the end! . . . We opened in Manhattan at the Ethel
Barrymore Theater, Christmas week of 1942.

I sat backstage during the performance, which I have
always done at every metropolitan opening of mine since
The Dover Road. Tired, unshaven — I dug my nails into my
palms and silently prayed. When the first curtain rose on
Kit and Judith, the applause was tremendous. Then the
scene started. There was no coughing out front. They were
listening. They were laughing. When the curtain fell on that
scene the audience was cheering. When the final curtain
fell they were still cheering.

Lewis Nichols, who was then pinch-hitting for Brooks
Atkinson during his wartime leave of absence, ended his
paean in the *New York Times* like this:

> *The Three Sisters* is a tightrope walk with carnage
> waiting those actors who fall off. Naturally they do not
> fall off at the Barrymore Theater for Miss Cornell and
> Guthrie McClintic, her director, have found the perfect
> person for each role. With so many players of renown
> it would have been easy for Mr. McClintic to let all go
> on their own but he doesn't work that way. His di-
> rection is a careful blend as to mood and the whole
> emerges as a play and not a group of players.

While Burns Mantle in the New York *Daily News* wrote:

> At the Barrymore Theater now is *The Three Sisters*
> with great Katharine providing a cast of players several
> degrees better than the average best. This Cornell lady
> not only revives the theater's modern classics she is

reviving the modern theater. More power to her. Her performance, and that of her present company, is much the best of any we have seen since Stanislavski and his Moscow Art Company gave it here twenty years ago. The direction by Guthrie McClintic is fluid and interesting.

With one lukewarm exception all the critics were enthusiastic about the play and players. We were very happy and gratified. Then on the Friday night of the first week, Christmas Day it was, the telephone rang around five o'clock in the afternoon and Teddy Gwenn's dresser, Ernest, told me that Teddy had been rushed to the hospital with double pneumonia. For an hour I frantically tried to locate the understudy. The three weeks on the road had been largely devoted to smoothing and polishing the production and there was little time left for understudy rehearsals. When at 6:30 the stage manager told me he was extremely dubious as to whether the understudy was secure in either lines or business, I decided to play it. Secure was the one thing I was. I knew every line, every movement in the play. Kit shook like an aspen leaf when I announced my decision. The cast was apprehensive but marvelously co-operative. Strange to say, I had no nerves at all.

I was a filler-in and my job was to hold the performance in shape. I got through without a hitch. During the following four weeks I continued in the part and before I bowed out I thought I was very good indeed. There was a certain excitement and satisfaction to me to be acting before an audience again, but I had no regrets in retiring when Teddy came back. Ruth Chatterton, Jane Cowl, Grace George, Sascha, Clifton Webb, Mildred Natwick, Lillian Hellman and Dorothy Gish all saw my performance at various times and came back to my dressing room to voice their approval. It seems odd that the only times I have ever played a good part anywhere have been under my own management or the family's, without benefit of rehearsal and with no direction — even my own. On second thought, maybe it isn't so odd!

After one hundred and twenty-two performances in New York we took it on the road. Everywhere we were acclaimed. (That sounds like every actor but it was true nevertheless.) It improved with every performance. These actors were concerned about the play as a whole. I saw it during its final week in Chicago and as I sat in the audience, which was rapt in attention and filled the theater to overflowing, I became starry-eyed. It was so good that I forgot I had anything to do with it. . . . None of the principals in the cast had anticipated this phenomenal success and all of them had new commitments, so with our banners flying high and capacity business we closed. *The Three Sisters* had run in all thirty-nine weeks. That is the longest run any Chekhov play has ever enjoyed in this country . . . and the longest run *The Three Sisters* ever had anywhere.

Casting problems, like the poor, are always with us in the theater. We begin by thinking of the ideal cast and end up thanking God they can all stand up. A "name" cast is by no means a guarantee of a fine performance but neither is it to be implied they can't give a fine one. I think all of the many "name" casts we've had have been good. I have never chosen an actor for his name value — always for his rightness for the role. Casting is contingent on so many things: the temperaments of the players involved — the author's wishes — the producer's reservations — the star's approval as well as the director's. An author's contract contains a clause that gives him the right to approve of every actor in the play, and there is a further line that says the approval may not unreasonably be withheld. That, of course, is to protect the producers in case a particular player the author desires is unavailable, or too expensive — or even committed to outside activities such as the radio or TV, which many times makes it impossible for the actor to rehearse properly. However, in my years in the theater, I have yet to run across a really difficult author. I have heard of them but I have never had to deal with one. . . . Well — only once! . . . They realize the casting question is a mutual problem and are usually only too eager to come more than halfway in meeting it. When it seems advisable that the services of a star be required for a play, the only difficulty as a rule is the financial arrangement. You see, there are many people who enjoy the dubious privilege of having their names in electric lights above that of the play, but out of that plentiful group there are only eight people at the most whom I rate as being actually stars in the legitimate theater.

To me a star is one thing and one thing only, and that is an individual who is blessed with some indefinable chemical element that makes great masses of the public willing to pay money to see him or her irrespective of the play the star is appearing in. That doesn't mean that stars are the greatest actors. If they are fine actors as well — and curiously enough seven of the eight I just referred to are — it's so much gravy, so to speak. Stardom only means that they draw the greatest number of people into the theater. Stars, therefore, are a definite asset to any play in which they appear . . . and as a rule are rather canny in their selection of plays. These particular people are worth what they are being paid, which is quite considerable, because they not only enhance any play they appear in but are a financial insurance. Even in plays that are not big successes, the presence of a money-drawing star can enable a producer to pay back some of the cost of his production. Now with these eight stars no producer quibbles about the high salary. But there is a sizeable group of other players who are accomplished actors too, who have had flattering — and justly so — criticisms from the press, yet who do not draw a great public. Why? I can't explain beyond the fact that the chemical element I've just mentioned is missing in them, and when they are approached one faces intricate problems of juggling financial arrangements. For through the grapevine this particular group or their representatives have an inkling of the approximate earnings of the few who are "draws," and they are inclined or advised to ask the same terms. Days and weeks are sometimes consumed in smoothing down the vanities and adjusting the stipends to something that approaches the players' actual worth. More times than not this is successfully done. Bruised feelings are healed, and tranquillity reigns.

Visual adherence to the author's description of a character as a rule is complied with, but not always. All of us in the theater — stars, managers, authors and directors — are apt to forget that a good actor is supposed to act and that a photographic exactness to any character is of less importance than the fact that he can play it. When Kit played *The Green Hat* the author, Michael Arlen, O.K.'d her —

although her appearance was the direct opposite of the tawny tiger, Iris March, he had described in his book. Casts just don't come on Christmas trees. A capable, large cast represents months of work. If the large cast turns out to be brilliant it can only mean your astrological chart is in the ascendant.

Both my parents died in the late '20s.

It was during Christmas week of 1927 that my mother passed on. I rushed from an opening in Boston and arrived in Seattle just too late (no planes then). The train had been held up thirty-six hours by a blizzard. My little mother — who had built a fence around herself or around me, I never knew which — was gone. Twelve years before she had written me a letter imploring me to support W. A. in all he did, as if she feared I might be prey to a certain restlessness that she thought had destroyed my father or that I might offend by an exhibition of my temper which, in its way, is quite as good as dad's was. Yet, in the early days of my recognition, although I knew she was happy for me, it seemed I could never awaken any interest in the activities that constituted my life. I was hurt and baffled. On the day after her funeral, as I was going through her desk, I found a scrapbook tied with a special ribbon in which she had pasted all my press notices!

XVIII

The Third Juliet

I<small>T WAS</small> on a Saturday morning during Lent in 1922
that I had a phone call at the office telling me that Mrs. Fiske
was attending the matinee of *The Dover Road* that afternoon and wondered if it would be convenient for me to
speak to her after the second act. Was someone kidding?
Would it be convenient? Minnie Maddern Fiske represented
the finest our American theater had to offer. No one to this
day has assembled a better group of players than those that
surrounded her in the heyday of her "Manhattan Company,"
as it was called: George Arliss, Holbrook Blinn, Emily
Stevens, and John Mason were a few of the notables. She
was a pioneer in presenting Ibsen in this country and proved
him to be good box office as well. She produced *Salvation
Nell*, the first play of Edward Sheldon, a young American
of brilliant promise whose career was curtailed by a baf-
fling illness but who remained a potent influence in the
lives of many of us in the theater until he died a few years
ago. Would it be convenient? ! ! ! I phoned back I would
be delighted and rushed to Beekman Place to don my good
suit — more truthfully, my other suit. Although I had made
a down payment on a house and bought a couple of new
plays, I hadn't invested in any much-needed wardrobe for

myself, as Kit and I were planning a belated honeymoon abroad during the coming summer and Allan Pollock, who I thought looked well turned out, had given me the address of his tailor on Savile Row. So I was content to remain shabby until this famed London firm would risk their reputation by fitting me out in my first made-to-order clothes.

My suit changed, my hair slicked down, I taxied over to my matinee. The house was sold out and I wandered among the standees at the back trying to spot Mrs. Fiske. In the first intermission I found her. She didn't move from her seat in the fifth row on the center aisle. The play was going marvelously, thank Heaven, but I found I was having an attack of stage fright at the thought of actually meeting this great lady of the theater as myself. How different this one was from the brash imposition of that fake interview I had subjected her to in Seattle years before! *She* had asked to meet me, Guthrie McClintic. The second act over, I went down the aisle to greet the lady in the fifth row who was lowering her veils as the house lights were coming up. I leaned towards her. "Mrs. Fiske," I murmured.

She looked up and stood up, holding out her hand, "My dear — my dear . . . dear Mr. . . . Mr. MacGuthrie — this is very nice of you," she said in her best staccato tones. The "MacGuthrie" left me a little abashed. I wanted to laugh but I restrained myself. I had to be on my best behavior. She continued, "Dear Mr. MacGuthrie, to come here and see me when you have so many other things to do. Is there anywhere we can talk?" And she looked around the crowded aisles as if we might seek refuge under the seats. The sad fact is that very few New York theaters have anywhere you can talk — certainly not the Bijou. So we pushed through the aimless audience, stretching its legs in the lobby, to 45th Street and walked up and down in the afternoon sunlight. Her low voice, her rapid, jerky utterance and extraordinary vitality, were as fascinating and arresting as ever.

"Dear Mr. . . . Mr. MacGuthrie," she was saying, with her arm linked in mine, "I wanted to ask you if you would consider reviving *Becky Sharp* for me." (She had made a sensation in it over twenty years before.) And she went on, "You know I would like to do it again while I still keep," and she was bubbling with laughter. Wonderful Mrs. Fiske!

Why didn't I do it? For one thing, I had two plays on my schedule for the following season; and then, she had already created the part: there would be little for me to do beyond acting as impresario, which I suspected was all she wanted — as her husband, Harrison Grey Fiske, was still about and had done most of her directing since she distinguished him by becoming Mrs. Fiske. After that matinee I saw her many times and there were occasions when she got my name right.

"My dear boy," she said to me once, "I am so tired of hearing this new breed of actors say they can't go on the road, they must play in New York. Pish, tush and nonsense. New York, indeed! To me New York is just a 'stand,' like St. Louis, Kansas City and San Francisco. If you could see my audiences on the road — the aristocracy of America!" And shaking her finger at me — "When your Katharine is a star don't ever let her play only in New York."

And so, when "my Katharine" became a star, she went on the road and when she became a manager as well she still went on the road. In fact her great tour of 1933–1934, at the height of the depression, when she covered some 17,000 miles and played 77 cities, has been credited by many as bringing the road back. It certainly revealed to the booking office then and to other stars and managements that there were great eager hungry audiences throughout the country that would crowd theaters for fare that was good. That was the season we first did *Romeo and Juliet*.

It was the sainted Ray Henderson who kept after me when I first talked the idea over with him as I was pondering on plays and parts that Kit should enact. Ray was our ambassador to the press. I think the whole profession as well as the newspaper world regarded him as an ambassador rather than a press agent. In his quarter of a century's service to the theater he *selected* those he wished to be associated with. He began with Sir Johnston Forbes-Robertson on his farewell tour, then on to William Faversham in the days of his splendid revivals, then with E. H. Sothern and Julia Marlowe, later to W. A., Ethel Barrymore and finally with Kit. (He was killed in an airplane accident in Greece as he was completing an around-the-world survey of a tour we were planning for Kit in 1937.) He expected — in fact demanded — your finest effort and was never satisfied until you gave it. He kept saying to us "Shakespeare will never let you down," following it up with "There has never been a truly great actress in the English language who has not played one or another of Shakespeare's heroines and received her greatest praise from doing so."

Despite the constancy and reassurance of his enthusiasm I think, in the beginning, he was a shadow over my vision. He talked so persistently about Marlowe and Sothern's production that I ended up thinking their abbreviated version was Shakespeare. Miss Marlowe was *the* Juliet of the early part of this century. Beautiful Julia Marlowe, with the

almost too beautiful voice — she and E. H. Sothern had
made a fortune from the Bard in their coast-to-coast tours. I
never saw them as a team. *Romeo and Juliet* I had seen only
twice — once in England at Lillian Baylis's Old Vic with
Jean Forbes-Robertson and Eric Portman enacting the title
parts, and again in 1923 when Jane Cowl had her successful
revival with Rollo Peters as Romeo and Dennis King making
his first big success as Mercutio. Miss Cowl was lovely to
look at, lovely to hear and had great acclaim. She was the
second outstanding Juliet of the twentieth century.

After I read *Romeo and Juliet* again, on our decision to
do it, Ray, from out of nowhere, unearthed Sothern and
Marlowe's prompt book and pushed it under my nose. I de-
voured it, which was too bad. For over a year it stood between me and Mr. Shakespeare's text. Also I consulted the
Variorum and eventually found out that that was not my
way of approaching the immortal Will. All of this intensive
research and study influenced me even as to scenery. Wood-
man Thompson, who had done lovely decor for W. A.'s
Gilbert and Sullivan operettas, I engaged to do my sets. He
designed according to my wishes, exceedingly practical and
beautiful backgrounds. We decided that year that we would
try out *Romeo and Juliet* along with our productions of
Candida and *The Barretts,* for a full season, on the road but
not touching Boston, Philadelphia or Chicago. Ray had
warned us that *Juliet* would be the weak sister of the three
at the box office, because, in Shakespeare, the great public
would not flock to novices — even when they were popular
stars. So to pay our expenses we carried a couple of spares,
so to speak. His prediction proved right.

Casting was something of a problem too, for I had to cast

three plays, using the same actors in all of them. Plenty of compromise went into selecting of the company. Not sympathetic in the first place, I was convinced that repertory was not for me. Here were two plays in which Kit had been phenomenally successful and a third in which she was trying her wings. Curiously enough, neither *Candida* nor *The Barretts* had been considered star plays until Kit played them. In England the accent in *The Barretts* had been on Father Barrett and Elizabeth, while here I put the greater accent on the love story of Elizabeth and Robert Browning. Certainly in *Candida* Marchbanks had always been considered the outstanding role. Ah, sez you, in real repertory there is no star. Pish, tush and nonsense, as Mrs. Fiske would say, who felt much the same as I do about repertory. In the famous Moscow Art Theater there were two who could be classified as stars; first and foremost, Katchaloff, and then Stanislavski. Whether they received star billing is quite another matter. They were the stars.

Our company was a good one and it was not the actors' fault that they were better in some parts than others. For example, Orson Welles, a youngster sent to me by Alec Woollcott, made his debut in America with us that season. He was effective in Shakespeare but left more than a little to be desired when he undertook Marchbanks in *Candida*. That he got by was by no means enough. A. P. Kaye was enormously effective as Candida's father, but brother! No one should have looked when he did Montagu in *Romeo and Juliet*. Basil Rathbone, I thought, was effective in all three plays. So, too, were Brenda Forbes and Charles Waldron — splendid actors both of them, who had played with Kit continuously since her debut as an actress-manager when she presented *The Barretts of Wimpole Street* with Brenda playing "Wilson," Miss Barrett's maid, inimitably, and Waldron giving a fine performance as Father Barrett — but they were the exceptions.

Equity allowed us five weeks' rehearsal then, and two plays were ready when we opened our season. All during the rehearsals of *Romeo* the menacing cloud of Shakespeare's commentators hung over me — the dictatorship of tradition had imposed on me a boundary over which I felt it treason to cross. In the second scene, between Lady Capulet and the Nurse, it is said that Juliet will be fourteen in a fortnight and odd days; but as Miss Marlowe, Jane Cowl, and other Juliets without number — going back to before Ellen Terry — had changed her age to eighteen, I decided Kit would be eighteen. The famous "rope scene" that begins with "Gallop apace, you fiery-footed steeds" had never been played since Adelaide Nielson did it in the mid-seventies; all the vignettes of the preparation for Juliet's wedding to Paris . . . the scene in which the Nurse discovers Juliet's body . . . the one just before the finale in which Friar Laurence learns that his letter to Romeo was undelivered — all of them, in this country, had almost never been done . . . certainly not by Marlowe nor by Cowl, according to their prompt books. And they were not played when we opened in Buffalo. Our notices were good. Our business wasn't. On "Big Time," so to speak, Shakespeare had been a box office graveyard since Barrymore's *Hamlet* and Jane Cowl's *Juliet* twelve years before. . . . When we substituted *The Barretts* the business leaped to capacity.

From Buffalo we jumped to Milwaukee. Now, the city that some beer has made famous is only two hours by train from Chicago; and to our dismay all the dramatic critics in the Windy City sharpened their pencils and, incidentally, their knives and journeyed over to witness our opening. Two days later, there appeared a set of notices in the Chicago papers that were unanimously bad and to our sensitive egos cruel. We weren't at our best that night, but we weren't as bad as one might think from reading them. And those criti⸗ cisms miraculously winged their way back to New York, but as a matter of fact it wasn't such a bad thing as it turned out. Meanwhile, we rolled up our sleeves and worked. We weren't taking it lying down. We had no more critical broadsides. Kit gained confidence and by the time we reached San Francisco not only were our notices good but, before we gave our last performance, *Romeo and Juliet* was playing to capacity houses along with *The Barretts* and *Candida* — BUT it wasn't right. The good notices didn't fool me. The bad ones from Chicago told me nothing beyond the fact that they did not like it. The cast, while acceptable, was far from ideal. I knew that my best directorial foot was not forward by any means. The production and costumes looked lovely; restrained and lovely. But more than that was wrong. What was it? Why didn't the play "send" me? I must confess that it never had in the two productions I had previously seen, but with me it should be different. With Kit it had to be. Looking at her in San Francisco, I knew she was potentially a great Juliet — potentially only. She couldn't stop at that. At one matinee I sat in front of two very chatty ladies and when the lights went up on the final scene, in the tomb of the Capulets, I heard one of them remark: "I knew it! When the curtain went up on this show I knew it would have a bad end." My first impulse was to say "Sh-h" emphatically. But I caught myself as I was turning my head. Out of the mouths of babes . . . profound criticism! Could she be right? She obviously knew nothing about the play but she should not have known, when the first curtain rose, that it would have a bad end. I hurried to the nearest bookstore and bought an ordinary copy of the play, like the one I'd first read before being influenced by the improvements of my predecessors. I wanted to find out who tipped their hand, Mr. Shakespeare or me. I avoided like the plague all the marked copies and the prompt books I had diligently assembled. As nearly as I could, I was going to sweep away all the cobwebs of other days from my brain and walk untrammeled through that script avoiding the many footprints the great performers of other years had left there. I would try to read it as a play by a new, unknown author — completely unaware that it had a "bad end." When I had read it over and over again, a faint flush of discovery overcame me. Into the discard went all the bosh about scanning the verse. Just read the verse for meaning and the poetry would take care of itself. Mr. Shakespeare had seen to that. And what a good play it turned out to be when it wasn't amputated. Previous presentations might have been better described as excerpts from Shakespeare's *Romeo and Juliet*. The Prologue, which also was rarely done, refers to the story as "the two hours' traffic of our stage." The events of the entire play occur in just seventy-two hours! Here was a drama of hot blood, high passion and exhilaration! Tragedy, springing from recklessness — from youth's fervor — its refusal to turn back — to pause and reflect; had either one of the lovers ever stopped to think, there would have been no tragedy. This was no museum piece steeped in tradition.

Its "two hours' traffic" must be breathless with headlong action, not an actor's holiday — a play to be played as written. I had approached this play through the eyes of past performers and there could not have been a worse approach. Put me down as backward and let it go at that.

I started back at the beginning again. Everything in my present production had been wrong: first me, and my cutting of the script, and — with the exception of Kit and Basil, Brenda Forbes, Charles Waldron and Orson — the cast. Then the scenery! My fault again: I had leaned towards a quiet, almost somber background. I needed a fresh mind; so I straightaway sent for Jo Mielziner, who joined me in the Middle West; I told him of my newly conceived idea of décor: light, gay; hot sun, hot passions; young, swift; and outlined my procession of scenes, every one in the play, including the Prologue. After several weeks Jo returned with the entire production designed; skillful as to the lightning-quick changes I wanted, breathtaking as to beauty — in effect, looking not unlike Giotto backgrounds — light, gay, spacious, and ending with a marvelous dark Capulet tomb where, as Shakespeare indicates, "no healthsome air breathes in." Jo had captured the whole terror of this place, "where bloody Tybalt lies festering in his shroud — where for these many hundred years the bones of my buried ancestors are packed" — as Juliet says in the potion scene. When Paris descended into this vault at the opening of the final scene, he actually needed a torch — one couldn't tell which tomb was Juliet's. And later, when Romeo and Paris fought their duel in and out and around the tombs, the effect was both macabre and exciting. On one point only did I question Jo's designs. That was the balcony set. It was beautiful, but it seemed a thing apart — and possibly impractical. Jo convinced me it would work. Everything else he had designed seemed so miraculous that it wasn't overhard to persuade me. Then he started the drawings for costumes.

Romeo and Juliet was dropped from our repertory in Cincinnati. We gave all the scenery and the platforms of that production to the Little Theater there, and disposed of the costumes in New York. This represented a loss of many thousands of dollars but if we were going to do it at all we decided we would do it at the top of our resources, financial and otherwise. Martin Beck put his theater at our disposal. In my opinion it is the finest-equipped legitimate playhouse in New York. Our opening was set and announced during the summer for December 20, 1934, at 8:15 sharp. I spent most of my waking moments thereafter steeping myself in the text — making new discoveries at almost every reading — that is, when I was not interviewing literally hundreds of actors for the new cast. There were the revelers for the ballroom scene to be found, the street crowds in Verona — in addition to innumerable small parts, *all* of whom attended every rehearsal and went on the road with us. Of the major parts I had to get the Nurse, Mercutio, Benvolio, Lady Capulet and Capulet. Thanks to some lucky refusals, the gods smiled on our endeavor. Edith Evans (not a Dame then but as brilliant an actress as the English-speaking world can boast of) came over to play the Nurse as it had never been played before. Brian Aherne, our original Mr. Browning, was handsome, high-spirited and swashbuckling as Mercutio; Moroni Olson, a towering and expansive Capulet; Irby Marshall, patrician and beautiful as his Lady. George Macready was Paris; John Emery, Benvolio. Add to these, Cornell as Juliet; Rathbone as Romeo; Orson Welles as Tybalt; Waldron as the Friar and Brenda Forbes as Lady Montagu. Quite a cast! Paul Nordoff composed enchanting music. Martha Graham staged, with exquisite style, the dance in the fairy-story ballroom Jo had designed. And Santelli arranged the hair-raising duels that were fought in the street scenes. The youth and enthusiasm of the cast were inspiring to work with. It was the only time I ever saw a Nurse that you believed could have been Juliet's. They are usually so ancient they creak. I had managed to crase not only all my mistakes of the year before from my mind but my conception as well. The turn-about had been mine but the added incentive came when I saw the cast beginning to form, heard the music, saw Jo's costumes being fitted and the scenery on the frames being painted at the studio. I was staging an exciting new play by a man named William Shakespeare. I had decided to play all twenty-three scenes (otherwise structurally the story falls apart), cutting only the obsolete comedy of the musicians and servants, to bring the playing time — including one twelve-minute intermission — to within the three hours the stagehands' union allows. Juliet's age was to be as Master Will indicated — fourteen. It was no greater strain to be fourteen than eighteen. It was simply a question of being. The actors must be made to forget they are playing Shakespeare. The look that comes on the average actor's face — what happens to his body — when he starts reading Shakespeare is something that has to be seen to be believed. They must be rehearsed in costumes, so they will look as if they are wearing clothes and not appear as stuffed dummies. The tempo must be fast — no stilted pauses to let an audience be depressed by the fact that they are witnessing a

Shakespearean production; warmth, gaiety — JULIET IS THE SUN! — and there must be no waits between scenes. For instance, after you hear Romeo's lines at the end of his first scene, Lady Capulet immediately speaks as the lights are quickly dimming out: "Nurse, where is my daughter? Call her forth to me." Then the lights are coming up and you are in Capulet's hall, with the Nurse entering. . . . This overlapping of scenes gave the performance not only great pace but stopped distracting applause at the end of them. The lighting was beautiful. I never troubled about the factual sources of a light but I troubled a great deal about the effect of a light. We rehearsed for over two weeks with our platforms and props. It was truly exciting. The handful of our last year's company looked with incredulous and unbelieving eyes at this magic we were suddenly enmeshed in. Edith Evans, who had quite rightly held out for, and received, a high salary, after the first few days of rehearsal said to me, "As I see what you're aiming for with this production I want to say I will take the figure you offered me instead of the sum I asked for." A touching and warming gesture from a great artist . . . We did not take advantage of her generosity.

As we were nearing the dress rehearsal, Kit and I became very much concerned about the dress she made her first entrance in and we couldn't seem to make Jo understand what we wanted. The first gown he had designed had been discarded. The next one was in the making. At the dress parade practically everybody looked better than we hoped, which was saying a great deal. All of the girls in the ballroom were quite bewitching and right. Kit's costume for that scene was still not right. She seemed a person apart — more a star

than one of the girls. It was very discouraging. Jo seemed
to have run dry of ideas when, with more concern than I
cared to show, I mounted the stairs to the stage and, approaching one of the girls in the ensemble, told her to go
into Kit's dressing room and divest herself of her charming
frock and then told Kit to put it on. It was perfect. Juliet,
sartorially, was no different from any of the other girls at
the party. The total cost of Kit's two discarded gowns was
one thousand dollars. The one she wore cost eighty-five
dollars. There are certain disadvantages in being a star!

Twenty years ago I was graciously permitted by the scene
designer to "light" my own productions. This was primarily
because I insisted that my actors be lit wherever they were
on the stage, regardless of what it might do to the scenery.
In most cases it would do nothing — for I had explained be-
forehand where I wanted scenes played, and where I wanted
light, and what volume of light I wanted thrown on the actors. From certain scenic artists I have had screams of
anguish about what they think is overlighting on my part.
I light for the back row of the balcony, and those lesser-
priced seats from which I am a graduate member — and,
therefore, feel they have a right to see clearly, possibly a
better right than those preferred folk who buy the front-
row stalls and who, alas, are many times the late arrivals at
a play. They haven't queued up in the rain to get the balcony
and gallery locations for two and sometimes three hours or
had to conform to any time a seat was available. It is an old
story that the balcony and gallery are the true support of
the theater. They have done well by me throughout the
years and I in turn feel an obligation to them.

The best of our modern theaters make lighting a harrowing, exhausting, nervewracking ordeal. It incites violent tempers, frustration and ulcers. I will take you backstage for a moment where behind the proscenium arch, you will find, on either side, what we call "the tormentors" — great iron pipes extending high in the air — loaded with eight to twelve lamps or "spots" on each one. Overhead there are the borders: the first pipe, second pipe, and third pipe. In the front of the theater balcony are the "front spots," twelve to thirty depending on the production. All of these lights are numbered. All of these are controlled according to the size of the production by one to three or even four switchboards which are worked by the master electrician and his assistants. To focus any one of these, giant ladders are brought out on the stage and an electrician climbs up with an assistant steadying it while he perilously teeters as he endeavors to identify the spotlight that is wanted with a number on the switchboard. Then the spot has to have the right color medium and be focused. For a tricky show this can go to thirty spots for one scene alone, and they all have to be focused — with the ladder and electrician moving for each one. That goes for the "tormentors," the "spots" in front of the house and the borders. And to say nothing of those very special things known as "baby spots" or, as we constantly hear them called at rehearsals, "babies." All lights have to be checked for effect from every part of the theater: sides, center, front of the orchestra, back of the orchestra, back of the balcony.

I start my light rehearsal of *Romeo and Juliet* at eight in the morning. Everyone is there except the actors. They are represented by a small group of understudies, who are going to serve as stand-ins for the principals; that is, they assume the exact positions of the principals on the stage and as the lighting proceeds we see that they are properly lit. The entire crew, that means the carpenter department, all of the property men and, naturally, all the electricians are on hand; and in a production of the magnitude of *Romeo* that involves a considerable number of men. We may not need or use any of the carpenters or prop crew but the Union says "hot or cold, you have them." You see they are paid and paid well. It's not at all unusual to see some of the more exalted members of the stage crew arrive in their cars while the stage manager and his assistant and the stand-ins have trekked in from the subway; the scene designer and his assistant and myself have modestly arrived by taxicab. The whole production has been mapped out in regard to light, and I hope to be through in twelve hours, knocking off an hour for lunch and an hour for dinner.

I start off the perfect gentleman. "Good morning, Jimmy" (Jimmy is my stage manager); "Hello, Trell" (his assistant). I go absolutely overboard for the heads of the departments, and I am filled with solicitude for the stand-ins. "I am sorry you had to get up so early." (A lie! The only person I am sorry for is myself.) "Now take it easy until I call you on the set. You can come out front, if you want to." I go out front. "Are you ready, Jimmy?" I call. I have never had to use one of those telephone contraptions. They can usually hear me two blocks away. "Not yet, Boss, it won't be long," is Jimmy's reply. I exchange a few pleasantries with the stand-ins who are sitting behind me. I hear the box-office telephone ringing and I hope it is business, not gossip. A half hour passes. Another half hour drags on. Another! The carpenters are engrossed in a hot game of pinochle in the basement; the religious property man is reading his Bible; the electricians seem to be having trouble. . . . They are all being paid so what does it matter?

I am getting testy. "Jimmy," I call with a phony cheerfulness, "what's wrong?" "Nothing, boss, we can't find three babies." I raise my voice. "What do you mean you can't find them? You have a diagram of the whole set-up haven't you?"

"You don't understand, Boss, there are three babies we can't find on the Number Two switchboard. Don't get impatient, we'll locate them. . . . Kill that baby," he shouts to the master electrician and lights are going on and off as they continue. I am obviously a nuisance. Why should I get impatient? Only an hour and a half gone! It's our party. We are paying for it — Lord knows what the head carpenter has lost by now at pinochle. But I must stop worrying about that. Maybe I should find the religious property man and read the Scriptures with him? Better not.

I walk out of the auditorium and go downstairs to the men's room. I study my unshaven face in the mirror. Good God! Could it be possible that once I thought I looked like Edwin Booth? Well, that phase is over for me; but I *am* in the theater. Yes — down in the men's room on a bleak morning, stewing my guts out over this blankety-blank delay. In my wildest dreams in Seattle I could never have imagined the me, of now. The colored cleaning man comes down with his mop and pail. I cover by looking at my notes. "I must remind Kit to stay on the balcony when the scene is over and be wheeled off with it. It will make the change quicker. It is imperative Orson remain on stage for the curtain call. The stage manager can't go up three flights to fetch him. Who the hell does he think he is? Waldron must pick up his cue quicker. . . .

"Mr. McClintic," calls one of the stand-ins from the theater auditorium, "they are waiting for you on stage!" Waiting for ME! I have been in the theater for over two hours. But why argue? I am glad we can start. Those three errant babies being found, we proceed. . . .

Things were going remarkably well, until we got to Jo's pet, the balcony scene. I stopped cold in my tracks. . . . It is beautiful, but can Juliet act on it? — I ask myself — It looks so tiny! . . . But for once I didn't want to be too hasty, so I suggested that he light it while I retired and glanced at a sandwich. . . . I didn't look at it again until I saw it at the dress rehearsal.

That started at eight o'clock in the evening. Before our beautiful sage-green curtains with the crest of the Capulets embroidered on one side and the Montagus' on the other, Orson — resplendent, shielding his face with a gold Benda mask — came through and in his magnificent voice began the Prologue: "Two households both alike in dignity . . ." When he finished, his spot dimmed out, the curtains parted, and there was the first scene exactly as I hoped it would be: the vivid yellows, reds, mauves and browns of the peasants' costumes as they drowsed in the noonday sun of the public square; the contrasting elegance of the wealthy of Verona as they passed through — it oozed vitality, passion and humor. No chattering female could predict how this one would end. . . . Now comes the first scene with Juliet, the Nurse and Lady Capulet. Kit is radiant, light and gay. Next Mercutio and the Queen Mab speech, Brian looking unbelievably handsome. Every scene change is working without a hitch. I am getting frightened — it is going too smoothly. The ballroom in the Capulet house bursts upon us. White satin, gold and red, with its one great chandelier being lit by pages. A spacious and handsome background for the lovely costumes of the revelers. The dance starts. Juliet is dancing with Paris. Romeo sees her. Her heart skips a beat as she meets his eyes. She loses her step. Romeo turns to ask who she is. She disappears. The dance goes on. Romeo turns back. She is not there. He exits, trying to find her. The candles gutter and the dancers are dancing in moonlight. Suddenly Romeo meets Juliet face to face in a downstage arch. "If I profane with my unworthiest hand this holy shrine . . ." This brief scene of ecstasy is highlighted, presumably by an off-stage torch. They stand out against the shadowy figures behind them, dancing in the moonlight. Her vigilant nurse interrupts them. "Madam, your mother craves a word with you." The party is breaking up. Father Capulet is saying, "Honest gentlemen, good night."

Jo steals up the aisle to me in the darkened theater and whispers, "It is thrilling, Guthrie. I never dreamed it would be like this." I am feeling pretty good myself. Lights out and on again. Then follows the brief scene before Capulet's garden wall. Again the lights dim out and come up on the balcony. No person is on stage. We hear Benvolio's voice fading away in the distance. "Romeo, my cousin Romeo." It is a delight to the eye. Exquisite! Now Romeo is over the wall — "he jests at scars who never felt a wound." A bull in a china shop! The whole thing is out of scale. No actor should invade it. It is like Gulliver and the Lilliputians. "But soft, what light through yonder window breaks? It is the east and Juliet is the sun." She appears on the balcony. Kit, the little fourteen-year-old girl of the previous scene, now looks not unlike some massive Wagnerian soprano. There is no room to move. Juliet looks as broad as the balcony. I close my eyes. There are magic sounds in the air. I open my eyes again and my vision shuts them out. I light a cigarette and inhale to the bottom of my lungs. Dear God, I think, why should this happen to Me? Why didn't I yell my fool head off at the time of my first misgivings? Why did I bend the knee? Why did I acquiesce? Why? Why? Why? . . . On and on and on. "Parting is such sweet sorrow that I shall say good-night until it be morrow." The scene is almost over. No time to dawdle now in a purgatory of recriminations. We have to open Monday. This is Thursday night. What *can* be done before the opening "Now the grey-eyed morn smiles on the frowning night." They are in the Friar's cell. Waldron is saying his first lines. They must not go on. We have got to fix that balcony! "Jo," I yelled, more in anguish and pain than in temper — more a tonal wail at my own inadequacies. "What can we do about that God-awful balcony? Kit has no room. She can't move. It is the greatest love scene ever written, and we are playing it in an elevated telephone booth." Waldron has dress-rehearsed with me before. He sits quietly down on the Friar's cot. So has Kit. But she shuts her dressing-room door and goes into the farthest corner to avoid hearing me. For one quarter of an hour I indulge myself in a series of sounds that shake the walls of the theater to indicate that I don't like the balcony; while Jo, with that courtesy and sympathetic understanding that never seem to desert him, patiently tells me we can paint it down for the Detroit opening, light only the faces of Romeo and Juliet, and it will serve. Then we will plan a new one for the New York opening, three weeks hence. I am getting back into the land of reasonableness, slightly mollified. The rehearsal goes on. The final curtain falls just before 2 A.M. Not bad really, but everybody is tired. The stagehands are dismantling the scenery, getting it ready to load on the trucks that will take it to Grand Central Station where a couple of cars will be waiting to receive it and take it to Detroit for our next dress rehearsal on Sunday night. As Kit and I are leaving the theater it is snowing. My friend, the stage carpenter, no doubt to pacify my misgivings about the balcony, says, "Boss, some of this stuff (the scenery) is bound to get snow on it. That's good luck, you know. You couldn't have a better sign. Good night."

During the train journey to Detroit Jo and I discuss the new balcony set. It will not be literal — just beautiful. It is to be ten feet across to provide ample space for movement; it is to be made of blue velvet so it can absorb the light, yet have the actors plainly visible even though the "mask of night" is on their faces. It is the illusion I want. It will be ready for the New York opening. For the time being we shall do our darnedest with what we have. There is a general feeling of optimism in the company. . . . But the Detroit opening-night audience managed to dispel that altogether. They sat on their hands. There were moments when the actors wondered if the curtain were really up. I felt a little bit as if I were dressed to kill and my pants had split and my shoes squeaked. However, the town of our courtship didn't let us down, the notices were brilliant. Ray Henderson was transported and the subsequent audiences enthusiastic and big. By Wednesday matinee, we all thought we were as good as we thought we were. In Cleveland and Pittsburgh the notices were excellent — business, too.

Our New York opening was set for a Thursday evening, but we played two performances in Toronto — Monday night plus a Tuesday matinee — because we did not wish to be without an audience until then. It was impossible with our big production to make the regular train that left Toronto at seven o'clock for New York, so a special one was arranged that arrived in Buffalo in time to connect with the 20th Century which would put us in Manhattan the following morning, a Wednesday. We were scheduled to open the next night. The new balcony was waiting for us. It was the stuff that dreams are made of. Although Basil and Kit rehearsed on it the night before I wasn't able to light it until the day of the opening. I was posing her "stand-in" in every attitude that Juliet had and checking every spotlight that hit her for accurateness of focus, color of light, volume of light, when out of the magic moonlight of Verona Kit appeared and said "Is it all right if I take Ruth March's place now?" (That was her stand-in.)

"Why aren't you resting?" I asked.

"I'd rather be here," she replied. She took Ruth's place and we proceeded with the lights.

Shortly after four, we are finished at the theater. The crew and the stage managers are doing their final checking-up. Many boxes and baskets of flowers have already arrived. The stage-door man is assorting scores of telegrams that have come for the company from friends wishing them luck. In the car going home, I hold Kit's hand. We are both very quiet. Suddenly Kit breaks the silence with, "Guth, I

don't think I'll be nervous tonight. They may not like me
out front. That's their privilege, but I think I know more
about Juliet than anyone out there." After the most meager
of dinners we are back at the theater at 6:30. Kit visits
every dressing room to wish them luck — from extras to stars.
I am getting restless. Right or wrong, this is it. I have a two
days' growth of beard. My suit is old and shiny. I never
"dress" for an opening of mine (another superstition!). I'm
getting in everybody's way so I go out on 45th Street and
wander towards Ninth Avenue and then saunter back to the
stage door. The first-nighters are beginning to arrive now
. . . dressed up, and distinguished-looking they are too.
Ninety-five per cent of them are in their seats by 8:15. One
minute later Jimmy gives the signal to the house electrician
to dim the house lights. "Down to half," says the electrician.
"Hold it," says Jimmy, then he looks through the pass-door
and pauses a second to give a few stragglers who are hurrying down the aisle a chance to get seated. Then he signals
the electrician to take the house out. "House out," says the
electrician. Jimmy looks at his watch, warns the curtain man,
the warning light is off — the curtain is going up. There is
applause for Jo's front curtains and then through them
Orson appears and the Prologue begins. I go through my
usual ritual — digging my nails into the palms of my hand
and saying a prayer. The curtains part and the show is on!

It seems to me I walked many miles in the blackness
of backstage that night, dodging stagehands in the quick
changes, stepping out of the way of actors hastily exiting
or of crowds waiting to make an entrance. My work had
been done. Nothing would have been gained by my being
out front — plain masochism if anything went wrong and

embarrassing to any who might know me out there. This night represented three years of preparation, of learning, of unlearning, of learning again. It was a pivotal one in Kit's career. So much that might lie ahead for both of us depended on it. Yet I suddenly felt impotent — spent. My impressions were blurred — like looking out of a window when rain is beating against the pane. As I waited on the side lines, the actors — denizens of Verona and Padua — were like people out of a dream. I vaguely recall the gasp that came from the audience when Kit winged her way across the stage in her vivid red dress at the beginning of the garden scene. I felt the audience were held. No accident marred the evening. And when the final curtain fell, there was a stillness out front such as I never experienced before or since in a theater. Kit, clear-eyed and curiously beautiful and girlish in her great purple cape which she wore for curtain calls, was looking as if she were trying to determine if the heart of a loved one whose chances of life were touch-and-go was still beating. She whispered to me, "We can't take calls if no one applauds." Then it started. We took calls all right! There were cheers for the company. Bravos for Edith Evans. And when Kit appeared alone there were more bravos. As the curtain closed on her I noticed tears in her eyes. She said to Jimmy in a choked voice, "There will be no more curtain calls." The company were protesting, "You must, it is thrilling." "No," said Kit very firmly with the tears running down her cheeks. "If the audience sees me like this, it will look as if I am asking for something. I am sorry!" She walked off the stage. The house lights went up and the audience were still cheering. I thanked everybody — the crew, the actors, and the extras — as the stage began to overflow with milling people offering congratulations. When the last of them had gone and only our official family were sitting around Kit's dressing room, Gert Macy, who had been opening telegrams, handed one to Kit. "Read it to me," said Kit. Gert read: HIE TO HIGH FORTUNE — and it was signed Jane Cowl.

The next day's criticisms were heart-warming and magnificent. Burns Mantle gave it his highest rating — four stars. Brooks Atkinson of the *Times* said in part:

> Miss Cornell has hung another jewel on the cheek of theater nights. Her *Romeo and Juliet,* which she put on last evening, is on the highest plane of modern magnificence. Probably no one expected anything less radiant from her resourceful workshop where she and Guthrie McClintic prepare the dramas for her repertory, but the result is no less exalting to those who sit before the footlights. For this is an occasion. When it is produced and played with romantic and tragic candor, *Romeo and Juliet* is a drama that drains the playgoers' emotion. In those circumstances all a reviewer can say is "Bravo." Shakespeare has a vital servant in Miss Cornell.

Richard Lockridge mentioned my direction thus:

> Guthrie McClintic, who staged the play, has somehow managed to persuade all the members of the cast that the word Shakespeare is one which need not of necessity freeze the lips.

John Mason Brown filled our cup to overflowing with this:

> It is not often in our lifetime that we are privileged to enjoy the pleasant sensation of feeling that the present and the future have met for a few triumphant hours. We know as we enjoy the passing moments of the pres-

ent that most of them are destined to slip by unre-
membered. They have not the importance or the beauty
or the intensity out of which the kind of abiding memories are made to which we return, boastfully or wist-
fully, in the future when the present has been swal-
lowed up into the past.

Yet it was this very sensation — this uncommon sensation of having the present and the future meet by witnessing the kind of event to which we will be looking
back with pride in the years to come — that forced its
warming way, I suspect, into the consciousness of many
of us last night as we sat spellbound at the Martin Beck
in the presence of the acting wonders and the scenic
splendors of Katharine Cornell's production of *Romeo
and Juliet.*

To say that she emerged triumphantly from the evening both as an actress and a manageress is but to state
an agreeable truth. To add that beyond any shadow of
doubt she is today "The First Lady" of our stage is but
to state another and no less agreeable truth.

As a manageress she has given *Romeo and Juliet*
one of the most beautiful, most spirited and best-acted
Shakespearean productions of our time. Her arrangement of the text (which is fuller than is customary and
which includes not only the first prologue but also the
final scenes of reconciliation after the death of the star-
crossed lovers) is as generous to the various actors who
appear in it as Shakespeare meant it to be. It moves forward breathlessly with an Elizabethan swiftness. And
as it does so, it is at all times enhanced by the vigor
and pictorial effectiveness of Mr. McClintic's direction
and the superlative loveliness of Mr. Mielziner's set-
tings.

The century's third Juliet had arrived!
Out of all the dailies, weeklies and monthlies, there were

only two unfavorable notices — George Jean Nathan wrote one and Robert Garland the other — but like Mother God-dam we survived. The engagement was twice extended. The standees were limited to the number the fire laws sanctioned. The following autumn we took it on the road for a brief season with some new faces in the cast: Florence Reed was the Nurse, and what an ingratiating one she was; we brought an unknown actor from England who read Romeo beauti-fully — his name was Maurice Evans; Ralph Richardson was our superb Mercutio; and a good-looking newcomer played Benvolio — Tyrone Power. Some values were different; oth-ers extended and expanded. I thought the production had gained in richness.

Remembering the Milwaukee opening of two years before it was not without misgivings we played Chicago. But the gentlemen of the press there hailed the new Juliet as a miracle. They tossed their hats in the air and ordered dancing in the streets. We closed our tour by doing a special return engagement in New York, once again at the Martin Beck at Christmas-time. I sat out front at the last perform-ance. All in all, Kit had played Juliet over two hundred fifty times, and at her farewell performance she had the fresh-ness of an opening one, and the grace and effortless sim-plicity with which she played had the hallmark of all great acting. And when she took her final curtain call, this time there were tears in my eyes. From now on, it would be a memory. . . . However, we had the satisfaction of feeling we had done a good job. . . . Already we were in the throes of our next one — the hills were getting steeper — but we couldn't stop — just catch our breath and say gratefully, "Merry Christmas."

XIX

Broadway — East and West

I WAS about to say that the Christmas season has almost always provided a time of theatrical rejoicing, but memory has stepped in to give that statement the lie. One Christmas I was engrossed in a stinker called *The Lady Who Came to Stay* which proved to me that we live but never learn. Quite rightly it drew the wrath of the fourth estate and did not survive its opening week. Another Yuletide offering of mine was an imperfect but beautiful piece by Gustav Ekstein called *Christmas Eve*. It concerned the emotions of a young girl just passed eighteen who is shocked and ashamed to discover that her mother, after many years, is about to have another baby. The baby was born on the stage. I thought my handling of that scene was one of the finest and most sensitive directorial jobs I had ever done. The New York critics with the sole exception of Arthur Pollock, however, thought otherwise as they floundered about for new adjectives to bludgeon me with, for producing the play in the first place and for my chore of directing in the second. Regardless, in my chronicle it remains an achievement that gives me pride. There was another Christmas offering that Kit and I participated in: André Obey's *Lucrece*, adapted by Thornton Wilder; music by Deems

Taylor; scenery by Robert Edmond Jones; direction by McClintic; and starring Katharine Cornell with Brian Aherne, Blanche Yurka and Robert Lorraine. As you may have guessed, it was the story of the rape of Lucrece, and maybe Monsieur Obey did go a little arty in the telling of it, and more than likely we smothered it to death with too much affection; but I can never agree with Mr. Nathan's summing up of the rape scene between Aherne and Kit "as a couple of Vassar girls having a pillow fight." Kit and I laughed along with others who read it, but I at least didn't agree. The press on the whole was respectful but unimpressed. It was withdrawn after five weeks. If the opening night was not one of electric enthusiasm, the closing night was. An audience that filled the theater to overflowing remained seated with the house lights up for twenty minutes after the final curtain fell, until Kit came out and in a scarcely audible voice thanked them. No sir, not every Christmas were we rereading our notices!

I have been frequently asked, "What is your favorite production?" Out of the many that I have done there are obviously ones that I care about more than others, but I have no favorite. However, I can say I am proud to have presented *Hamlet* with John Gielgud, Judith Anderson, Lillian Gish and Arthur Byron; *Winterset* with Burgess Meredith, Margo and Richard Bennett; *High Tor* with Meredith and Peggy Ashcroft; *Saturday's Children* with Ruth Gordon, Roger Pryor, Beulah Bondi and later Humphrey Bogart. The last three were written by Maxwell Anderson. Then there was Sidney Howard's *Yellow Jack*, a moving dedication to the men who served as guinea pigs for Walter Reed in his fight against yellow fever during the Spanish American War, done against Jo Mielziner's stunning functional set, with James Stewart, in his first big part on Broadway, running neck-and-neck with Sam Levene and Myron McCormick, who were also guinea pigs. It was great fun restaging *Crime,* and doing *The Trial of Mary Dugan* in London and on the coast; and taking Mrs. Leslie Carter in and out of that house in China and depositing Florence Reed there for keeps had its exhilarating moments too. That is called Operation *Shanghai* [*Gesture*] on my boards. And the interlude which brought beautiful Elsie Ferguson in *Scarlet Pages* across my path. She solemnly explained to me she could not do a piece of business I had given her because she was a "star"! Some things have to be explained! . . . I remember with sadness the bubbling effervescence of tragic Margaret Lawrence. I am happy in recalling those brief days of rehearsal with Tallulah in *Jezebel,* which her illness, unfortunately for me, prevented her from appearing in. Proud I am, after the many years that intervened between my apprenticeship to Grace George as her stage manager, to have presented her at long last in three plays, all of them successes. And I thank whatever gods may be that Pauline Lord came my way and that I was privileged to direct this unique and complex actress in four plays. This woman of the half-gesture, with the stumbling utterance and low voice that seemed to come from the inside of a storm — with a strange off-beat and wild humor that was like wind on the prairie — and her indirect approach to a part that was so sensationally right when it was right and so sensationally wrong when it was wrong . . . This indirectness naturally enough was her nature. I recall a letter she wrote me about a play she was appearing in out of town which was about to close because she refused to go on with it. In part she wrote, "There's nothing really wrong with the whole setup. It's just a little matter of bad direction, bad lighting, bad actors and bad management." To all of you who never saw this smallish woman with the unbobbed, honey-colored hair and the soft voice from the center of a whirlwind play *Anna Christie,* or as Amy in *They Knew What They Wanted* or Zenobia in *Ethan Frome,* I can only say I am sorry — you missed something! It's hard to believe she's no longer here. Whenever there is a stiff wind blowing I fancy I can hear her whispering, hesitant voice saying, "Don't worry about me, Guth, it's not so bad over here after all."

The endless sea of faces that have been at my first rehearsals of the ninety and more productions which have appeared on the metropolitan stage in the last thirty years come before me — either smiling or puzzled, frowning or glum, men with their ties off, sometimes shirts off, men well groomed, the ladies dressed to kill or just with clothes on — all with pencils sharpened, parts in hand, waiting for the signal to begin — Charles Cherry, José Ruben, Sylvia Field, "Ted" Emery, Blanche Bates, Madge Kennedy, Cyril Keightly, Estelle Winwood, Ina Claire, Fay Bainter, Jacob Ben-Ami, Constance Collier, George Abbott, Kent Smith, Lee Tracy, Uta Hagen, Paul Muni, Jane Cowl, Howard Lindsay, Dorothy Stickney, J. C. Nugent, Ann Andrews, Franchot Tone, Diana Wynward, Charles Bickford, Francine Larrimore, Tom Ewell, Walter Hampden, John Williams, June Walker, Dan Duryea, Jessica Tandy, Aubrey Smith, Helen Menken, Charlton Heston, Mildred Natwick, Burgess Meredith, Julie Harris, Montgomery Clift, Jean

Dixon, Louis Calhern, the Gishes — Lillian and Dorothy — Arthur Kennedy, Gregory Peck, Marian Seldes, José Ferrer, Maurine Stapleton, Marlon Brando, Barbara Bel Geddes, John Kerr — all of these and many more are a part of the vivid tapestry that has been my working background from December 23, 1921, until now.

I make a special bow to Judith Anderson. It's a mere twenty years ago since she succumbed to my managerial wiles and played in a production of mine that expired after a brief four weeks' run in Manhattan, *Divided By Three* it was called. But that four weeks plus the time of rehearsal only whetted my appetite for more of Miss Anderson, and at every opportunity since then that the two of us can agree on a script and at the same time be available to each other we have gladdened ourselves, and I hope a number of play-goers, by her participation at one time or another in my productions of *Hamlet, The Old Maid, The Three Sisters, Medea* on tour and at the Berlin Festival in 1951, and a revival of *Come of Age.* A supreme actress — a joy to work with!

It was a rewarding occasion when I directed and presented Ethel Waters in her first dramatic role, Hagar in *Mamba's Daughters* — a true actress as well as a remarkable woman. A distinguished colored cast supported her: Georgette Harvey, Willie Bryant, Fredi Washington, Canada Lee and Georgia Burke. José Ferrer headed the noncolored support. Then there was Gladys Cooper, still a beauty but also an actress now, in Emlyn Williams's play *The Morning Star* — which also served as a springboard for Gregory Peck's leap to movie glory. And Emlyn Williams himself, who made his first appearance in this country under my banner in

Criminal at Large; and Alexander Woollcott, who made his
debut as an actor in my production of *Brief Moment.* Only
once in all these star-spangled years did I act as an impresario and nothing else. That was when I presented the Greek
National Theater Company in *Electra* and *Oedipus,* and
very proud I was too. The production of *Electra* was particularly impressive — the chorus was the only integrated one
I have ever seen in the presentation of a Greek play. It
seemed extraordinary, as I attended their final performances
in the huge Mark Hellinger Theater and watched the capacity audiences and standees respond to the emotional
grip of these twenty-five hundred-year-old plays being
played in modern Greek . . . It seemed extraordinary when
I remembered the fuss and fume, the worry, anxiety and
lost tempers that accompany an out-of-town opening of almost any new play . . . Yet there before us was a road map
of the eternally successful drama — as new as the most
advanced moderns — imperishable. There was a curious se-
renity about these plays, as if they were smiling with amused
tolerance, saying: Can you do better? Have you done as
well? . . . That was the trend of my thinking when, at a
party given by the Greek Ambassador, I was startled to hear
a vehement young Greek saying, "I wish the war had wiped
out every vestige of ancient Greece — it's not an inspiration
to those of us who live there. We've been rotting through the
years on glories that were won three thousand years ago.
We are nothing but ruins for tourists to inspect." He was a
passionate Greek patriot. His emotion had a certain validity,
but I could never agree with his point of view.

Once I directed Ethel Barrymore. It was a play that she
brought to me. It was not a success but I would have pre-

sented her doing the multiplication table if she had asked me to. She was radiant, glamorous, unerringly right in everything that she did, but, as we too frequently find out, "The play's the thing," and in this instance it was not there. But I would do it again for the privilege of presiding at her rehearsals.

And now I come to my greatest pride — Kit. No, I'll heed Bernard Shaw this time, and say Katharine Cornell. Since the days of *The Green Hat* (you look up how many years ago) I have directed with two exceptions all of her plays and actively participated in her productions. From the moment of her becoming a manager she has assembled casts that few have equaled and none surpassed — Leslie Howard, Ann Harding, Franchot Tone, Burgess Meredith, Margalo Gillmore, Robert Lorraine, Effie Shannon, Cedric Hardwicke, Grace George, Raymond Massey, Ruth Gordon, Dudley Digges, Clare Eames, Basil Rathbone, Florence Reed, Ralph Richardson, Edith Evans, Philip Merivale, Judith Anderson, Maurice Evans, Godfrey Tearle, Mildred Natwick, Jean Pierre Aumont, Brian Aherne, Brenda Forbes, Laurence Olivier, Edmund Gwenn, Robert Flemyng, Tyrone Power, Orson Welles and a host of others. And her productions — *Romeo and Juliet, The Barretts of Wimpole Street, The Three Sisters, No Time for Comedy, The Doctor's Dilemma, Candida, Saint Joan, Antigone, Antony and Cleopatra, The Wingless Victory, The Constant Wife.* The theater was well served in all of them.

I have run the whole gamut of English authors from Shakespeare to Shaw and most of the American group — S. N. Behrman, Maxwell Anderson, Elmer Rice, Sidney Howard, Philip Barry, Tennessee Williams, Mary Chase and many others. I have never had a disrupting argument with any of them. Bernard Shaw, about whom many stories were circulated concerning his being adamant against the deletion of a single line, I cut ruthlessly in *Saint Joan* and *The Doctor's Dilemma*, and, though he knew it, he made no objection or comment about it. Of the scene designers, I have worked more consistently with Donald Oenslager and Jo Mielziner but there have been times that I have used such men as Robert Edmond Jones, Harry Horner and Leo Kerz.

The American theater has been blessed with many fine directors from David Belasco and Winthrop Ames to Elia Kazan and Joshua Logan. We all work in our different ways to achieve our own approximation of perfection. Although I am never out front at a New York opening of mine I never miss a performance of any out-of-town breaking in. I try, as a rule, to be apart from the audience although I have had some helping hints by sitting among them. In the beginning I like to have a mass reaction rather than an individual opinion, so for that reason I sit in a box — that is, if the theater has them — watching the performance and listening to the audience response — whether restless, quiet or demonstrative. Years ago Arthur Hopkins presented a musical play called *Deep River* which opened, I think, in Harrisburg, Pennsylvania. It represented an investment of $130,000 of his own money, and at its initial performance he felt his actors were letting it go down the drain; and, as the evening progressed, he found himself cursing his performers individually and collectively, when he was tapped on the shoulder by the lady sitting behind him who whispered, "If you don't like this show why don't you leave and get your money back?"

"I wish to God I could," murmured Hopkins as he made for the nearest exit.

We all have our individual conceits but if we truthfully look at our glorious past — the theater's, that is — we will find that most of the great stars and managements have done the finest plays of their time and the great classics as well. Certainly in the early part of this century Richard Mansfield is an outstanding example with his presentations of Ibsen, Shaw, Rostand and Shakespeare. Charles Frohman, who, to use a cheap phrase, was dubbed "commercial," also presented Ibsen, Shakespeare, Galsworthy, Maugham, Rostand and Pinero. We who are following in the footsteps of our illustrious predecessors are only carrying the torch on.

I shudder when someone tells me of an actor — or an actress — who is "dedicated to his art" but I'm afraid if one is not dedicated, or its equivalent, one should stay out of the theater. I am filled with envy and criticism, but when I see a superlative performance or a magnificent job of directing I am lost in admiration and cannot help saying so. My appraisal is not everybody's nor is everybody's mine. I loathe a phony and the fact that a phony may be the success of the moment does not stop my too, too articulate judgment of same.

The critics? I agree and I disagree with them. Naturally, when they praise something I have done I put halos around their every head, but when they don't . . . ! I think I feel as Julia Marlowe did when she penned a note to George Arliss consoling him on his bad notices after he had played Shylock. She wrote, "When they [the critics] are good, believe them. When they are bad, they just don't know. Edwin Booth comforted me with this when I was a youngster."

I remember a phone conversation I had with Gustav Ekstein on what he thought the function of a critic was. He said, "It always seems to me the critic's job is not to miss anything truly right or original. I simply cannot believe that his function is to lead people in or out of the theater. The untrained audience can be counted on to do that pretty well for itself. Certainly the critic ought, for instance, to get behind a bad performance to a good script, or behind a bad script to a brilliant performance or a brilliant direction. I think especially that he ought to be ashamed ever to hold a wet finger into the air, feel how the wind is blowing, and with that protection speak out cleverly or brutally. That certainly is too easy. Because his highest function can be to contribute to the future of the theater by pointing to the positive or to the beautiful, thus guiding creativeness and the general taste." Whether they conform to this Utopian concept or not, I venture to say that by and large, through the years, our American theater has been well served by the gentlemen of the press who have sat in judgment on us.

It's a long time since I first sat in Rose Glass's classroom boning up on ancient history and dreaming of New York. The memory of her — her red hair, warm smile — is still vivid. A week or so ago (June 1954 that is) I journeyed into town to meet her at Idlewild where she was due to arrive by plane from Seattle to attend a convention of retired teachers being held in New York. On arriving there I was more than a little put out to find her plane had been rerouted to Washington, D.C., because Idlewild was closed in. By phoning Washington I discovered she was on a plane coming into LaGuardia. I hurried through dense traffic, expecting to find her exhausted (I was). But, no. She bounced off looking as young as I remembered her over forty years ago, telling me how wonderful the Capitol looked when it was floodlit. Her high spirits were a shot in the arm for me. I suddenly felt this emanation of youth of hers was due to the fact that she was never bored. She doesn't get annoyed as I do, at inconveniences, but takes them in her stride. We talked all the hour-long drive we had back to the country. Her energy and zest for life are undiminished. Her presence brought to mind a few lines of a poem by Hilaire Belloc:

> From . . . first beginning,
> Out to the undiscovered ends
> There's nothing worth the wear of winning
> But laughter and the love of friends.

XX

Square-cuts

THE SPRINGTIME of 1922 was one of continuous sunshine. On a sparkling Saturday afternoon Geraldine Farrar gave her final performance at the Met in the role of Zaza. Thousands and thousands of "Gerry Flappers" overflowed the opera house, the streets adjacent, the fire escapes, and the buildings opposite the stage door, to wave a tearful farewell to the glamorous Geraldine who was leaving an empty place in their hearts by her retirement. I attended that matinee and wormed my way out of the reluctantly departing crowd at the end, and walked slowly towards Beekman Place. It seemed so extraordinary to me that that magnetic, beautiful young woman (she was forty then) should be putting a period to her operatic career. I began thinking about myself — about Kit — and our careers, if one could be so presumptuous in mentioning them as such then. Would we have farewells? What do you do afterwards? Certainly we had just been showered with a lot of attention and praise. *The Dover Road* had been chosen as one of the ten best plays of the year by Burns Mantle. Kit's performance in the *Bill* had been on every critical list of the ten best. By many I was singled out for special praise.

I grew skeptical as I walked along, apprehensive: Suppose all this acclaim, I queried, should be for this waning season only? . . . I recalled personalities of the past who had captured the public fancy briefly and then faded into obscurity. That could happen to me. Maybe my notices of the season past would be just things written on paper that no one but myself would remember — aging pieces of yellowing paper that fall apart when you take them out to read them again.

I found myself talking out loud — "No, I refuse to believe it!" — as if in reply to the other questioning me. *"The Dover Road* was no accident for me. It was the result of ten years of discouragements, of work, of living. I had chosen my route, I knew where I was going. That lady called Luck would smile on me again and maybe she smiled when your work was good and Luck was just a name we gave her, or your friends gave her." Anyway, there it was — and I was remembering those sighs of complacent vindictiveness from my childhood, when the elders in their rocking chairs would sum up the activities of "him or her" with the words, "Time will tell." And how right they were! It does.

Just before Easter that year of 1922, *A Bill of Divorcement* called it a day and left the Times Square Theater after a run of twenty-six weeks to play a brief season on the road. Kit went with it. She had signed to play Mary Fitton in *Will Shakespeare* (also by Clemence Dane) the following season, with Winthrop Ames. As for myself, being on my own now with W. A.'s investment paid back many weeks before, I was getting ready to leave the Little Theater and move to offices that would have only my name on the door. Johnson Briscoe was stepping into my room at 244. Despite the solid sensation of a current success, I felt a little bit as I did when I swam out beyond my depth for the first time.

✻　　✻　　✻

With Kit away the phone bill at Beekman Place began to assume astronomical figures as we talked to each other every day, sometimes more than once and never briefly. I was meeting her at the end of her second week on tour in Montreal and proceeding with her from there to her home town, Buffalo. I wanted to give her a present — I had always wanted to give her a present — a present worthy of her — an indication of what she meant to me (I have never yet succeeded).

On examining my newly acquired bank balance I began looking at advertisements in the higher-priced magazines in search of a suggestion of a suitable gift for a bride. Jewels, I thought, but what? I found myself fascinated by opulent pictures of square-cut diamonds and that I decided would be the offering. I tapped the till for five thousand dollars. I was dealt five crisp bills bearing the likeness of Alexander Hamilton — a face I'll never forget. I looked at them in wonder — five of them and all mine. I had never seen anything larger than a hundred-dollar bill before. I slipped the pictures of Mr. Hamilton into the pocket of my jacket, figuring that if any light-finger frisked me he'd never attack a jacket pocket; but notwithstanding I couldn't resist thrusting my right hand in to clutch with a vise-like grip those thousand-dollar bills.

Cartier's was my destination. It seemed to me to have an edge over similar establishments that dispense square-cuts. To me it reeked of the rarified atmosphere of Bond Street and the Rue de la Paix. I had never been in such an establishment in my life, rarely even looked in the windows of one. . . . I arrived at Cartier's. The smiling, uniformed attendant opened the door. I entered, right hand still in jacket pocket. A poker-faced fellow in a short black coat and striped trousers inquired what I wanted.

I replied, "Square-cut diamonds."

"Mr. MacKie will take care of you," he said. "Mr. MacKie, the gentleman wishes to see square-cut diamonds."

Mr. MacKie's smile might have been painted on; his Scotch accent was real. I detected a certain tenseness in the air as I was seated at a small table facing the painted smile. It never occurred to me that that right hand of mine clutching the bills gave the impression that it might have been clutching a gun instead. I was conscious of men behind me. I didn't look — I felt out of place, but, by Jiminy, I was sticking. Mr. MacKie was courtesy itself as various messengers arrived with black velvet trays of sparklers when suddenly my eyes opened wider and my pulses started racing as I looked at a diamond and sapphire bracelet (square-cuts, of course). I thought it exquisite. My first feeling was I didn't have enough money to pay for it; but when Mr. MacKie examined the hieroglyphics on the tiny tag attached and informed me it was a mere forty-five hundred dollars, I heaved a great sigh of relief knowing I would have five hundred dollars for peanuts when I got outside. But as I tried to extricate my right hand from the pocket — its protection of the precious pieces of wampum had been so intense that it had become frozen, paralyzed, and I was quite conscious of the startled stares of the onlookers as my left hand went over to help my right hand out. Those bright new bills were a mess — sweaty and crinkled.

Mr. MacKie smoothed them out, counted them — then he smiled at me, a real smile this time. I smiled back — I don't know why. Just silly . . . ! The air about was calmer now.

"May I have your name?" he asked.

"Mr. M'Klenk," I replied, sounding not unlike a harelip victim. I have never been able to pronounce my last name (Mr. Psychiatrist, tell me why). It's most unfortunate!

"I beg your pardon?" said Mr. MacKie.

Taking a deep breath, and slowly as if I were speaking in a strange language, I replied, "My name is Guth-rie Mac-Clin-tic." I got it right that time.

"Oh," replied he, "Mr. McClintock . . . hm . . . hm . . . Would you mind waiting just a minute?" and he disappeared with all my pictures.

Presently he was back with another gentleman who came at me with hand extended, saying, "How do you do, Mr. McClintic, I don't think you've been here before — I am trying to recall why your name is familiar."

"I am a theatrical producer," I found myself saying.

"Of course," said the gentleman. "Have you anything on at the moment?"

"*The Dover Road*," said I.

"How stupid of me to have forgotten," replied the gentleman; and, as if trying to solve a puzzle, he queried, "You're married to . . . ?"

"Katharine Cornell," I answered. I was beginning to get hot under the collar and deciding to damn well ask for my money back and go elsewhere to get square-cuts when my inquisitor stopped me with:

"Mr. McClintock, why pay cash? Cartier will be glad to have you charge them."

I had never had a charge account in my life, and here was Bond Street and Rue de la Paix asking me to leave without paying. My mind shot back to those other days on tour when

I left without paying to save a few dimes, but I quickly gained my equilibrium and stammered, "I'd rather charge them."

Mr. MacKie gave me back my straightened-out bills and a few seconds later the bracelet was handed to me in a distinguished embossed leather box that I pocketed as I was being ushered to the door by a group of respectful and bowing gentlemen. I walked down Fifth Avenue in a delirious haze.

The sad part of this story is that no voices told me that my bride didn't like jewelry — never wore any — and, although she received the square-cuts with expressions of delight and wore them proudly in Buffalo, I am sorry to relate that that first-important-wedding-gift-of-mine's greatest service has been its visits to various pawnshops, where it was "doing time" for some unfortunate extravagance of ours. It's out of hock now and reposing in the safe-deposit vault, but it is always on call. I have suggested that she sell it but she hangs onto it for sentimental reasons.

Women are funny that way!

These are the plays I remember were directed by me in the years
indicated, many under my own management and many for others.

December, 1921 – June, 1955

William Shakespeare	ROMEO AND JULIET, 1933–34–35
	HAMLET, 1936
	ANTONY AND CLEOPATRA, 1947
George Bernard Shaw	THE DOCTOR'S DILEMMA, 1941
	CANDIDA, 1933, 1937, 1942, 1946
	SAINT JOAN, 1936
Anton Chekhov	THE THREE SISTERS, 1942
S. N. Behrman	BRIEF MOMENT, 1931
	NO TIME FOR COMEDY, 1939
Maxwell Anderson	SATURDAY'S CHILDREN, 1928
	WINTERSET, 1935
	HIGH TOR, 1936
	STAR-WAGON, 1937
	KEY LARGO, 1939
	WINGLESS VICTORY, 1936
Sidney Howard	ALIEN CORN, 1933
	YELLOW JACK, 1934
Owen Davis	ETHAN FROME, 1936
	JEZEBEL, 1933
	BEWARE OF WIDOWS, 1925
	LAZYBONES, 1924

Kate O'Brien	THE ANTE-ROOM, 1936 (London)
	THAT LADY, 1949
Clemence Dane	THE WAY THINGS HAPPEN, 1924
	MARINERS, 1927
	COME OF AGE, 1952
Edward Sheldon &	AGE OF INNOCENCE, 1928
Margaret Barnes	DISHONORED LADY, 1930
Howard Lindsay &	LIFE WITH MOTHER, 1948
Russel Crouse	
Somerset Maugham	THE CONSTANT WIFE, 1951–1952
	THE LETTER, 1927
Dodie Smith	LOVERS AND FRIENDS, 1943
Robert Ardrey	HOW TO GET TOUGH ABOUT IT, 1938
Thomas Job	BARCHESTER TOWERS, 1937
Noel Coward	FALLEN ANGELS, 1927
Elizabeth Ginty	MISSOURI LEGEND, 1938
Tennessee Williams	YOU TOUCHED ME, 1945
John Colton	SHANGHAI GESTURE, 1926
Henri Bernstein	ROSE BURKE, 1942
Friedrich Hebbel	HEROD AND MARIAMNE, 1938
André Obey	LUCRECE, 1932
John Van Druten	FLOWERS OF THE FOREST, 1935
Philip Barry	JOHN, 1927
Philip Barry &	COCK ROBIN, 1928
E. L. Rice	
Jean Anhouil	ANTIGONE, 1946
Michael Arlen	THE GREEN HAT, 1925
Bayard Veiller	THE TRIAL OF MARY DUGAN, 1928
Samuel Shipman	CRIME, 1927
	SCARLET PAGES, 1929
Lewis Beach	SQUARE PEG, 1923
Emlyn Williams	MORNING STAR, 1947
Edgar Wallace	CRIMINAL AT LARGE, 1932

A. A. Milne	THE DOVER ROAD, 1921
	THE TRUTH ABOUT BLAYDS, 1933
Rosemary Casey	THE VELVET GLOVE, 1950
Bertram Bloch &	SPRING AGAIN, 1941
Isabel Leighton	
Rudolf Besier	THE BARRETTS OF WIMPOLE STREET, 1931
John Synge	THE PLAYBOY OF THE WESTERN WORLD, 1946
George Batson	PUNCH AND JULIA, 1942
Elsie Schauffler	PARNELL, 1935
Mary Chase	BERNADINE, 1952
Robinson Jeffers	MEDEA, 1948–1951, 1955
Thomas Mitchell	GLORY HALLELUJAH, 1926
Mary Kennedy &	MRS. PARTRIDGE PRESENTS, 1925
Ruth Hawthorne	
J. P. McEvoy	GOD LOVES US, 1926
Mark Reed	SKYLARK, 1929
	THE LADY WHO CAME TO STAY, 1945
Vincent Sheean	INTERNATIONAL INCIDENT, 1940
Du Bose Heyward	MAMBA'S DAUGHTERS, 1938
William Marchant	TO BE CONTINUED, 1952
Sophie Treadwell	GRINGO, 1927
Dennison Cliff	SCOTLAND YARD, 1929
Howard Richardson &	DARK OF THE MOON, 1945
William Berney	
Dan Totheroh	DISTANT DRUMS, 1933
Martin Flavin	CROSS ROADS, 1930
Gustav Ekstein	CHRISTMAS EVE, 1939
Arthur Richman	ALL DRESSED UP, 1925
Eleanor Belmont &	IN THE NEXT ROOM, 1923
Harriet Ford	
Lynn Starling	IN HIS ARMS, 1924

Euripides	ELECTRA, 1951	(Greek National Theater Company; I presented them only.)
Sophocles	OEDIPUS, 1951	
Greer Johnson	MRS. PATERSON, 1954	
Christopher Fry	THE DARK IS LIGHT ENOUGH, 1955	
Zoë Akins	THE OLD MAID, 1935	
Denis Cannan	CAPTAIN CARVALLO, 1950	

Index